THE
PERSIAN GULF
WAR

THE
PERSIAN GULF
WAR

Lessons for Strategy, Law, and Diplomacy

Edited by Christopher C. Joyner

Contributions in Military Studies, Number 99

GREENWOOD PRESS

New York • Westport, Connecticut • London

Library of Congress Cataloging-in-Publication Data

The Persian Gulf War : lessons for strategy, law, and diplomacy /
   edited by Christopher C. Joyner.
      p.   cm. — (Contributions in military studies, ISSN 0883–6884 ;
   no. 99)
   Includes bibliographical references.
   ISBN 0–313–26710–3 (lib. bdg. : alk. paper)
   1. Iran-Iraq, 1980–1988.   2. Persian Gulf Region—Politics and
government.   I. Joyner, Christopher C.   II. Series.
DS318.85.P46   1990
955.05′4—dc20   89–25730

British Library Cataloguing in Publication Data is available.

Library of Congress Catalog Card Number: 89-25730
ISBN: 0–313–26710–3
ISSN: 0883–6884

First published in 1990

Greenwood Press, Inc.
88 Post Road West, Westport, Connecticut 06881

Printed in the United States of America

The paper used in this book complies with the
Permanent Paper Standard issued by the National
Information Standards Organization (Z39.48-1984).

10 9 8 7 6 5 4 3 2

For Nancy, Kristin, and Clayton

Contents

Preface

For nearly eight years, the war between Iran and Iraq defied diplomatic efforts to reach a cease-fire, much less a solution. The tragic result was an immense loss of life and tremendous waste of resources on both sides. This volume critically examines the Persian Gulf conflict with the aim of clarifying the causes of that war, appraising the military and political strategies pursued by both belligerents, and gauging the relative efficacy of various diplomatic means used to bring about an end to the hostilities.

Several of the contributions to this volume were originally prepared as papers for two panels at annual conferences sponsored by the International Studies Association in St. Louis in 1988 and in London in 1989. I would like to express my gratitude to the Department of Political Science at the George Washington University for the support to attend those professional meetings and the opportunity to organize those panel sessions.

Thanks are also due to Dartmouth College for the opportunity to spend the summer of 1989 in the Department of Government as a Visiting Professor of International Law. The quiet and serene environment of Hanover, New Hampshire, made it easy and pleasurable to think seriously about this project. As a consequence, it was during this summer that most chapters for this volume were initially edited and prepared for publication.

Special thanks are due to Nathan Brown, whose advice in selecting forms of Arabic transliteration was very helpful, and to Robin Epstein, who assisted in proofreading the final version. Last and surely most, the greatest appreciation is owed to my wife, Nancy, my daughter, Kristin, and my son, Clayton. Without their loving support, patience and understanding this work would never have been completed. It is accordingly to them that this volume is dedicated.

THE
PERSIAN GULF
WAR

1

Introduction

The Geography and Geopolitics of the Persian Gulf

Christopher C. Joyner

The Persian Gulf region since World War II has appreciated markedly in strategic importance for the international community. The security and stability of the Gulf have become prominent considerations in gauging global energy needs and in calculating the superpowers' policies in the Middle East and Southwest Asia. During the 1980s the geopolitical importance of the Gulf became even more magnified as the protracted Iran-Iraq War increasingly threatened to upset the political, economic, and military balance of power in the region.

On September 22, 1980, following intermittent skirmishes over sovereignty of the disputed Shatt al-Arab waterway, Iraq launched an all-out armed attack against Iran. While Saddam Hussein's immediate military objective was to regain control over the Shatt al-Arab, his ultimate political aim was to bring about the overthrow of Ayatollah Ruhollah Khomeini. The timing seemed propitious. Iran looked vulnerable in the fall of 1980: No single group or person appeared to be in full control of Iran's policy; the Iranian military was in disarray after purges of officers loyal to the Shah; and with student militants holding 52 Americans hostage, military assistance to Iran from either the United States or the West was improbable. Clearly, however, Saddam Hussein underestimated the staying power of the theocratic regime in Iran and the political will of the Persian people to fight for God and country. The war dragged on for 94 months.[1]

The war between Iran and Iraq consequently became the dominant issue in the Gulf region during the 1980s. This conflict, as one commentator described it, was "a war between two barely distinguishable four-letter countries. It was fought with the weapons of the 1980s, the tactics of World War I, and the passions of the Crusades."[2] Iran and Iraq battled each other for nearly eight years, but the war was not confined to their land territories. Fighting spread to the Gulf waters and along the shores of neighboring states. A constant danger was that the war might spill over into other Gulf countries.

The end of hostilities between Iran and Iraq in July 1988 left an altered political landscape in the Gulf and invites reevaluation by scholars and policy analysts of the political, security, and diplomatic opportunities and problems there. In a broad sense, this reflects the chief purpose of the present work. The contributions to this volume are intended to place in clearer perspective the political, security, and diplomatic dimensions of the Iran-Iraq War. The aim is to produce a gauge for better assessment of those factors and forces that affected the conflict's outcome and that will influence future political and security developments in the region. This chapter sets the stage by examining the Gulf's geographical milieu and the prominent geopolitical considerations that influenced local and international perceptions of the region during the Iran-Iraq War, as well as in its aftermath.

GEOGRAPHY OF THE GULF

The Persian Gulf, known to Arab riparian states as the Arabian Gulf, is a shallow marginal sea of the Indian Ocean lying between the Arabian Peninsula and Iran (see map). The Gulf extends northeast 614 miles from the Gulf of Oman in the south through the Strait of Hormuz to the Shatt al-Arab in the north. The Gulf is bordered by the United Arab Emirates (UAE), Saudi Arabia, Qatar, and Kuwait on the southwestern shore, with Iraq on the northwestern tip and Iran along the northeastern shore. The island state of Bahrain lies off the western shore.

The Gulf occupies 92,254 square miles in area and contains 11.3 million cubic yards of water in volume. It stretches 210 miles at its widest point, from Bandar-e Maqam in Iran across to Ra's al-Sila on the coast of the UAE. The Gulf's narrowest mainland point reaches 35 miles across in the Strait of Hormuz.

Regarding bathymetric character, the Persian Gulf is practically a land-locked epicontinental basin. It is remarkably shallow, with an average depth of only 150 feet. The deepest waters range between 270 and 300

Persian Gulf Region

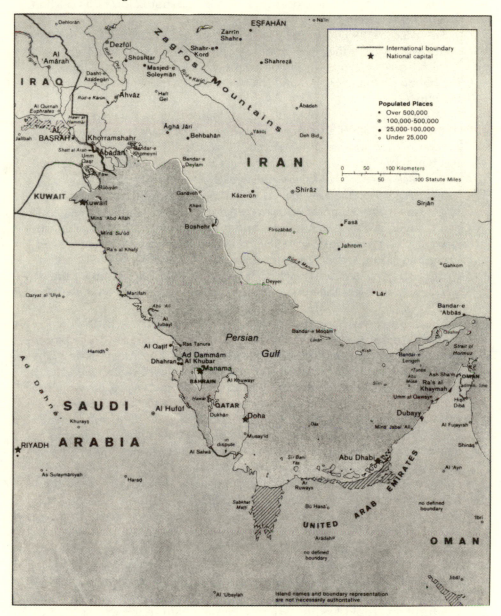

Source: U.S. Department of State, *U.S. Policy in the Persian Gulf*, Special Report No. 166, July 1987, frontispiece.

feet and lie off the Iranian coast. The shallowest areas, less than 120 feet deep, are along the UAE portion of the Gulf. Ships exceeding 5,000 tons displacement can sail no closer than 5 miles offshore along this portion of the Arabian coast.[3]

The head of the Gulf contains the low, swampy delta of the Shatt al-Arab waterway, which is formed by the confluence of the Tigris and Euphrates rivers with the Iranian Karun River. The Shatt demarcates the boundary between Iran and Iraq for some 120 miles before emptying into the Gulf.

The physiography of the Gulf littoral is mostly a narrow coastal plain with sandy beaches and small estuaries. Numerous small islands dot the shoreline, among which Bahrain and Qeshm are the largest. The Iranian shore is mountainous, with cliffs in some places. The largest peninsulas are those of Qatar and Oman.

With regard to climate, the Gulf is arid, subtropical, and notoriously unpleasant. The summer is characterized by high temperatures, little cloud cover, scanty precipitation, and high humidity. Dust storms, carried by winds from the south called *khamsins*, blow sand across the Gulf. Haze and mirages are common along the Arabian shore. Winters are considerably colder in the northern Gulf. Most of the region's rainfall, which averages less than one inch annually, occurs between November and April in the form of sudden downpours.

The southern entrance to the Persian Gulf connects with the Gulf of Oman through the Strait of Hormuz. Oman and Iran are the riparian states, and each claims territorial waters out to 12 nautical miles. The narrowest part of the strait, a distance of 24 miles, lies between Larak Island (owned by Iran) and the Quoin Islands (owned by Oman). The principal navigation channels in the strait run 210 to 270 feet deep. While these channels may be difficult to obstruct physically, they lie sufficiently close to Oman's Musandam Peninsula to be vulnerable to attack. In an age of missile warfare, it remains of critical importance which government controls the shores of strategic waterways.[4]

As many as 80 vessels transit the strait daily, including among them the world's largest supertankers. After the Iranian Revolution and the Soviet invasion of Afghanistan, widespread concern surfaced that the Strait of Hormuz might be closed to international shipping. These anxieties were most acute in the United States, Western Europe, and Japan, who are heavily dependent upon imported oil that passes through Hormuz. Short-term interruptions to Gulf oil supplies would create national inconvenience and higher prices; over the long term, however, those interruptions could lead to serious international economic disruptions. It is this realization that highlights prominent geopolitical considerations in the Gulf region.

GEOPOLITICS OF THE GULF

Geopolitics concerns the relationship between geography and politics, an interplay that is multifaceted and interdependent. Geopolitical considerations include variables of space, population, national interests, and natural resources. The strategic location of states and forward projection of national power are also involved.

The Persian Gulf region is characterized by precarious stability. Within the last decade, three profound shocks to the area have thrust the Gulf into geopolitical prominence: first, the seizure of power by revolutionary forces in Iran in February 1979; then the Soviet invasion of Afghanistan in December 1979; third, the war between Iran and Iraq that erupted in September 1980. Western concerns about the Persian Gulf remained preoccupied largely by these events during the 1980s. Placed within the context of these shocks, four principal geopolitical considerations presently distinguish the Gulf as an especially dynamic and volatile region: (1) the vast petroleum resources located there; (2) the particular geographical situation of each local Arab state; (3) the recent rise of Islamic fundamentalism; and (4) the geostrategic ambitions of the Soviet Union.

Petroleum Resources

Petroleum plays a key geopolitical role as the region's superabundant resource. The economic stakes in the Gulf for Western states are therefore high indeed. The economies of the Gulf states are dominated by the production of petroleum, which is the major export of the region and its link to the Western world and Japan. Oil remains the chief source of revenues for Gulf governments, and consequently it has made possible rapid socioeconomic development and the advancement of modernization programs.

Throughout the 1970s petroleum exports established the Gulf states as a salient influence in international commerce and world politics. While the world price for oil since 1980 has fallen considerably and new discoveries of petroleum have been made elsewhere, the geopolitical importance of the Persian Gulf today still remains vital: Gulf states currently furnish 25 percent of all petroleum moving in international commerce, and the region contains 65 percent of the known petroleum reserves in the non-Communist world. Nearly 30 percent of Western Europe's oil imports originate from the Gulf. Approximately 65 percent of Japan's petroleum is imported from the Gulf; for the United States, in late 1989 the figure for imports as part of petroleum consumption climbed to 52 percent, with around 18 percent of those imports—or 9 percent of total consumption—coming from the Gulf producers.

For both Western Europe and the United States, geopolitical concern about Gulf oil production extends beyond the region itself. Security considerations require not only ensuring access to the wellhead, but also securing routes to refineries and consumers. The need exists to protect sea lines of communication to and from the Gulf, around the Cape of Good Hope, to Europe and North America. Geostrategically, the West must preserve the sealanes through the Gulf from regional instability and be prepared to deal with the contingency that the Soviet Union might challenge international sealanes through the Indian and South Atlantic oceans.

International dependency on oil imports from the Gulf is likely to grow. As world demand for petroleum accelerates, so too will the need for greater supply. The Persian Gulf furnishes the greatest readily available source of those petroleum supplies. Consequently, Western states that might be most severely affected must pursue policies designed to enhance the security of oil supplies. Promoting peace and political stability in the Gulf region would contribute substantially to that objective.

Local Geography

A second principal geopolitical consideration concerns the particular situation of each Gulf state. Saudi Arabia, Iraq, and Iran are the three regional powers with strongest influence in Gulf activities. The other five local powers are Kuwait, Qatar, the United Arab Emirates, Bahrain, and Oman. Physical location, demographic characteristics, resource availability, and government capabilities of these polities all figure into the Gulf's geopolitical calculus.[5]

Saudi Arabia. Saudi Arabia covers a land area of 839,996 square miles— about one-fourth the size of the United States—and occupies four-fifths of the Arabian Peninsula, a strategic location reaching from the Persian Gulf to the Red Sea and the Gulf of Aqaba. The desert kingdom shares borders with every Arab state in the region—Kuwait, Iraq, and Jordan in the north; Yemen, South Yemen, and Oman in the south; and the United Arab Emirates and Qatar on the east. A 15–mile causeway links the Saudi mainland with Bahrain.

The population estimated for Saudi Arabia in 1989 is 12,678,000, of whom 99 percent are Sunni Muslims who follow the puritanical Wahhabi doctrine. Saudi Arabia has some 2 million expatriate workers, mostly Yemenis, Koreans, Indians, Pakistanis, and Egyptians. This large influx of foreign labor presents a dual problem for the Saudis in that first, it creates a certain dependence on foreign countries, and second, this group conceivably might foment internal dissent against the Saudi regime.

The government of Saudi Arabia is a monarchy, headed by a king with a crown prince as heir apparent. There is no modern constitution or parliament. Since 1982 the head of government and head of state has been King Fahd ibn Abdul Aziz, and the current heir apparent is Crown Prince Abdullah, Fahd's half brother.

The key to Saudi Arabia's economy is its petrochemical industry, a development naturally flowing from the country's vast oil resources. With a pumping capacity of 10 million barrels per day and reserves estimated at 170 billion barrels—the largest in the world—Saudi Arabia has assumed a prominent role in the international economy.

Saudi Arabia is considered a moderate in the Arab world. It maintains close ties with the United States and favors a collective Arab approach to policies and peace in the region. During the Gulf War the Saudis contributed as much as $25 billion to the Iraqi cause, largely out of apprehension over the revolutionary regime in Iran. From the Western viewpoint, the role of Saudi Arabia retains particular importance because of its tremendous oil reserves and production capability. At issue here not only is Saudi Arabia's ability to protect its vast oil fields from external attack, but also the need to guard against the threat of internal disruption by Islamic fundamentalism and disgruntled minorities.

Iran. Iran, the only non-Arab state in the region, encompasses 636,293 square miles, an area slightly larger than Alaska. Iran's population in 1989 was estimated to be 51,005,000, far greater than all the Arab Gulf states combined. Its people are 98 percent Muslim, with a 93 percent majority of the Shi'ite sect. Iran's neighbors include Turkey and Iraq to the west, the Soviet Union in the north, and Afghanistan and Pakistan in the east. The entire eastern littoral of the Gulf is Iranian. Critical for geopolitical consideration in the West is that Iran's long northern border with the Soviet Union leaves it vulnerable to Soviet encroachment.

In February 1979, Ayatollah Ruhollah Khomeini ended nearly four decades of rule by Shah Mohammed Reza Pahlavi. Iran became an Islamic republic, and Khomeini became the symbol of revolution and its spiritual leader. Although Iran has a parliament—the 270–member Majlis—and a head of state, the driving feature of the nation's unification is Islam. Iran adheres to the Twelver Shi'a sect of Islam. From early 1979 until his death on June 3, 1989, Ayatollah Khomeini served as the *faqih*, the enlightened individual responsible for making final decisions regarding matters of religious principle. His mission was to keep the government on the path of the true believers. As the head of Shi'ite institutions and the dominant authority in temporal affairs, Ayatollah Khomeini consequently exercised preeminent power during the 1980s in shaping Iran's foreign and domestic policies.

Iran's most valuable resource is oil. With some 93 billion barrels in proven reserves, Iran ranks fourth in the world, behind Saudi Arabia, the Soviet Union, and Iraq.[6] It also ranks as the world's second-largest producer of natural gas, after the Soviet Union. Most of Iran's oil fields are located in the northwest corner of the country, beyond the reach of Iraq's conventional military attack, and hence they escaped much damage. However, Iran's production facilities were severely affected by the war. Six refineries, the largest of which is located at Abadan, are situated only 20 minutes away from Iraq's border. Iran's principal sea terminal at Kharg Island, 20 miles off the southern coast, was repeatedly exposed to Iraqi air raids. During the conflict, bombings and attacks by Iraq on tankers in the Gulf attempted to cripple Iran's oil industry in order to cut off revenues needed to finance the war effort. This strategy was largely unsuccessful. Iran's petroleum production actually increased from 1.37 million barrels per day (b/d) in 1981 to a high of 2.606 million b/d in 1983 and leveled off at 2.34 million b/d in 1987. The war, however, took a devastating toll on Iran in human terms. Iran suffered more than a million casualties in the conflict, and some estimates of property damage run as high as $200 billion.[7]

Iraq. Iraq covers 167,924 square miles, an area larger than California. Iraq is located at the northern end of the Persian Gulf and borders on Jordan and Syria in the west, Turkey in the north, Iran in the east, and Kuwait and Saudi Arabia in the south. Its postwar population in 1989 was estimated at 17,610,000. Of these, 95 percent are Muslim, with some 60 percent being Shi'ites and 30 percent Sunnis.

With 30 miles of Gulf coastline being its only access to the high seas, Iraq has but two major ports—Umm Qasr on the Gulf and Basra, located inland at the confluence of the Tigris and Euphrates rivers that forms the Shatt al-Arab. South of Basra, the Shatt forms the international border between Iraq and Iran, which has remained the source of tension between these two Gulf powers since the early 1800s.

Three major groups constitute Iraq's population. The majority of the people are impoverished Shi'ites who remain politically excluded but are highly politicized. Sunnis constitute a second group, which dominates Iraq's political structure. Arab Sunnis furnish most of Iraq's political rulers and military leaders. The third group is the Kurds, a non-Arab people who are Sunni Muslims, but whose Kurdish nationality is salient. Comprising 15 percent of Iraq's population, Kurds inhabit the mountainous northern regions of Iraq, as well as portions of Iran, Turkey, Syria, and the Soviet Union.

The guiding political philosophy in Iraq is Baathism, a pan-Arab movement that espouses that national borders are artificial barriers set by Westerners. Baathists advocate a national socialist approach in which all Arabs are conceived as an indivisible polity, that is, an Arab nation. In Iraq the Baath Party controls all important facets and functions of society and government.

The highest executive organ in Iraq's government is the National Council, which is overseen by a 15-member Revolutionary Command Council. The Revolutionary Council effectively constitutes Iraq's executive and legislative branches. Since 1979 the central figure in Iraq's government has been Saddam Hussein, who serves as president, commander in chief, and head of the Baath Party. Hussein virtually controls Iraq's political system.

The Gulf War exacerbated Iraq's economic difficulties. With the ports of Basra and Umm Qasr closed, and the world price for petroleum depressed, Iraq's annual oil revenues dropped markedly, from $21 billion in 1980 to less than $10 billion in 1988. Nonetheless, important new discoveries of petroleum reserves over the decade substantially enhanced Iraq's role as a major player in international petropolitics. In 1981 Iraq's reserves were put at 29.7 billion barrels; by 1988 those reserves had climbed to 100 billion barrels. Furthermore, new overland pipelines facilitated continued expansion of Iraq's production capability during the 1980s, from 892,000 b/d in 1981 to 2.096 million b/d in 1987.[8] Perhaps paradoxically, the Gulf War also prompted certain political benefits for Iraq in the region, particularly in its relations with other Arab states. Save for Syria, Libya, and South Yemen, all the Arab governments supported Iraq in its war effort, politically and rhetorically if not materially or militarily. In large part this pro-Iraqi attitude stemmed from anxieties that Iran's Islamic fundamentalism might spread throughout the region, infecting neighboring Gulf states with domestic unrest.[9]

Kuwait. Situated in the northern end of the Persian Gulf between Iraq and Saudi Arabia, Kuwait covers 6,880 square miles, an area slightly smaller than New Jersey. In 1989 Kuwait's population was estimated to be 1,967,000, of whom 85 percent were Muslim (70 percent Sunnis, 30 percent Shi'ites). Kuwait operates as a constitutional monarchy and is experimenting with parliamentary democracy under the ruling al-Sabah family. Independent since 1961, Kuwait was the first of the conservative sheikhdoms to establish diplomatic relations with the Soviet Union, although in recent years, Qatar, Oman, and the United Arab Emirates have done so as well.

The Iran-Iraq War elevated national security to paramount concern among Kuwaitis.[10] Early on in the conflict, Kuwait came out on the side of Iraq, largely because it viewed the spread of Iran's revolutionary ideology as a threat to its internal stability. Less than one-half the population are native Kuwaitis; most inhabitants are Iranian, Palestinian, Pakistani, and Indian immigrants who have come to Kuwait as foreign labor. This demographic fact highlights Kuwait's concern over external Islamic fundamentalism and its disruptive potential in fomenting dissent among the nonnative population, particularly the sizable community of

Shi'ites. As a consequence, throughout the conflict Kuwait remained susceptible to terrorism by Islamic extremists. Several terrorist bombings in December 1983 demonstrated the reality of that threat.

Qatar. The sheikhdom of Qatar is 4,247 square miles in area—smaller than Connecticut—and juts northward on a peninsula on the west coast into the Gulf. It is bordered by Saudi Arabia and the United Arab Emirates to the south. The 1989 estimated population of Qatar was 342,000, making it the least populated of the Gulf states. Some 95 percent of the people are Muslims, mostly Sunnis of the Wahhabi sect. Only 70,000 of Qatar's population are native born. Foreign workers from Egypt, Pakistan, Korea, and Bangladesh comprise 80 percent of the Qatari labor force. Largely because civil rights and political liberties of foreign residents are severely restricted by the ruling family, the government remains concerned about expatriate workers becoming a possible source for domestic unrest.

The government of Qatar, a traditional emirate, functions under the staunchly religious and politically conservative ruling al-Thani dynasty. Independent since 1971, Qatar deliberately maintains a low international profile and tends to follow the lead of Saudi Arabia in regional policy.

The United Arab Emirates. The United Arab Emirates embodies a confederation of seven Arab emirates that merged into an independent polity in December 1971. Formerly known as the "Seven Trucial States," the UAE stretches for 750 miles along the southern shore of the Gulf and covers 32,280 square miles, about the size of Maine. Its neighbors include Qatar to the north, Saudi Arabia to the west and south, and Oman to the east.

Sheikh Zayed ibn Sultan al-Nahayan has been president and head of state since the UAE's inception. Of the seven autonomous emirates, Abu Dhabi, Dubai, and Sharjah are the most influential, largely on account of their oil wealth. The four remaining emirates include Ajman, Ras al-Khaimah, Fujairah, and Umm al-Qaiwain.

The combined population of the emirates in 1989 was estimated to be 1,455,000, of whom some 94 percent are Muslims (80 percent Sunnis, 20 percent Shi'ites). Indigenous inhabitants account for less than one-quarter of the confederation's population, and nearly 90 percent of the UAE labor force is foreign. Egyptians, Jordanians, Omanis, Pakistanis, Indians, Iranians, and Yemenis supply a substantial community of immigrant residents.

The regional instability caused by the Iran-Iraq War, the fundamentalist upheaval stemming from the Iranian Revolution, and acute proximity to Iran across the Gulf—only 35 miles—provoked serious concern for the emirates during the 1980s. As a result, the UAE government sought to forge closer security links with Saudi Arabia, while also adopting policies designed to keep the confederation neutral during the conflict.

Bahrain. Bahrain is the smallest of the Gulf states. It covers an area of 258 square miles, slightly smaller than New York City, and consists of an archipelago of 33 islands in the Gulf. Six of these islands are inhabited, and they lie 15 miles off the southern shore, between Saudi Arabia on the west and the Qatari Peninsula on the east. In 1989 the estimated Bahraini population was put at 483,000, nearly all of whom are Muslims. The government has been a constitutional monarchy since independence in 1971 under the dynastic rule of the al-Khalifa family.

Of the Gulf states, Bahrain remains the most vulnerable to Shi'ite radicalism. Although it is the only Gulf sheikhdom where the native population outnumbers immigrants, 70 percent of Bahrainis are Shi'ites, while only 30 percent are Sunnis. Consequently, real governmental concern exists about the spread of Iranian-inspired fundamentalism among the Shi'ite population. Aggravating this situation is the fact that Iran holds claims to Bahrain going back to the eighteenth century. Although these claims were dropped under the Shah's regime, they were reasserted without governmental authority by Ayatollah Sadeq Ruhani in 1979. The gravity of the Iranian threat was revealed in December 1981 when an alleged Iranian plot to overthrow the Bahraini government was exposed and thwarted.

Bahrain was especially concerned during the 1980s about the impact of the Iran-Iraq War on Gulf oil shipping. While being openly threatened by Iran, Bahrain continued to operate one of the largest crude refineries in the region, which was located midway on the Gulf tanker route between the two belligerents. Bahrain, consequently, became particularly distressed over the "tanker war" phase of the Gulf conflict.[11] Due to its small size, Bahrain remains heavily dependent upon regional security arrangements, principally the Gulf Cooperation Council (GCC).[12]

Oman. The sultanate of Oman occupies a strategic position above the vital chokepoint at the Strait of Hormuz, through which Gulf oil tankers must pass as they enter the Arabian Sea. With an area of 82,030 square miles, about the size of Kansas, Oman reaches some 1,000 miles from the mouth of the Persian Gulf, around the southeastern coast of the Arabian Peninsula. Its neighbors include the United Arab Emirates, Saudi Arabia, and South Yemen, all to the west. Oman's 1989 population was estimated to be 1,389,000, some 75 percent of whom are Ibadhi Muslims. More than 200,000 expatriate workers are counted among the Omani labor force.

The government of Oman is an absolute monarchy under the control of Sultan Qabus bin Said. There is no modern constitution or parliament; the sultan legislates by decree. In terms of economic policy, Oman's opportunities are linked to oil. Oman, however, is neither a member of the Organization of Petroleum Exporting Countries (OPEC), the price-setting cartel, nor the Organization of Arab Petroleum Exporting Countries (OAPEC), which imposed the Arab oil embargo in 1973–74. In foreign policy Oman pursues an independent line, albeit with strong ties to the West, particularly the United States. In a 1980 agreement Oman gave the United States access to military facilities and emergency landing rights in its territory. Importantly, Oman's dealings with the United States are those of an ally and clearly not akin to any client-state relationship.

Over the past two decades the Gulf states have been caught up in the transition from traditional societies to those experiencing the process of rapid modernization in the Western sense. Authoritarian political rule is exercised largely by tribally based ruling families whose leaders are wary of innovative, participatory political systems. Relatedly, in several Gulf states, notably Kuwait, Qatar, and the United Arab Emirates, the expatriate labor force outnumbers the indigenous population. Many expatriates are well-educated Palestinian Arabs.

The rise of a revolutionary regime in Iran launching an anti-Western crusade, aggravated by the onset of the Iran-Iraq War, presented the Arab Gulf states with a serious security challenge. Apprehensions rose that Iran's brand of religious zeal might infect local populations and that Iran might attack other Arab states in the region. Gulf states came to recognize dual threats of subversion and direct military attack from Iran. They also recognized that political complexities and uncertainties accompanied reliance on Western governments, particularly the United States, for defense from Iranian attack. By the end of the Gulf War in mid–1988, the effectiveness of the defensive role played by Western governments against the Iranian threat had tempered those doubts.[13]

Islamic Fundamentalism

A third contemporary geopolitical force operating throughout the Gulf region, and indeed throughout the Muslim world, concerns the revival of Islamic fundamentalism. The power and saliency of the phenomenon was clearly demonstrated in early 1989 by the severe international reaction of Muslims against Salman Rushdie's novel, *The Satanic Verses*. Often fundamentalism is viewed as dangerously radical, terrorist, or militant. In broad scope, it actually personifies a more moderate trend. Fundamentalism generally represents a populist movement coming in response to poverty and unequal distribution of wealth in society. Islamic fundamentalism is rooted in frustrations of coping with modernity and embodies a vibrant reaction to the postcolonial introduction of material goods and secular Western beliefs into traditional Muslim societies.

It is in the profound rejection of Western materialism and secular values that the dramatic impact of Islamic fundamentalism is felt, and it is in Iran where that message has emanated most fervently since 1979.

During the 1980s the Iranian theocracy preached revolutionary fundamentalism, principally aimed to appeal to underprivileged and impoverished Shi'ites in the region. Large Shi'a communities in Iraq, Saudi Arabia, and Bahrain supplied opportunities for asserting Iranian hegemony throughout the Gulf, and this realization raised serious concern among local Gulf sheikhdoms during the war. Not surprisingly, the Gulf states tended to support Iraq politically in the conflict.[14]

The Soviet Union

A fourth geopolitical concern in the Gulf focuses on the regional ambitions of the Soviet Union. It is fair to conclude that the Soviet Union displayed restraint in the Gulf region over the past decade, which may be largely explained by its preoccupation with Afghanistan and internal domestic problems. Still, the Soviet Union retains great vested interest in restraining Islamic fundamentalism in the Gulf, especially given rising Islamic consciousness and nationalistic restiveness in Soviet republics with large Muslim populations, for example, in Soviet Azerbaijan.

The principal Soviet geopolitical interest in the Persian Gulf has been to achieve sufficient influence there to reassure its own security concerns. Soviet strategy involves denial of the region to the West, or at least the diminution of Western influence there. Soviet policy in the Gulf is aimed principally at reducing the influence of the United States and undercutting the predominance of the conservative states. This latter point becomes evident if one realizes that Soviet influence holds far greater sway with Baathist Iraq and Marxist South Yemen than with Iran, Saudi Arabia, or the Gulf sheikhdoms. Nevertheless, Soviet policy during the Gulf War was pragmatic, flexible, and generally cautious in avoiding confrontation with the United States.[15]

A secondary interest of the Soviet Union in the Gulf is to gain access to the petroleum supplies for itself and its East European allies. Very possibly, Soviet interests in the region will correspondingly shift and expand as the Soviet Union's own oil reserves dwindle in coming decades.

CONCLUSION

The war between Iran and Iraq highlighted the geopolitical interests at risk in the Gulf. There are long-standing desires by Western states to preserve friendly relations with moderate Gulf states by encouraging regional security and maintaining a stable balance of power in the region. During the 1980s the Iran-Iraq War threatened to upset that arrangement. By broadening the regional conflict, greater opportunities were opened for Iranian hegemony to spread throughout the Gulf. Likewise, the possibility was created for the Soviet Union to become more politically and militarily involved in the region. Such developments, calculated in geopolitical terms, could radically alter the balance of power in the Gulf, threaten local moderate Arab governments, and jeopardize access by Western states to oil from the Gulf.

Western concern and awareness over the Persian Gulf region significantly increased during the 1980s. Unimpeded access to Gulf oil remains crucially important for the economic well-being of the United States, Western Europe, and Japan. During the early 1980s these geopolitical stakes assumed greater saliency as the Gulf became perceived as a potential region for superpower rivalry, given the loss of U.S. influence in Iran and the Soviet Union's costly invasion of Afghanistan in 1979. Since the advent of Mikhail Gorbachev to power in 1985, however, the Gulf situation has been characterized more by a mixture of quiet U.S.-Soviet cooperation and traditional competition. Important also is that since March 1985 the conservative Gulf states have moved to abandon the traditional view of the Soviet Union as a pariah state; witness the recent opening of diplomatic ties with the Soviet Union by Qatar, Oman, and the United Arab Emirates. No less significant is that Soviet-Saudi and Soviet-Bahraini relations have warmed noticeably. Similarly, in mid-June 1989 Iran also undertook an initiative to better ties with the Soviet Union, as then Speaker of the Parliament and now President Hashemi Rafsanjani visited Moscow. Rafsanjani's discussions with President Gorbachev centered on improving cooperation in economic, scientific, and technical relations. Reportedly, much was accomplished by Rafsanjani during his visit, including agreement on reopening Iran's natural gas pipeline to the Soviet Union, restoration of railroad service across the border, and securing possible arms sales. The pattern here is clear: The Soviet Union is markedly improving its diplomatic and economic standing with the Gulf states, a development that over the long term could present serious geopolitical problems for Western governments.

Legal and diplomatic interests remain at stake in the Gulf. Preserving freedom of navigation and open sealanes in the Gulf, with oil commerce flowing through the Strait of Hormuz at reasonable prices, endures as a vital concern of Western governments.[16] Maintaining regional stability through the efforts of the Gulf Cooperation Council is viewed as being diplomatically desirable as well, although the GCC states staunchly refuse to act as a surrogate for Western or U.S. interests in the region.[17] Underlying these ambitions is the need to bring the Iran-Iraq War to a negotiated conclusion, with neither side emerging as declared victor in order to allow both governments to save political face.

In sum, there is good and bad geopolitical news for the Gulf region. The good news is that Iran and Iraq have now agreed to a U.N.-sponsored cease-fire.[18] This situation has raised hopes in Western Europe of the greatest construction bonanza since the Saudi Arabian petro-dollar rush of the 1970s. The eight-year-long Gulf War left both belligerents with devastating damage that must be repaired. There are still massive amounts of petromonies available in underground oil reserves. With estimates for work and equipment needed by Iran and Iraq ranging as high as $500 billion, tremendously lucrative opportunities for Western firms appear to be at hand. The death of Ayatollah Khomeini in June 1989 has fueled optimism that these prospects may become reality.

The bad news is that the Gulf remains a crucible of fragile stability, challenged by ambitious radical regimes. In Iran the passing of Ayatollah Khomeini has prompted hopes of more moderate Iranian policies toward the West, but that remains to be seen. Concern by moderate Arab governments still hangs over uncertainties inherent in Iran's new theocratic government and the likelihood that Islamic fundamentalism will be used to propel its international influence throughout the Muslim world.

In Iraq President Saddam Hussein continues to pursue his personal quest to make Iraq the hegemonic power in the Gulf and to replace Egypt as the leader of the Arab world. Both Iran and Iraq (as well as other Middle Eastern states) are now armed with chemical weapons and ballistic missiles, a situation that invites horrific scenarios in the event all-out war in the region should once again erupt. When the ingredient of nuclear weapons, presumably possessed by Israel, is added to the regional military mix, a recipe exists for massive conflagration.[19] The fact that both superpowers rely on arms sales as a principal instrument of regional influence does little to alleviate concern. The mutual unwillingness of the United States and the Soviet Union—as well as their allies—to agree to limit the quantity and quality of weapons exported to the Gulf region exacerbates the already-high levels of intraregional tensions. Given these trends, policies by Western governments should be driven less by long-standing assumptions about the Gulf and more by informed geopolitical considerations that protect Western interests and contribute to regional stability. While certain states must take a leading role, none should assume a unilateral one.

During the 1980s the war between Iran and Iraq underscored the extravagant cost of political, economic, and social dislocations caused by personal animosities and historical antagonisms in the Gulf. The future challenge for Gulf governments and the international community will be to intensify efforts dedicated to resolving political disputes before they are permitted to erupt into regional warfare. The most profound revelation from the Gulf War experience is plainly obvious: War is a wasteful human tragedy, with no real victor. It is a geopolitical lesson that begs not to be forgotten.

NOTES

1. For elaboration of the causes of the Gulf War, see Edmund Ghareeb, "The Roots of Crisis: Iraq and Iran," Chapter 2 in this volume.

2. Mark A. Heller, "Turmoil in the Gulf," *New Republic*, April 23, 1984, p. 16.

3. Alvin J. Cottrell, ed., *The Persian Gulf States: A General Survey* (Baltimore: Johns Hopkins University Press, 1980), pp. 541–48.

4. Gerald Blake, "Bab al Mandeb and the Strait of Hormuz" (map 47), in John Dewdney and Jonathan Mitchell, *The Cambridge Atlas of the Middle East and North Africa* (Cambridge: Cambridge University Press, 1987), p. 97. On the strategic importance of the Strait of Hormuz, see generally A. H. Cordesman, *The Gulf and the Search for Strategic Stability* (Boulder, Colo.: Westview Press, 1984), and R. K. Ramazani, *The Persian Gulf and the Strait of Hormuz* (The Hague: Martinus Nijhoff, 1979).

5. Much of the following country data is drawn from Mark S. Hoffman, ed., *The World Almanac and Book of Facts, 1989* (New York: Pharos Books, 1989), pp. 654 (Bahrain), 684–85 (Iran), 685–86 (Iraq), 692 (Kuwait), 704–5 (Oman), 710 (Qatar), 712–13 (Saudi Arabia), and 727 (United Arab Emirates). See also David R. Tarr and Bryan R. Daves, eds., *The Middle East*, 6th ed. (Washington, D.C.: Congressional Quarterly, 1986), pp. 217–24.

6. "World Survey," *Oil and Gas Journal*, December 26, 1988, p. 48.

7. See Eric Hooglund, "Strategic and Political Objectives in the Gulf War: Iran's View," Chapter 3 in this volume.

8. "World Survey," *Oil and Gas Journal*, December 28, 1981, p. 86, and "World Survey," December 28, 1987, p. 86.

9. See Phebe Marr, "The Iran-Iraq War: The View from Iraq," Chapter 4 in this volume.

10. See the discussion in David D. Caron, "Choice and Duty in Foreign Affairs: The Reflagging of the Kuwaiti Tankers," Chapter 10 in this volume, and Thomas L. McNaugher, "U.S. Policy and the Gulf War: A Question of Means," Chapter 7 in this volume.

11. Tarr and Daves, *The Middle East*, p. 218.

12. See Joseph A. Kechichian, "The Gulf Cooperation Council and the Gulf War," Chapter 6 in this volume.

13. See Maxwell Orme Johnson, "The Role of U.S. Military Force in the Gulf War," Chapter 8 in this volume.

14. See generally Kechichian, "The Gulf Cooperation Council and the Gulf War."

15. See Mark N. Katz, "Moscow and the Gulf War," Chapter 9 in this volume.

16. See Boleslaw Adam Boczek, "The Law of Maritime Warfare and Neutrality in the Gulf War," Chapter 11 in this volume, and McNaugher, "U.S. Policy and the Gulf War."

17. I am indebted to Professor R. K. Ramazani for highlighting this point. See also his contribution to this volume, "Peace and Security in the Persian Gulf: A Proposal," Chapter 14.

18. See Anthony Clark Arend, "The Role of the United Nations in the Iran-Iraq War," Chapter 12 in this volume, and Charles G. MacDonald, "Iran, Iraq,

and the Cease-Fire Negotiations: Contemporary Legal Issues,'' Chapter 13 in this volume.

19. See Bernard Reich, ''Israel and the Iran-Iraq War,'' Chapter 5 in this volume.

PART I

STRATEGIC AND POLITICAL DIMENSIONS

2

The Roots of Crisis

Iraq and Iran

Edmund Ghareeb

On July 17, 1988, Iran surprised the world, and probably most of its own citizens, by accepting United Nations Security Council Resolution 598, which called for an end to hostilities and a negotiated solution to the Iran-Iraq War. This dramatic development was received with some skepticism by the outside world since it appeared to contradict the Iranian leadership's perception of the conflict as a battle between "Islam and blasphemy" and its avowed goal of overthrowing and punishing Saddam Hussein and his ruling Baath party in Baghdad. The decision contradicted pronouncements made only days earlier by both Iran's prime minister and interior minister that denounced any negotiated end to the war as an insult to Islam and its defenders, and it ran counter to everything Iran's leaders had proclaimed for close to eight years of war.[1]

Three days later the decision was grudgingly confirmed by none other than Ayatollah Khomeini, Iran's supreme leader, who nevertheless compared the action to "swallowing poison." In fact, Khomeini proved himself to be more cognizant of the changing political and military realities than many of his followers and critics had assumed. It is widely believed that Khomeini made the decision once he was convinced by his son, Ahmad, and his closest aide, Ali Akbar Hashemi Rafsanjani, not only that Iran could not win the war, but that the survival of the Islamic regime itself was perhaps at stake.

In the end, the guns fell silent for a combination of domestic, regional, and international factors. By 1987–88 the war had entered a new phase, with growing Iranian and Iraqi missile and air attacks against each other's capitals and civilian centers, and with attacks against tankers in the Gulf. The ruin and terror caused by the "war of the cities" and the use of chemical weapons left a devastating impact, not only on an increasingly war-weary population, but more importantly on Iran's soldiers, who seemed unwilling to continue the war. Iranian leaders became convinced following a string of Iraqi battlefield victories (al-Faw, al-Shalamjah, Mehran, and the Majnun Islands) that they had no chance of achieving a military victory over Iraq.

Furthermore, Iran's economy was in shambles and its military and economic reserves were depleted at a time when Iraq's superiority in weapons, manpower, and morale was becoming quite evident. The increasing regional and international isolation of Iran, the changing attitudes of the two superpowers—particularly the United States in the wake of the Iran-Contra affair—and the effort to contain the war and to bring it to an end were also contributing factors.[2]

The end of the fighting, which came two months before the eighth anniversary of the war, was only the latest of many surprises accompanying a conflict surrounded by much confusion and uncertainty. The war had surprised specialists and contradicted many of their predictions about its causes, outbreak, development, impact, and duration. It has probably even confounded the analyses and expectations of the protagonists themselves.

Almost to its end, the war generally appeared to be a distant and largely irrelevant conflict between "two barely indistinguishable four-letter countries."[3] Only intermittent fears about the impact of the fighting on the West's oil supplies grabbed headlines. Interest appeared to recede when the threats proved groundless. Besides direct U.S. involvement, other issues that brought the war before public attention, directly or indirectly, were the hostage crisis, allegations about the use of chemical weapons, the use of children in shock-wave attacks, important battles with high casualty figures, the Iran-Contra scandal, and the U.S. escorting of Kuwaiti tankers.

There has also been a natural tendency in the West to ignore the uncertainties surrounding the war and the Iranian Revolution. The uncertainty was greatest when it came to analyzing the two most critical factors affecting the war, that is, the course of the Iranian Revolution and the outcome of the war.[4] What is certain, however, is that this has been the longest and bloodiest conflict since World War II. Accurate figures of the casualties and the economic costs of the war are difficult to obtain. Some experts have estimated the number of casualties on both sides as high as one million dead and three million wounded, in addition to tens of thousands of prisoners, millions of homeless, hundreds of billions of dollars in material damage, and inestimable human suffering.[5]

THE ROOTS OF CONFLICT

The roots of this tragic conflict have been deeply embedded in confusion. The war has been described as a conflict over territory, or portrayed as a Sunni versus Shi'i religious struggle, or depicted as a personal conflict between Iraq's Hussein and Iran's Khomeini. It is clear that these characterizations are inaccurate oversimplifications. The quarrel between the two countries is deep and complex and goes beyond a mere territorial dispute. This dispute, in fact, may have been the justification needed to reopen a conflict of historic, territorial, political-strategic, and legal proportions that has been accentuated in recent times by nationalism and by disputes over power and ideas.[6]

Some researchers have looked deep into history in their search for the roots of this conflict, tracing it back to the days of antiquity.[7] While it may be a bit farfetched to reach several thousand years back into history to search for causes of a modern war, it is nevertheless significant to point out that tensions and rivalry (as well as close cooperation) have long characterized relations between these two countries, their predecessors, and their peoples. The two countries lie on a geographic and cultural divide. Some historians have viewed the conflict in terms of Arab versus Persian and have traced origins of the conflict to seventh-century Arab-Muslim invasions of Iran, which converted most Persians to Islam, and to the period preceding these invasions.[8] For others, roots of the contemporary conflict began in the religious struggle between the Sunni Ottomans and the Shi'i Safavids in the sixteenth century and in their confrontation over the borders.[9] Others, however, see the present conflict in terms of strategic and political competition for regional hegemony and control of economic resources in a war heavy with religious and ideological symbols.[10]

Iraqi leaders and analysts have looked at this conflict as the last phase of a historic struggle between two civilizations and peoples that goes back to the Sassanid-Babylonian rivalry and has continued, following the conversion of Persians to Islam, down through the Ottoman-Safavid conflict to the present day.[11] They present the conflict as part of a historic, national, and cultural conflict before and after Islam. They point to the battles of Thi Qar (pre-Islamic), Nahawand, and Qadisiyyah and to the Persian General Abu Muslim al-Khurasani's role in bringing down the Omayyad dynasty, the conflicts between the Caliph Harun al-Rashid and his Barrmacid ministers, and the struggle between al-Amin and al-

Mamun for the caliphate as manifestations of Persian efforts to undermine the Arab state and Islam. They further point to the rise of the
Shu'ubiya (ethnicism) movement, which aimed at seeking equality between non-Arab, particularly Persian, Muslims and Arab Muslims, taking pride in the Persian heritage and civilization and asserting its
superiority over the Arabs and their culture. Furthermore, the conflict
was seen not only as a manifestation of national consciousness, but also
as a means to undermine Islam and Arab rule by introducing pre-Islamic
practices and espousing creeds aimed at undermining Islam.[12]

The conflict is also viewed in historic terms by Iranian scholars and
historians, both secular and religious. The secular nationalist element
believes that "the roots of the Arab-Iranian ethnic and religious animosity lie in the Arab defeat of Iran in the 7th century A.D. The Arabs'
military conquest of Iran, however, was not accompanied by a cultural
victory, and it did not eliminate the Iranian spirit of independence. Thus
despite the Islamization of Iran, the Arabs and the Persians remained
ethnically and culturally apart."[13]

Other scholars have argued that the destruction of the Sassanid empire
by the Muslim Arabs at the battle of Qadisiyyah in 637 A.D. has been
viewed as a "great calamity" that "has not been forgotten by the Persians," as other invasions had been.[14] Another cause is attributed to the
"Arabs' proprietary attitude towards Islam's cultural legacy including
the part contributed by non-Arab nations—especially Iranians."[15] These
and other scholars contend that Iran has been able to maintain its distinctive character and identity and has been able to adapt and remold
Islam to suit its own cultural particularism.

The religious leaders of Iran have also used mostly Islamic symbols
and events to refer to the conflict as one between Islam and blasphemy,
between the martyred Hussein and his persecutor Yazid. Furthermore,
President Bani-Sadr, during the battle for Dezful in the fall of 1980,
summoned imprisoned air force officers who had been jailed for plotting
against the Islamic Republic and implored their help to defend Iran by
comparing them to the legendary pre-Islamic hero, Rustum, who had
fought against foreign invaders.[16]

During the early days of the Gulf War, each side resorted to the use
of pejorative characterizations loaded with negative historic symbols to
describe the other side. The Iraqis described the battle as the "second
Qadisiyyah" against the "racist" Persian maji (Zoroastrian priests) who
"harbor rancor against the Arabs," while the Iranians spoke of "back-
stabbing" and "uncouth Arabs" who drink "camel milk and eat lo-
custs."[17]

The historical tensions between Iraq and Iran began as early as the
sixteenth century, when Iraq was the focus of Ottoman-Persian rivalry.
The emergence of Persia as a Shi'i state under the strong leadership of

Shah Ismail al-Safawi paved the way for a series of bitter confrontations with the entrenched Ottoman state, which upheld Sunni Islam. The adoption by Persia of Shi'ism as the state religion reflected a strong, latent ethnocultural identity at a period preceding modern nationalism, as well as a desire to separate itself from the Sunni Ottoman state and control Iraq and the northern Gulf area. Sunni-Shi'i schism had become a territorial as well as a communal rift. Both Ottomans and Persians viewed the area in strategic terms. The Persians, however, viewed it in religious terms as well. Nearly all of the Shi'i shrines and holy places are located within Iraq, and the Persians sought to extend their domination over the southern Euphrates and the northern Gulf area.[18] This point became especially important when the radical Islamic regime, led by Khomeini, came to power in 1979.

The territorial conflict, which existed regardless of the nature of the regime in power in either of the two countries, dates back to the struggle between the Ottoman and Safavid dynasties, which had manifested itself in clashes over the border. Bruce Hardcastle has provided an ironically amusing historical sketch of this territorial-legal dispute:

Historians of diplomacy will find in the Iraqi decision to continue diplomacy by other means the failure of the 1975 Algiers Agreement, an accord which was to have rectified what Iranians saw as the intolerable one-sidedness of the treaty of 1937, which the Iranians had agitated for, to adjust what they claimed was the patent unfairness of the 1914 border demarcations, which were called for in the protocols of 1911 and 1913, which were to implement the 1847 treaty, which was negotiated to amplify certain articles of an 1823 treaty, which reconfirmed a 1746 treaty which confirmed the 1639 treaty of Zhigad, which left basically intact the 1555 treaty of Constantinople, an Ottoman-Safavid treaty which roughly defined what is the international if somewhat violated border between Iraq and Iran.[19]

The main point of contention over these agreements dealt with the issue of the Shatt al-Arab waterway, a narrow but strategic body of water formed by the confluence of the Euphrates, Tigris, and Qarun rivers as they flow into the mouth of the Gulf. The second Erzerum treaty signed in 1847 is viewed as the first treaty concluded between two sovereign Islamic states in accordance with Western practices and rules. As such, it established a precedent for future agreements based on the principles of peace and coexistence, territorial sovereignty, and noninterference in internal affairs. This treaty, while ceding the entire eastern bank of the waterway to Persia, was not deemed satisfactory by the Persian leaders, who later considered it "inequitable" and "foreign imposed" because it only ceded sovereignty over Abadan and its port and anchorage, but not over the waters of Shatt al-Arab.

Differences arose in the early twentieth century over interpretation of the 1847 Erzerum treaties. The Shatt al-Arab became an important issue to Iran with the growth of the port of Khorramshahr and the discovery of oil in 1908. Iran was displeased over the payment of Ottoman import duties by ships carrying oil-drilling equipment and other cargo into Khorramshahr and began to call for a revision of the agreement. With Britain and Russia mediating, the two sides signed two protocols in 1911 and 1913 that recognized the growing importance of Khorramshahr and accepted the *thalweg* (the navigable midchannel boundary) principle across its port. The rest of the river stayed under British control.

Following World War I Iraq emerged as the eastern Arab successor to the Ottoman state. Consequently, the question of frontiers surfaced again as a matter of dispute between the two parties, along with a number of other issues, particularly Iraq's recognition by Iran. The recognition problem was resolved in 1929 when Iraq abrogated a judicial agreement with Britain over special privileges. Iran had sought unsuccessfully to apply this agreement to tens of thousands of Persian Shi'is who had settled in and around the Shi'ite holy places in Iraq.

Iran, under the leadership of the nationalist Reza Shah, also began to question the Constantinople protocol, claiming that it had been signed under duress when Iran was weak and had no choice but to accept. Border incursions occurred in the 1930s, and Iraq ultimately brought the issue before the League of Nations. In arguments before the League's Council, Iraq's foreign minister, Nuri al-Said, underlined clearly the strategic importance of the Shatt for Iraq. He pointed out that Iran had a long coastline, a deep-water harbor, and many ports, while the Shatt remained Iraq's only access to the sea; he further added that Basra was Iraq's only port, and that Iraq thought it undesirable that another power should command this channel from one base.

Iran responded that it had not formally ratified the treaties involved. Turkey and Britain finally helped mediate the dispute, which led to a new treaty that fixed the frontier between the two countries in 1937. The new treaty recognized Iraqi sovereignty over the Shatt, but Iraq accepted that the *thalweg* principle should apply across from Abadan as well as Khorramshahr.

The ability of the two countries to overcome their differences was undoubtedly affected by a number of domestic, regional, and international factors, including the Italian invasion of Ethiopia in 1935 and the rising Kurdish nationalist activity in the region as a whole. These events contributed to the signing of the Sa'dabad pact in 1937 among Turkey, Iran, Iraq, and Afghanistan. The close relations that had developed since 1937 between Iran and Iraq, however, were unable to withstand the far-reaching consequence of the 1958 Iraqi revolution, which overthrew the monarchy and changed the direction of Iraq's domestic and foreign policies.

The struggle against Western colonialism, World War II, and the creation of Israel unleashed new currents and social forces in the region that separated the two countries and pitted them on opposite sides. The Iraqi military that had overthrown the Hashemites followed a different path from that of the Iranian military, which remained loyal to the monarchy and continued to defend it until 1979. In addition, a new generation had begun to demand political participation and to question the direction of domestic and foreign policies adopted by the ruling groups of both countries. In Iraq, as the attempt by civilian reformers to achieve change by peaceful methods failed, the military became the means to achieve social, economic, and political reforms.

The 1958 military revolt in Iraq brought a bloody end to the ruling family and sent shock waves throughout the region not unlike those felt in the wake of the Iranian Revolution almost twenty years later. The new Iraqi regime's goal of radical social and economic policies and its opposition to Western-dominated alliances were perceived as threats to regional stability by Iran, conservative Arab governments, and the West.

Relations between Iraq and Iran deteriorated rapidly as hostile propaganda erupted in the media of both countries. In 1959 the two countries entered into a new phase of conflict, which manifested itself by Iran's demands to alter the 1937 Shatt al-Arab treaty and its support for Iraqi dissidents, including Iraq's Kurds in their struggle against Baghdad.

The situation worsened with the coming of the Arab Baath (Renaissance) Party to power in 1968. Iran viewed with suspicion the Socialist pan-Arab regime in Baghdad that advocated Arab nationalist goals, preservation of the Arab character of the Gulf, and rejection of security arrangements dominated by Iran. The antagonism between the two sides was fueled further by Iran's aid to the Kurdish leader, Mulla Mustafa al-Barzani, and by its collusion in a conspiracy to overthrow the Iraqi regime in 1969. Iran renewed its claims to the Shatt and on April 19, 1969, unilaterally abrogated the 1937 treaty, claiming that it had been imposed on Iran by the British.

Superpower rivalries further divided the Iraqi and Iranian governments and pushed the conflict to a higher level of intransigence. In the wake of Britain's decision to withdraw from the Gulf by 1971, Western powers appeared to be developing a regional security policy aimed at excluding Iraq. The Nixon Doctrine advocated reliance on Iran and, to a much lesser extent, on Saudi Arabia to maintain security in the Gulf. To this end, the United States began a massive supply of arms to Iran. These developments were viewed with much suspicion by Iraq, which envisaged them as serious challenges to its own interests and ambitions in the Gulf. Furthermore, these events were occurring at a time when Iraq's interest in the Gulf—and particularly in the Shatt al-Arab—had been greatly enhanced as a result of a number of domestic economic and political events and concerns. The Baathist regime's quest for security—a matter of basic priority since the Baath ouster in 1963—required creation of prerequisites for stability by developing a strong military, by improving the living standards of the people, and by diversifying Iraq's vast industrial and agricultural potential.[20]

In order to achieve these objectives, the government needed to increase revenues by fully exploiting its oil wealth. The nationalization of the Iraqi oil company in 1972 and the increase in oil prices in 1973–74 had a dramatic impact on Iraq's oil economy and consequently spurred major infrastructural developments in the southern part of the country near the Gulf. Iraq's growing economy and its increasing reliance on the Gulf implied an enhanced strategic importance for the Shatt al-Arab and the Gulf. The country is confined to 38 miles of coastline on the Gulf and mostly shallow-water ports. Consequently, during the 1970s Iraq's economic security became vulnerable to the increasing power and demands of Tehran.

As Iraq attempted to gain control of its oil wealth by nationalizing its oil, it turned to the Soviets and signed a 15–year treaty of friendship, largely because the United States was backing the Shah and encouraging him to play the role of Gulf policeman. Iraq's radical nationalism was perceived as a threat by Iran, which sought to isolate or overthrow the increasingly stable Baath regime. As a result, the Shah, with U.S. and Israeli aid, used the Kurdish weapon to undermine the Iraqi government.

The Kurds' quest for autonomy in oil-rich northern Iraq has been a recurrent nightmare for the central government in Baghdad for many years. The Kurdish problem is both an internal and external problem. It is internal in that the Kurds are ethnically and linguistically distinct from the Arab population of Iraq and as such have for many years desired to have special status and even autonomy from Iraq. Yet, these concerns for national expression were exploited by external powers which had interests in destabilizing Iraq. With the help of these foreign powers, and in the face of inept resistance by successive Iraqi governments since 1958, the Kurdish rebellion smoldered and blazed until 1968, when the Baath party was restored to power. The Baathists made conciliatory overtures to the Kurds in the form of offers of national rights and limited autonomy. However, Mulla Mustafa al-Barzani, encouraged and supported by the United States, Iran, and Israel, insisted on control over Kirkuk and its oil resources and a separate Kurdish army as well as an independent Kurdish foreign policy. All these demands were rejected by the central government, and heavy fighting ensued.

In 1974–75 a new threat of war emerged between the two countries because of Iran's escalated support for the Kurdish forces, the increasing border clashes, and the shelling of each other's towns following a series of significant Iraqi military successes. The growing gravity of this situation prompted mediation efforts by Jordan's King Hussein, Egypt's President Sadat, and Algeria's President Boumedienne. These mediation efforts succeeded, and an agreement was signed that netted gains for the two sides. For Iran, the agreement meant Iraq's acceptance of the demands that the boundaries between the two countries in the Shatt al-Arab run along the *thalweg* line, and that Iraq end aid to Iranian dissidents and Arab and Baluchi secessionists. For Iraq, the agreement signified an end to the Kurdish rebellion and upholding the status quo for the land frontiers, which translated into returning to Iran 76 square miles of land borders. One article of the accord, however, stipulated that violation of any of the treaty's provisions would render it null and void.

Relations between Iraq and Iran improved markedly after 1975 as both governments appeared to carry out their agreement in good faith. Furthermore, both sides avoided any disruption of oil production and established a strong front within the Organization of Petroleum Exporting Countries that called for increasingly higher prices.

THE IRANIAN REVOLUTION

It was the Iranian Revolution that brought down the Shah in 1979 that, more than any other event, kindled new ideological, territorial, strategic, political, and personal disputes and led to the longest and bloodiest war between the two countries. The emergence of a radical and revisionist Islamic regime in Tehran altered the regional military and political balance of power, sent psychological shock waves throughout the region, and ushered in an era of violence and turmoil that sparked the bloody war between Iraq and Iran. Iran appeared to pose serious challenges to the status quo.

To begin to understand the regional impact of the Iranian Revolution in its early days, it is useful to consider an assessment of it published in 1980 by Nasif Nassar, a prominent Arab nationalist intellectual. He described the revolution as "an extraordinary phenomenon in the history of the Islamic and the Third World. It is extraordinary in its populism, in its deep-rootedness and in the manner it brought down the Shah. Because of these factors it is awesome, breathtaking and puzzling."[21]

The Iranian Revolution, at least during its early days, tended to show that Islam, as a way of life, had the ability to reassert itself and to pose challenges to the control of the superpowers. It posed serious military, economic, ideological, and strategic challenges to the states of the region. The revolution challenged existing governments and appealed to the frustrated and angry masses.

The Iranian Revolution was able to tap important religious sentiment by presenting itself as a Muslim, not merely as a Shi'i, revolution. It was able to carry its appeal to Arab countries because it portrayed itself as the voice of the "Mustadhafin" as well as the real challenge to Zionism and to the "Mustakbirin," the force of international arrogance. Strategically, Iran's size, economic resources, population, and geography made the country an important regional actor. Even under the Shah, Iran had been able to extend its influence beyond its borders; but by toppling the man considered to be the most powerful ruler in the region, closure of the Israeli embassy, support for the Palestinian cause, and above all, its Islamic ideology, the revolution had widespread appeal and posed serious challenges to neighboring regimes. Success of the revolution created a new security environment. A revolutionary government determined to spread its ideology replaced a regime selected by the United States to play the role of regional policeman. The disputes that had been set aside by the Algiers accord were acutely revived.

For Iraq, the Iranian Revolution could not have occurred at a worse time. As a result of its internal stability, increased oil revenues, and a more pragmatic foreign policy, the country had begun to come from its isolation and to emerge as a major regional player, particularly in the wake of the Camp David Accords. Internally, the regime had adopted ambitious development programs that had significantly improved the standard of living for the average Iraqi.

After the Shah's departure, Iraqi leaders welcomed Iranian statements declaring that Iran no longer would play the role of Gulf policeman. Foreign Minister Hammadi praised this stand as a "positive step toward the establishment of cordial relations toward the Arab Gulf states."[22] Similar views were echoed by Saddam Hussein, who declared: "We are keen on cooperation with Iran in a way that will ensure the interests and security of the people in the area as well as preserve the historic ties of non-interference and respect for national sovereignty. . . . Any system which does not side with our enemy, respects our independence and whose oil policy is consistent with the interest of our two peoples will certainly command our respect and appreciation."[23]

Deputy Prime Minister and Revolutionary Command Council member Nai'm Haddad told this writer in the spring of 1979 that Iraq welcomed Iranian stands opposing the superpower presence in the Gulf and Iranian support for the Palestinian cause. He added that some Iranian leaders had been attacking Iraq, but that the Iranian government was still in its infancy and should not be prematurely judged. He also expressed hope for economic cooperation between the two countries.

These hopes for better relations did not materialize, however. Deep personal, ideological, and political differences continued to divide the two countries. The bad blood between the leaders of Iraq and Iran may have started with Iraq's expulsion of Iranian leader Ayatollah Khomeini after he had begun to escalate his activities against the Shah's regime in the spring of 1978. In accordance with the Algiers agreement, Iraq asked Khomeini to cease his activities or leave the country after protests from Iran's prime minister.[24] Khomeini and his followers interpreted this move as a hostile act against their revolution and harbored resentment against the Iraqi leadership, believing that "every opponent of the Imam must be punished." Khomeini was offended by and condemned Saddam Hussein for receiving Iran's queen in November 1978 at the height of the revolution and turmoil.

In addition, Khomeini and other religious leaders appeared to believe that their revolution was not simply an Iranian event but the beginning of a world revolution, with Iran only being the starting point. The Islamic Revolution must spread to neighboring countries. They believed that Iraq, because of its religious composition and geography, was an obvious place to start.

Khomeini and his followers believed that the existing international system is essentially unjust because the superpowers (the oppressors) arrogantly dominate the world at the expense of the oppressed, who consist mainly of Muslims and other Third World people. Under his concept, the *faqih*, or the supreme jurisprudent, has the obligation to pave the way for the return of the mahdi. All religious and political authority (except that which belongs to an infallible imam) belongs to the *faqih*.[25] Khomeini felt that Iran, as the first country where the *faqih* rules, should lead the way toward the establishment of an Islamic government of the disinherited in other parts of the world. Khomeini thus asserted: "We should try hard to export our revolution to the world. We should set aside the thought that we do not export our revolution, because Islam does not regard various Islamic countries differently and is the supporter of all oppressed people of the world. If we remain in an enclosed environment, we shall definitely face defeat."[26]

For Khomeini and other clerical leaders, the concept of the "nation-state" was alien and anti-Islamic. In addition, Khomeini saw nationalism as un-Islamic. "There are no nationalities in Islam. Islam supersedes and abolishes all of them. Nationalism is a pre-Islamic legacy." By denouncing nationalism, particularly Arab nationalism, and declaring his intent to export the revolution, Khomeini set himself on a collision course with the secular nationalist Baathists of Iraq.

Ideologically, the two regimes are at opposite ends of the spectrum. Iran is run by a theocratic, internationalistic (pan-Islamic) regime whose leaders insist on implementing the Shari'a as the supreme law of the land and make no attempts to hide their intention of exporting their Islamic ideology to other countries. Iraq is ruled by a secular, nationalist (pan-Arab) party that sees Arab nationalism at the core of its system of beliefs and views and hopes to establish a united Arab nation-state, not an Islamic one.[27] The conflict with Iran was perceived as an act aimed at defending the area from foreign interference and encirclement. Islam is seen as the "finest expression of the genius of Arabism and as a symbol of its identity." According to Baath party founder Michel Aflaq, Islam and Arabism have expressed the "inner spirit" of the Arab nation. But while emphasizing the organic link between Arabism and Islam, Aflaq stressed that revering the spiritual, historic, and cultural aspects of the religious heritage does not mean enslavement to the past and to tradition. Baathist views on the issue have been emphasized by Saddam Hussein, who stressed that Baathists oppose the "use of religion for political purposes" because adoption by the state of religious policies in dealing with secular affairs will only lead to "sectarian and religious conflicts that result in national division and disunity."[28]

Obviously aware of the religious and sectarian diversity of Iraq and of the Arab world, Hussein made it clear that politicization of religion "will lead to the division of our people not only between the religious and the non-religious but among the faithful themselves according to their various religious and sectarian affiliations and interpretations." He further warned that the use of religion as a cover for politics would be met with the iron fist of the revolution. Consequently, it was inevitable that such radically divergent ideologies toward sensitive issues of religion and nationalism would lead to conflict between the two regimes.

Use of Islam by Iranian leaders, their explicit call for a jihad to overthrow the "evil and atheist" Iraqi leadership, and their talk of exporting the revolution raised suspicions in the minds of Iraqi leaders, who felt that this could not occur except through interference in the ethnosectarian structure of Iraqi and Arab society. As a result, the Iraqis resorted to using the other major force in Arab politics—Arab nationalism. Charges by some Iranian leaders that Arab nationalism contained not Islamic but "Zionist, Fascist, and Nazi doctrines" added fuel to the fire. But the crunch came in April 1980 when Iran began to support the Kurdish rebels, led by the sons of the late Mulla Mustafa al-Barzani, who had resumed their activities in the Kurdish regions, and to provide military aid and training to the Iraqi Shi'ite Da'wa party (the call). Iraq accused Iran of border violations and of seeking to stir ethnic and sectarian divisions to overthrow the government. These acts were viewed by Iraq as direct violations of the Algiers accords. The Iraqis further charged that Iran was committing cross-border attacks and airspace violations, was refusing to return the 400 square kilometers in land area as agreed to by the Shah's government, and was seeking to maintain the Shah's gains while attempting to export its revolution to Iraq. Iraq also accused Iran of committing acts of sabotage and assassination in Iraq, including attacks on Information Minister Latif Nusayf al-Jasim and Tariq Aziz, a member of the RCC and the National and Regional Commands of the party. Hussein declared that such acts would not go un-punished, and Iraq responded by expelling thousands of Iranian residents in Iraq. The Iraqis accused Khomeini of being a "turbaned Shah" who was using Islam to cover his "Persian racist designs" to destabilize and dominate the Gulf.

Iran, in turn, accused Iraq of supporting Baluchi, Kurdish, Arab, and antiregime Persian groups in Iran, in addition to harboring monarchist opponents of the regime. Iran further charged Iraq with committing acts of spying and sabotage in Khuzistan and Kurdistan, inciting racial and sectarian hatred. Iraq accused Iran of engaging in cross-border attacks and airspace violations.[29] In addition, both sides appeared to be locked in a dispute over oil wells in Ilam, along the Iran-Iraq border.

The political dispute focused on the desire of both countries to assume a leading role in the region. Iran sought to play this role through emphasis on exporting its Islamic ideology. Iraq, on the other hand, did so in the name of Arab nationalism. Its government was stable, its economy was broadly based and expanding, and its military was strong. As the competition between Iraq and Iran intensified, Iraq also appeared to take up the role of the defender of the small Gulf states and of Gulf Arabism. Saddam Hussein articulated the charter of national principles on the anniversary of the Baathist coup of 1963 as a clear attempt to formulate a common Arab strategy, to offer the Arabs a third way as opposed to superpower tutelage, and to guide relations between the Arabs and their neighbors.[30]

Iran's growing hostility to Iraq may have had an unintended effect in strengthening the hands of a hardline faction in Baghdad that ultimately contributed to the timing and eruption of the war. Two schools of thought in Iraq's Baathist leadership had existed in Baghdad regarding how to deal with Iran. One group, led by President al-Bakr, advocated taking a neutral or even a favorable attitude toward revolutionary Iran because the two countries advocated similar policies, such as nonaligned foreign policy, full independence, and opposition to Zionism and the superpowers. There was also the hope that Iranian moderates would win the day in Tehran. The other group, led by Saddam Hussein, advocated a wait-and-see attitude until the situation cleared in Tehran. The argument here supposed that Khomeini's Iran was unlikely to alter its regional ambitions and that knowledge of Khomeini's personality and the signs from Tehran were not very encouraging. Therefore, a firm and uncompromising policy was required.[31]

The debate between these two schools of thought purportedly occurred during the first six months of 1979. The unabating Iranian hostility and the fall of Iran's moderates strengthened the hands of the faction calling for a firmer line and may even have encouraged President al-Bakr, who was in ill health, to resign and ask the RCC to elect a successor.

Hussein's assumption of supreme power was accompanied by a purge of several top party leaders. While no definitive explanation for the purges has been forthcoming, some observers have linked the timing of Hussein's inauguration and the purges to the conflicts with the rival Baathists in Syria and to the crisis generated by the revolution in Iran.

The ascendancy of Saddam Hussein to the chief position of power in Iraq meant that both states were now headed by tough, shrewd, charismatic, and determined personalities who were extremely ambitious and deeply committed to opposing worldviews. The personality differences added another mix to an already-explosive situation.

The old territorial dispute over the Shatt al-Arab and the land border erupted anew as the two countries searched for and responded to opportunities to act against each other. Iraq made several attempts to resolve the dispute and reduce tensions by sending numerous diplomatic notes to Iran, without much success. During the nonaligned summit Hussein met with the Iranian foreign minister, Ibrahim Yazdi, and urged Iran to end the "unjustified vilifications and transgressions" against Iraq and to undertake a revision of the 1975 Algiers agreement, which "was concluded under special circumstances in 1975 in which you took part of the Shatt al-Arab and must be returned to Iraq."

These talks led nowhere. Relations deteriorated further following the assassination attempts on top Iraqi leaders by pro-Iranian elements and Iraq's execution of the leading Iraqi Shi'ite cleric, who had headed the al-Da'wa party. Border skirmishes and media attacks continued to escalate until September 4, 1980, when the dispute entered a new phase as Iranian heavy artillery shelled the towns of Zurbatya, Khaniqin, and Naft Khanah from Zain al-Qaws, an area that the Algiers agreement had required be returned to Iraq. The Iraqi Foreign Ministry sent a note protesting the shelling and stated that the area belonged to Iraq. On September 9 Iraqi forces occupied Zain al-Qaws and the Sayf Sa'd area. On September 17 Hussein publicly announced Iraq's abrogation of the Algiers agreement because Iran had violated its provisions in word and deed, specifically by supporting Kurdish rebels and refusing to return the specified land areas. Consequently, the treaty became null and void in accordance with Article 4. Iraq sent a notice to Iran of its decision through the Iranian chargé d'affaires in Baghdad. The note remained unanswered for 39 days.

THE BALANCE SHEET

On September 22, 1980, Iraq ordered its troops across the border with Iran to "deliver a fatal blow to Iranian military targets." Debates over when and why the war started and assessment of responsibility are likely to preoccupy historians and researchers for many years to come. It is well documented, however, that it was Iraq that launched its troops across Iranian borders in what Baghdad saw as a preemptive attack in response to what is generally accepted as heavy Iranian provocation.

It is safe to assume that Iraq launched the invasion in terms of its perception of Iran's threat to its territory, ideology, and national interests. After more than a year and a half of the Iranian Revolution, the decision by Iraqi leaders to launch the attack appears to have been motivated by several factors, among them the following:

1. The Iranian Revolution contained inherent threats to Iraq's stability in its advocacy by word and deed of a religious ideology that promised to undermine Iraq's ethnosectarian fabric and its national cohesiveness.

2. Iranian attacks on border towns and posts, the infiltration of arms and saboteurs into Iraq, and the training and arming of Iraqi dissidents had to be stopped.

3. The belief existed in Iraq that it was not possible to reach an accommodation with a clerical leadership determined to export its brand of revolution to other countries, the first being Iraq.

4. There was a widespread belief (encouraged by Iranian dissidents and others) that Iran was vulnerable and its army divided and incapable of defending itself. In addition, Iran was isolated regionally and alienated from its main arms supplier, the United States, because of the hostage crisis. These conditions would allow Iraq to score quick military victories that would weaken and overthrow the revolutionary regime.

5. Saddam Hussein was determined to redress what he may have seen as a humiliation for Iraq in the 1975 Algiers agreement.

6. Iraq wanted to fill the leadership vacuum in the Arab world created by Egypt's decision to sign the Camp David Accords.

7. Iraq wished to wage what it believed to be an inevitable conflict on Iranian rather than Iraqi soil.

Iran's interests in a confrontation with Iraq may be seen in terms of the following factors:

1. Iran's leaders believed that Iraq was ripe for an Iranian-type revolution and that Iraqi Muslims, especially Shi'is, would rise up and overthrow the government.

2. The decision was made to punish Hussein and his Baath party for the expulsion of Khomeini from Iraq and for the harsh measures against Shi'i opponents. Mehdi Bazargan, Iran's first prime minister after the revolution, hinted at Khomeini's motives when he said that the war is the result of the revolution "because it had prepared the mentality for revenge and destruction from before."

3. Iran's leaders wished to divert attention from Iran's economic problems and to mobilize support against growing political and ethnic opposition that threatened the country's unity.

The war proved costly, with far-reaching implications. It has shattered Iran's ambitions to be at the center of a new Islamic union and ended its role as regional policeman. Its dominant regional role has been taken by Iraq, Pakistan, and, to a lesser extent, Turkey. The course of future events depends on the policies and attitudes adopted by the present leaders of Iran and Iraq. Despite its defeat, Iran remains a regional actor to be reckoned with. Its size, vast human and natural resources, and military and economic potential assure its reemergence as a major regional actor in the not-so-distant future. Iran's future course, however, remains uncertain. It could play a positive and constructive role in the region or a negative and disruptive one, depending on the direction of its policies and the responses from Iraq and other Gulf neighbors. If Iran is made to feel humiliated and isolated, it is likely to play a disruptive role; if Iran's leaders are determined to export the revolution or to avenge their defeat, it is likely that regional tensions will continue.

The Iraqi "victory" has enhanced that state's role and capabilities and turned Iraq into a major regional actor. In the end, the war has shown that nationalist identities and loyalties supersede religious ones. But while the war has checked and undermined the power of religious fundamentalism in the area, it has not been able to stop it altogether. The war encouraged nationalist and separatist tendencies and movements in the area, particularly among the Kurds, and resulted in harsh measures against Kurdish opponents in both countries. The war also accelerated the trend toward greater cooperation and security coordination among the Gulf and other Arab states, leading to the establishment of the Gulf Cooperation Council and the Arab Cooperation Council. The war has also led to greater polarization in the Arab world and encouraged Israel to invade Lebanon without fearing a unified Arab response. That invasion produced untold consequences for Lebanon, Syria, the Palestinians, Israel and the United States.

Termination of the fighting has not, however, led to peace. Little progress has been made so far in the negotiations, as mutual hostilities and suspicions continue to run deep. The Gulf War has been one of the most tragic and unfortunate developments in the history of the Middle East. It has pitted two neighboring peoples with great civilizations and cultures against each other in a savage conflict that will only produce losers unless the protagonists learn to avoid previous errors and mistakes.

Historical lessons show that victories are hollow in the long run because it will only be a matter of time before the vanquished people rise up again to avenge their perceived humiliation. Consequently, peace and regional security cannot be achieved unless the causes that created the conflict are eliminated. The consent of all parties concerned is essential for arriving at a just and lasting peace. It is to be hoped that both parties will come to realize that their real national interests and the lessons of war require that they eliminate by mutual consent the sources of friction. In the end, the two sides must recognize that their interests require noninterference in each other's internal affairs and equal access to the Shatt al-Arab. If they fail to do so, this latest conflict with roots in history, security, sovereignty, ideology, religion, and nationalism is likely to remain but one in a long chain of costly and recurring Gulf wars.

NOTES

1. Mansour Farhang, "Khomeini and Postwar Iran," *Nation*, November 21, 1988, p. 522.

2. Iraq's strategy of internationalizing the conflict began to bear fruit when Iran's attacks against Gulf countries supporting Iraq led both the Soviet Union and the United States to offer protection to Kuwaiti oil shipments and contributed to the U.S. decision to vigorously pursue "Operation Staunch" aimed at curtailing the flow of arms to Iran.

3. Mark Heller, "Turmoil in the Gulf," *New Republic*, April 23, 1984, p. 16.

4. Jeffrey Record, "The U.S. Central Command: Toward What Purpose?" *Strategic Review* 19 (Spring 1986): 44.

5. For a variety of loss estimates, see Anthony Cordesman, *The Iran-Iraq War and Western Security, 1984–1987* (London: Jane's, 1988); Farhang, "Khomeini and Postwar Iran," p. 522; and Keith McLachlan, Safa Haeri, and Fida Nasrallah, "Ceasefire in the Gulf," *Arab Affairs* 1 (Summer–Autumn 1988): 23–51.

6. For an analysis of the historic, legal, diplomatic, religious, and ideological aspects of the conflict, see Majid Khadduri, *The Gulf War* (Oxford: Oxford University Press, 1988).

7. See Paul Balta, *Iran-Iraq: Une guerre de 5000 ans* (Paris: Anthropos, 1987); Charles Saint-Port, *La guerre du Golfe* (Paris: Proche Orient et Tiers-Monde, 1983); and Stephen Grummon, *The Iran-Iraq War*, Washington Paper 92 (New York: Praeger, 1982).

8. See Edmund Ghareeb, "The War in the Gulf: Why Did It Start, When Will It End?" *Arab Journal* 4 (1982): 12–19.

9. See Khadduri, *Gulf War*, pp. 6–13.

10. See Edmund Ghareeb, "The Forgotten War," *American-Arab Affairs* 5 (Summer 1983): 59–75, and Ron McLauren, "The Iran-Iraq War," *Korea and World Affairs* 8 (Summer 1984): 318–28.

11. For the Iraqi Baathist view, see *The Central Report of the Ninth Regional Congress*, June 1982 (Baghdad, 1983), 169–279. Also see Nazar al-Hadithi, *Arab-Persian Relations: A Historical Review* (Baghdad, 1986), pp. 23–57; Mustafa al-Najar and Najdat Safwat, "Arab Sovereignty over Shatt al-Arab in the Kaabida Period

in the Iran-Iraq War," in M. S. al-Azhary, ed., *The Iran-Iraq War* (London: Croom Helm, 1984); and the special issue on the war and its background in *Afaq Arabiyya* 7 (April 1982).

12. See Abd al-Aziz al-Duri, *Al Juthur al-Tarikhiya lil-Qawmiya al-Arabiya* (The historical roots of Arab nationalism) (Beirut, 1960), p. 35. See also Nazar al-Hadithi, *Arab-Persian Relations: A Historical Review*, pp. 23–42; Khadduri, *Gulf War*, pp. 3–13; and Jasim Abdulghani, *Iran and Iraq: The Years of Crisis* (Baltimore: Johns Hopkins University Press, 1984), pp. 2–3.

13. Shireen Hunter, "Arab-Iranian Relations and Stability in the Persian Gulf," *Washington Quarterly* 7 (Summer 1984): 68.

14. Yahya Armajani, *Iran* (Englewood Cliffs, N.J.: Prentice-Hall, 1972), cited in Abdulghani, *Iran and Iraq*, p. 2.

15. Hunter, "Arab-Iranian Relations," p. 68.

16. Ghareeb, "Forgotten War," p. 60.

17. Amir Taheri, *International Herald Tribune*, October 10, 1980; see also Bruce Maddy Weltzman, "Islam and Arabism: The Iran-Iraq War," *Washington Quarterly*, 5 (Autumn 1982): 181–88, and Khadduri, *The Gulf War*, pp. 3–13.

18. Khadduri, *Gulf War*, pp. 7–13.

19. Ghareeb, "Forgotten War," p. 60.

20. For details of Iraq's evolving Gulf policy, see Edmund Ghareeb, "Iraq in the Gulf," in F. Axelgard, ed., *Iraq in Transition* (Boulder, Colo.: Westview Press, 1987), pp. 59–83.

21. Nassif Nassar, "Al-Arab, al-Islam wa al-Thawra al-Iraniya" (The Arabs, Islam, and the Iranian Revolution), *al-Fikr al-Arabi al-Mu'asir* 2 (June 1980): 15.

22. *Al-Hawadith*, April 18, 1986.

23. For the text, see *al-Thawra* (Baghdad), February 14, 1979.

24. See *Central Report of the Ninth Congress*, pp. 172–74.

25. For Khomeini's attitude toward government and his worldview, see his *Ayatallah al-Khumaini's al-Hukuma al-Islamiya* (The Islamic government) (Beirut: Dar al-Tali'a, 1979). Also see R. K. Ramazani, "Revolutionary Iran's Open Door Policy," *Harvard International Review* 9 (January 1987): 9, and R. K. Ramazani, "Iran's Islamic Revolution and the Persian Gulf," *Current History* (January 1985): 11–17.

26. Cited in Ramazani, "Iran's Islamic Revolution," p. 6.

27. For details on the Baathist attitude, see generally *Central Report of the Ninth Congress*, and Tariq Ismail, *Iraq and Iran: Roots of Conflict* (Syracuse: Syracuse University Press, 1982).

28. *Al-Thawra*, June 6, 1977.

29. For details on Iran's charges, see Kzar Haydar, *Udwan al-Nizam al-Iraqi* (Aggression of the Iraqi regime) (No publisher given, 1982).

30. See Edmund Ghareeb, "Iraq: Emergent Gulf Power," in Husain Amir-sadeghi, ed., *The Security of the Persian Gulf* (London: Croom Helm, 1981), pp. 217–18.

31. For details, see Khadduri, *Gulf War*, pp. 68–70.

3

Strategic and Political Objectives in the Gulf War

Iran's View

Eric Hooglund

From September 1980 until mid-August 1988, Iran was preoccupied with trying to end what it termed the "imposed war" with Iraq. From the beginning, Tehran pursued both military and diplomatic strategies to resolve the conflict. The country's political elite never ceased hoping that a decisive military victory would terminate hostilities in Iran's favor, but the failure of several costly offensives to deal Iraq a crushing defeat convinced several policymakers to consider seriously a far less palatable alternative, a negotiated settlement. The July 1988 decision to accept United Nations Security Council Resolution 598 thus was the culmination of a gradual process whereby proponents of a diplomatic solution persuaded a majority of their colleagues that a military solution was not feasible. Comprehending the different perspectives of the supporters of diplomacy and the supporters of the military option is essential for understanding why Iran was prepared to accept a negotiated settlement of the war in 1988 and what its attitudes regarding peace prospects are.

Iran's war objectives evolved in response to conditions on the battlefront and to regional developments. This becomes evident when one examines goals during the different phases of the war. Dividing the Iran-Iraq War into stages naturally involves a certain degree of arbitrariness, but if the conflict is viewed from Tehran's perspective, then it is possible to follow the evolution of policy through five distinct phases. The first phase, from September 1980 to June 1982, corresponds to the Iraqi occupation of significant parts of western Iran and is a period when Tehran was on the defensive, both diplomatically and militarily. The second phase, from July 1982 to January 1984, marked a period of major Iranian offensives on Iraqi territory. The third phase, from February 1984 to February 1987, corresponds with the "tanker war" in the Persian Gulf, the intensified use of bombs and missiles against civilian targets (the "war of the cities"), and the general stalemate, despite several large and costly offensives, along front lines of the fighting. The fourth phase, from March 1987 to July 1988, is what Iran refers to as the period of American intervention. The coming into force of the U.N.-supervised cease-fire in August 1988 marks the beginning of the fifth phase of the war. Iran's military and political goals during each of these phases are analyzed in the following sections.[1]

THE FIRST PHASE

Iran was not prepared for war in September 1980 when Iraq's president Saddam Hussein sent his forces across the two countries' common border. The political turmoil unleashed by the 1978–79 revolution was still running its course. The ruling elite was deeply divided between those who advocated a return to relative normalcy, represented by then President Abol Hasan Bani-Sadr, and those who wanted to push ahead with radical social reforms, represented by the Islamic Republican party that dominated the Majlis (parliament).[2] Major political forces such as the Mojahedin-e Khalq openly challenged the legitimacy of the constitution, which vested ultimate authority in the clergy, and engaged in periodic street battles with supporters of the regime.[3] Approximately half of the Kurdish ethnic minority (Kurds constitute 7 to 9 percent of Iran's population and live predominantly in four western provinces) was in open revolt, and there were numerous disturbances among other ethnic and/ or religious minorities, including Arabs, Baluchis, and Turkomans.[4] Even more significantly, the military had been demoralized by a series of purges, the most recent in July 1980, when over 500 officers were arrested for alleged complicity in an abortive coup against the government.[5] Iran's foreign problems seemed to be as grave as its internal ones, for the Islamic Republic was isolated internationally on account of the still-unresolved hostage crisis with the United States.[6]

Given Iran's political problems in September 1980, it is not surprising that the initial Iraqi invasion, at several places along the two countries' 750–mile border, was successful. The Iraqis penetrated as deep as 50 miles at some points and captured several strategic border towns. Within a few weeks Iraq had occupied 5,400 square miles of Iranian territory, including the country's most important port, Khorramshahr on the Shatt al-Arab waterway, and was besieging the large industrial centers of Abadan and Ahvaz. The situation for Iran appeared so grim that even Washington, which had come to regard the Islamic Republic as an implacable foe, expressed official concern about and opposition to any "dismemberment" of the country. The Iranians rallied, however, and by mid-November they not only had contained the Iraqi advance but also had forced some of Saddam Hussein's troops to retreat from forward positions. In early 1981, much to the surprise of both Baghdad and international military analysts, Iran launched the first of several successful offensives that over the next sixteen months freed most of the occupied territory.[7]

Tehran's primary objective during the initial phase of the war was to compel a complete Iraqi withdrawal from all Iranian soil. The Islamic Republic also insisted that it would never accept Saddam Hussein's unilateral abrogation of the 1975 Algiers agreement that had established the middle of the Shatt al-Arab as the two countries' common border. (Under a 1932 treaty, the border had been established along the Iranian shore of the river.) After several months of fighting, Iran expanded its objectives to include compensation for damaged civilian property. In addition to military campaigns, Tehran sought to achieve its goals through diplomatic means. Initially, Iran was bitterly disappointed. The first U.N. Security Council resolution (Resolution 479 of September 28, 1980) called for a cease-fire but failed to mention Baghdad's resort to the use of force and did not demand an Iraqi withdrawal to international borders. Iran consequently lost confidence in the Security Council as a forum for redressing grievances and remained suspicious of this body's intentions throughout the rest of the war.[8] Ironically, even though Resolution 479 seemed biased in favor of Iraq, Saddam Hussein contemptuously dismissed it, promising that his forces would continue fighting until "every inch of usurped land was restored to Arab control," a reference the Iranians understood to mean the annexation of their oil-rich province of Khuzistan, which the Iraqis called "Arabistan."[9] Subsequently, Iran's political-spiritual leader, Ayatollah Ruhollah Khomeini, announced that there could be "absolutely no question of peace or compromise" with Hussein, a position he would reiterate frequently over the next seven years, contributing to a perception of Iranian intransigence.[10]

Khomeini probably expressed the attitude of many Iranians who were outraged over the invasion of their country. Still, in the initial phase of the war, most leaders did not have unshakable confidence in the prospects of an ultimate victory over Iraq, especially since very few of them had ever had any military experience. They continued to hope that diplomatic pressure could be brought upon Baghdad to pull all its forces back across the border. In mid-October Prime Minister Mohammad Ali Rajai personally went to New York to present Iran's case before the U.N. Security Council, but he failed to win sufficient international support for a new resolution calling for a cease-fire and simultaneous troop withdrawal. The unsatisfactory result of this trip only increased the sense of disappointment and frustration with the United Nations. Nevertheless, Iran remained willing to discuss ways to halt the fighting and in November agreed to discuss its position with Swedish statesman Olof Palme, whom Secretary-General Kurt Waldheim had appointed as his special representative to mediate between the two warring countries. Palme shuttled back and forth between Baghdad and Tehran at least five times between November 1980 and June 1981, but he was unable to work out a mutually acceptable cease-fire agreement.[11]

In addition to U.N. representatives, Tehran hosted mediation delegations sponsored by the Islamic Conference Organization and the Non-aligned Movement and initiated by other governments such as Algeria and Cuba. None of these efforts, however, succeeded in bridging the gap between Iraq's demand for a cease-fire in place and Iran's insistence on a cease-fire and simultaneous withdrawal. Iraq appeared to be in the stronger position militarily; even though Iraqi ground forces launched no major offensives after December 1980, Iran's army and Revolutionary Guards seemed unable to dislodge them from the territory they still occupied. Meanwhile, Iran's military problems were compounded by political ones, since the war failed to halt the progressively violent nature of the confrontation between proponents and opponents of clerical rule. Following the impeachment and dismissal from office of President Bani-Sadr in June 1981, thousands of youthful Mojahedin supporters staged an armed uprising against the government. The regime survived this major challenge, but the country paid a high human cost: at least 100 top leaders, including Rajai, were assassinated; hundreds of members of the Revolutionary Guards were killed; and at least 8,000 antiregime youths were executed or killed in street battles.[12]

The real impact of Iran's domestic political turmoil on its military effectiveness is probably impossible to measure. Even so, it is significant that during the summer of 1981, at the height of the conflict with the Mojahedin-e Khalq, no major offensives were undertaken on the war front. New campaigns were launched in the fall, however, and these achieved important successes, including the breaking of the twelve-month siege of Abadan at the end of September and the recapture of the town of Bostan two months later. These victories provided a much-needed boost to Iranian morale. Additionally, the tactics tested in these offensives were adapted and used again successfully in March and May

1982. Both military and political leaders now began to feel optimistic that all Iran could be liberated.[13]

The political turmoil of summer 1981 probably affected the diplomatic process more adversely than it did the military situation, since for several months little leadership continuity existed at the Foreign Ministry. After Ali Akbar Velayati became foreign minister in December 1981, however, he signalled Tehran's continued interest in a mediated cease-fire. The new U.N. Secretary-General, Javier Perez de Cuellar, responded to overtures from both Iran and Iraq by asking Olof Palme in January 1982 to resume his earlier efforts. Palme apparently made more progress in these discussions than he had in 1980–81, but he failed to get a cease-fire agreement: Iran's leaders mistrusted Baghdad's promises to withdraw its forces after a cease-fire had come into force, and they refused to recognize Iraq's claim that its riparian border was along the Iranian shoreline.[14]

Algeria also resumed its mediation efforts at the beginning of 1982 and actually may have been on the verge of achieving a breakthrough by early May. The Iranians believed that the Algerians appreciated their position on the necessity for a complete troop withdrawal and the reinstatement of the 1975 Treaty, an accord that had been achieved through Algeria's mediation. The Algerians seemed to understand the political complexities in both Baghdad and Tehran, and gradually they secured Iranian and Iraqi agreement to a number of secondary issues. Their method of mediating was to find compromises that would enable both belligerents to save face. The Algerians convinced some Iranian leaders in April that there were Iraqi officials, but not yet Saddam Hussein, who were prepared to accept a restoration of the status quo ante on the Shatt al-Arab in return for unspecified Iranian compromises on the issue of reparations. However, if there were any genuine prospects for a cessation of hostilities in May 1982, they were short-circuited when Algerian foreign minister Mohammad Benyahia and his entire team of negotiators were killed in a plane crash while en route from Baghdad to Tehran via Turkish airspace. The circumstances of this fatal crash have never been explained, although Iran accused Iraq of shooting down the plane with missiles. Lost with the Algerians was more than a year's experience of dealing with the emotional, legal, and political issues that fueled the Iran-Iraq War.[15]

Less than a week before the Algerian plane crash, Iran had launched its largest and most successful offensive to date and was recapturing an average of 100 square miles each day. This offensive culminated with the liberation of Khorramshahr on May 24 and the mass surrender of nearly 30,000 Iraqi soldiers. Iraq was now ready for a cease-fire, and in June Saddam Hussein announced a unilateral withdrawal of remaining sources from Iran. Tehran, however, now had no interest in a cease-fire. Convinced of Iraqi complicity in the destruction of the Algerian aircraft, intoxicated with a sense of invincibility from their latest victories, and incensed by the Israeli invasion of Lebanon, which they blamed on Saddam Hussein, Iran's political leaders adopted hardline attitudes and began to call openly for an invasion of Iraq in order to punish the perpetrator of all the evil that had been visited on the region since September 1980.[16]

THE SECOND PHASE

The second phase of the war began in July 1982, when Iran rejected the United Nations' second cease-fire resolution and sent its own troops into Iraqi territory. During the next eighteen months, military strategies dominated. Iran utilized "human-wave" tactics in its initial invasion, a series of offensives extending over three weeks. Despite the magnitude of their effort, the Iranians succeeded in occupying only a small strip of Iraqi territory. Although Iran retained the military advantage, it had failed to achieve a decisive victory. Additional offensives in the fall, and later throughout 1983, brought similar results: more slivers of land occupied by enduring high casualties without defeating Iraq.[17] The anticipated collapse of the "corrupt and godless" Baathist regime never occurred, and neither did the hoped-for uprising of the "oppressed" Iraqi Muslims.

The unexpected resiliency that the Iraqi military demonstrated during the latter part of 1982 and throughout all of 1983 caused the war's continuance to become controversial, dividing Iran's political elite into at least two groups. The first group, who can be called hardliners, dismissed the Iraqi ability to withstand Iran's offensives as temporary. The leaders in this faction advocated a military solution, were confident of ultimately defeating Iraq, and were reluctant to accord diplomatic efforts serious attention. The strength of their influence over policy was demonstrated in October 1982 when they persuaded their colleagues in the government to reject a new U.N. Security Council Resolution calling for a cease-fire and mutual troop withdrawals. Their expressed goals for ending the war became maximalist: the unconditional surrender of Iraq and punishment of its leaders. Saddam Hussein quickly emerged as the special target of their hostility. In November 1982 President Ali Khamene'i became the first Iranian leader to call openly for Hussein's overthrow, an objective subsequently embraced by Ayatollah Khomeini and several high officials.[18]

The second group comprised those leaders who believed in the feasibility of a diplomatic solution to the war. These leaders can be called pragmatists. Their skepticism about a quick military victory initially was aroused by the strategically undramatic results of the July 1982 offensive into Iraq. Similarly limited achievements in the fall and the 1983 campaigns tended to reinforce their doubts. Their goal was to obtain an acceptable, nonmilitary resolution of the conflict with Iraq. They gradually became convinced that the war was stalemated, that the hated regime in Iraq was not going to collapse or be toppled in a popular revolution, and that the war was a drain on Iran's own human and other resources. Many adherents of these views were found in the Foreign Ministry. Consequently, the pragmatists tended to be more sensitive than their hardline colleagues to foreign impressions of Iranian policy. In particular, they were concerned about Western journalistic fascination with the notion that Iran's precondition for peace was Hussein's removal, an objective that they considered unrealistic. As early as January 1983, Foreign Minister Ali Akbar Velayati tried to discourage such speculation about purported Iranian intransigence vis-à-vis the despised Iraqi president by stating in a press conference that "the overthrow of Saddam Hussein never was a main condition for peace negotiations with Iraq." He and other leaders reiterated this position publicly on many occasions in subsequent years.[19]

THE THIRD PHASE

The third, or "tanker war," phase of the Iran-Iraq War began in February 1984 and was characterized by both a major escalation of the conflict and an intensification of diplomatic efforts to end it.[20] During the next three years, intermittent but serious activity in three separate theaters of the war took place—on land, in the air, and at sea. Iran continued to maintain the advantage in land combat and gained additional parcels of Iraqi territory as a result of "human-wave" offensives in 1984, 1985, 1986, and early 1987. Nevertheless, these victories failed to blunt Baghdad's capacity to wage war. Iran fared less well in the air war, which became popularly known as the "war of the cities" because civilian population centers were the principal targets of random aerial bombing. Iraq had superiority in planes and missiles, and between 1984 and 1987 it bombed more than 50 Iranian cities and towns, primarily in the west; at least 4,000 civilians were killed in these raids. Iraq also controlled the war at sea, referred to as "the tanker war" since most of the "battles" actually were aerial strikes against neutral oil tankers or Iranian oil-export facilities in the Persian Gulf. The tanker war persistently interfered with Iran's ability to export petroleum.[21]

Tehran's objective during this phase was to end the war on favorable terms. The hardliners dominated policy in 1984, but in the following years their influence gradually eroded as each new "final offensive" failed to bring Iraq to its knees. Nevertheless, their faith in an ultimate triumph was constantly reinforced by Iran's steady, although strategically insignificant, gains in the land war. They argued that Iran's offensives were part of a strategy of attrition aimed at weakening Iraq and thus hastening its collapse. Victories such as the conquest of al-Faw Peninsula in February 1986 provided a tremendous boost to their morale. Iraqi tactics, such as the use of chemical weapons, aerial bombing of Iranian cities, and attacks on Iran's oil installations, only served to strengthen the hardliners' resolve to achieve a decisive military victory.

The pragmatists began to exert some influence on war policy in 1984. Their perception of a frontline stalemate was confirmed when Iran's capture of territory in Iraq's man-made Majnun Islands during a major campaign in February did not precipitate an Iraqi rout nor diminish Baghdad's ability to replenish its army with fresh troops and equipment. The pragmatists also were concerned about the consequences of Iraqi attacks on shipping and on cities, both of which escalated in 1984, since they recognized that their own air force had too few operable planes to counter effectively. In June they persuaded their hardline colleagues to accept a U.N.-sponsored moratorium in the aerial war of the cities, and for the next nine months, both countries honored this agreement. The pragmatists also convinced the government to offer to extend this moratorium to the tanker war, but Iraq refused to go along.

The pragmatists' objective during the third phase of the war was to find a face-saving, diplomatic solution that would permit Iran to extricate itself from the conflict. They sought consensus to renew diplomatic initiatives; in August 1984 Foreign Minister Velayati even called publicly for a more "positive and activist" foreign policy. The hardliners eventually acquiesced, although they did not abandon their military strategy and remained skeptical about the value of diplomacy. The pragmatists were able to gain support for their policy because they obtained the crucial backing of Khomeini, who agreed in the fall of 1984 to summon home all high-ranking diplomatic personnel and personally inform them of the need for more conciliatory foreign relations.[22] Thus Tehran once again welcomed mediation delegations, including those sent from India, the Islamic Conference Organization, and the United Nations. Velayati invited Perez de Cuellar to Iran to discuss the Secretary-General's modifications of an eight-point, step-by-step plan for ending hostilities that Palme had proposed in 1982. Perez de Cuellar did come to Tehran in April 1985, but he was unable to bridge the deep divide between Iran's insistence on a cease-fire in place and Iraq's demand for a cease-fire and simultaneous withdrawal of all forces to international borders. Iran also was adamant, probably due to the hardliners' influence, that Iraq accept responsibility for starting the war.

The pragmatists even made friendly overtures to the Arab countries of the Persian Gulf, all of which professed neutrality but generally were sympathetic to Iraq. The tanker war was a catalyst for these contacts. The Iranians believed that the other Persian Gulf states and neutral countries whose ships had been hit could be encouraged to pressure Iraq to halt its attacks. The pragmatists knew that the Arab governments of the Gulf countries actually had been concerned about the spread of the Iran-Iraq War since its inception. The war, in fact, had spurred six states to form a regional security pact, the Gulf Cooperation Council (GCC). By 1984 the attacks on shipping were alarming the GCC countries; their fears increased after a Saudi Arabian oil tanker was damaged by an Iraqi-laid mine in April, and again in May when Iran initiated a retaliatory policy against Arab shipping. The pragmatists sought to reassure the GCC states that Iran was as deeply committed to free navigation in the Gulf as were they. In addition, they stressed in numerous official meetings that Iran had no interest in subverting the GCC governments, that it wanted a negotiated end to the war, and that it generally shared the GCC strategic perspective about the need for political stability in the Gulf region. These efforts resulted in a major diplomatic breakthrough when the Saudi foreign minister made an official state visit to Iran in May 1985. Other high-level exchanges of visits followed with Oman and the United Arab Emirates.[23]

The pragmatists also aspired to end Iran's virtual isolation in international affairs. They believed that improved relations would lead to better understanding of Iran's position in the war and reduce sympathy for Iraq. In these efforts they obtained the crucial support of Khomeini, who admonished the public that failure to maintain good relations with other countries could lead to Iran's "defeat and annihilation."[24] One of the pragmatists' boldest initiatives, begun in 1985, was to engage in secret talks with American officials. These discussions culminated in the secret May 1986 visit to Tehran of a delegation headed by President Reagan's former National Security Adviser Robert McFarlane. The fact that none of the Iranians involved suffered reprisals after these contacts had been revealed is strong evidence that the overture had been approved at the highest levels of government. It is quite plausible that Khomeini had even given his blessing to the abortive negotiations, since in the spring of 1985 he had advised that it was possible for Iran and the United States to reestablish relations if Washington learned to behave properly.[25]

The one area where diplomatic progress eluded the pragmatists was the tanker war. In retrospect, the tanker war proved to be Iran's Achilles' heel. Iraq had initiated attacks on ships carrying Iranian oil as early as 1981, but this form of economic warfare only became systematic policy in 1984 following Baghdad's acquisition of French-made Super Etendard aircraft and Exocet missiles. The tanker war posed a major dilemma for Iran. Tehran viewed the Persian Gulf as its economic lifeline to the rest of the world: All of its oil exports—revenues from oil exports accounted for 90 percent of the government's budget—transited the Gulf through the Strait of Hormuz into the Gulf of Oman and beyond; a majority of the country's international imports arrived via this same route. Iran thus was unwilling to tolerate any threat to the free flow of trade through this strategic waterway. However, Iran was unable militarily to prevent Iraqi attacks on its shipping in the Persian Gulf sector.

Intensification of the tanker war forced an Iranian response. In the debate over an appropriate reaction, the hardliners persuaded their colleagues to adopt a policy of retaliating for Iraqi attacks by selectively striking tankers carrying Kuwaiti and Saudi oil. These countries' shipping was singled out because all Iran's leaders were convinced that both Kuwait and Saudi Arabia provided financial support and other assistance to Iraq. The objective was not to expand the war, although an inherent risk persisted of this happening; rather, the aim was to intimidate GCC states into exerting pressure on Baghdad to end its attacks on ships loaded with Iranian oil. Furthermore, Iran would not claim responsibility for any of its attacks, apparently hoping to confuse people into believing that they were the result of Iraqi error.

Iran's refusal to acknowledge its attacks did not fool anyone as to who the real perpetrator was. Nevertheless, for more than a year, Saudi Arabia, and to a lesser extent Kuwait, sought to resolve their differences with Iran through bilateral negotiations. The GCC states welcomed overtures from Tehran's pragmatists, interpreting these as signs of Iran's moderation. The tanker war, however, was not amenable to any diplomatic deal between the Gulf Arabs and Iran because it was an Iraqi war policy. Baghdad controlled the timing and intensity of attacks on Iran's shipping and oil installations; with far fewer operational aircraft and weapons, Iran had to make choices regarding when and against whom to respond. In the latter half of 1985, Iraq once again increased the level of its attacks, which continued at this accelerated rate throughout 1986.

Iran's retaliation policy deliberately had not been based on "an eye for an eye" but was designed to strike at one Arab tanker for every two or three Iranian ones hit. In 1984, the first year of the tanker war, Iran attacked only 18 tankers for 53 struck by Iraq; in 1985 Iran hit 14 for 33 attacked by Iraq. As Iraq increased the number of its strikes to an average of 5 per month in 1986, Iran felt compelled to escalate, attacking as many as 3 or 4 ships each month. Tankers carrying Kuwaiti oil became the special target of these attacks because of all the GCC countries, Iran had the least friendly relations with Kuwait; in addition, this small sheikhdom was a far weaker power militarily than Saudi Arabia. The Kuwaiti government responded to the increasing Iranian attacks by requesting Soviet and U.S. protection for its tankers. Internationalization of the tanker war was exactly what Tehran wanted to avoid, but in early 1987 that is precisely what happened when the Soviet Union agreed to lease three of its tankers to Kuwait, and then the United States agreed to reflag eleven Kuwaiti tankers.

THE FOURTH PHASE

The March 1987 decision to place Kuwaiti oil tankers under the U.S. flag marked the beginning of the war's fourth phase, a phase whose outstanding feature was American intervention. From the viewpoint of the pragmatists, this intervention was most unfortunate and inopportune. Since 1985 their influence over policy had grown steadily, and while they had not been able to discourage yet another major offensive in the Basra area—which began on Christmas Eve in 1986 and continued intermittently for nearly two months—the lack of victory had prompted further defections from the ranks of the hardliners. In addition, even though discussion of war policy was not permitted in the media, virtually all leaders were aware that the public's war weariness was fueling antiwar sentiment, particularly among an increasing proportion of the youth.[26] Thus when the pragmatists argued that the futility of continuing military campaigns justified a reappraisal of Perez de Cuellar's 1985 proposals, Velayati secured approval to approach the U.N. Secretary-General to discuss compromises even though the hardliners had remained suspicious of the Security Council since the war's beginning. Consequently, Iran had already initiated discussions with some members of the Security Council about a cease-fire resolution when the U.S. intervention occurred, interrupting this diplomatic process.[27]

The U.S. intervention, which was both diplomatic and military, was prompted by the November 1986 revelation that the Reagan administration had been secretly selling weapons to Iran, ostensibly in exchange for Tehran's promises to persuade Lebanese paramilitary groups to release American citizens they were holding as hostages in Lebanon. News of these covert deals deeply embarrassed Washington and put strains on relations with long-time allies such as Kuwait and Saudi Arabia. American foreign policy officials, who sensed a need to demonstrate the sincerity of U.S. friendship and loyalty, welcomed the opportunity presented by Kuwait's request for protection of its oil tankers. The new U.S. policy of defending freedom of navigation in the Persian Gulf quickly gathered an anti-Iranian momentum.[28] Indeed, since the Iranians had so recently held secret talks with representatives of the Reagan administration, they were baffled by the sudden turn of events that found Washington blaming Iran in May 1987 for an Iraqi attack on the USS *Stark* that left 37 American sailors dead. The United States then announced that it would provide escort service for reflagged Kuwaiti tankers. Infuriated by these U.S. actions, hardliners in June, either as a matter of official policy or as an independent initiative, ordered the sowing of mines in Persian Gulf waters. Discovery of the mines caused a further escalation of the U.S. military presence in the region.

On the diplomatic front, the United States took the lead in the United Nations to fashion a resolution advantageous to Iraq but unacceptable to Iran.[29] The diplomatic offensive caught Iran off guard and successfully frustrated Tehran's efforts to have its position heard. The result was Resolution 598, which passed the Security Council in mid-July 1987 and called on Iran and Iraq to begin negotiating a comprehensive peace, to be implemented in eight stages beginning with a cease-fire. This was a binding resolution with a mechanism for imposing sanctions on the belligerent who rejected it—and the prevailing assumption was that Iran would reject Resolution 598. The unexpected developments at the United Nations temporarily unified the pragmatists and hardliners. No one wanted to accept Resolution 598, but the pragmatists believed that re-jecting it outright risked providing Washington with the leverage to secure approval for sanctions from the Security Council.[30] To avoid such an outcome, the pragmatists persuaded their colleagues that the best course would be to try to outwit U.S. strategy by temporizing—that is, by neither accepting nor rejecting the resolution. Consequently, Velayati informed the U.N. Secretary-General that Iran was interested in dis-cussing how the order of the resolution's eight steps could be modified so that the country could comply with it.[31]

Washington's anti-Iran pressures at the United Nations and American military actions in the Persian Gulf convinced the Iranians that U.S. intervention posed a serious threat. The pragmatists believed that their country was neither militarily nor psychologically prepared for a major confrontation with the United States.[32] The hardliners preferred an ac-tivist policy that would demonstrate that Iran could not be intimidated; but after the mining incident, they agreed reluctantly to support the official, albeit not openly articulated, policy of avoiding clashes between Iranian and American forces. When Iraq resumed its attacks on neutral and Iranian ships serving Iran's ports—air strikes had been suspended for several weeks following the attack on the USS *Stark*—both prag-matists and hardliners decided to continue the retaliation policy. Never-theless, Iranian naval and air units generally stayed clear of American convoys in the Gulf. The Iranians were incensed that the U.S. armada, dispatched to the Persian Gulf ostensibly to protect neutral shipping, was effectively used as a cover for Iraq to bomb with virtual impunity neutral ships carrying Iran-related trade.

During the summer of 1987, Iran lost the international diplomatic leverage it had been cultivating for the previous three years. Although the United States had taken the initiative in marshalling opinion against the Islamic Republic, Tehran's mining of Gulf waters and intensified attacks on shipping greatly contributed to general perceptions that the country's policies threatened navigation and impeded the flow of oil to world markets. Iran's image was further tarnished when it became entangled in diplomatic disputes with Britain and France and when a political demonstration by its citizens on a pilgrimage in Saudi Arabia degenerated into a riot with Saudi security forces and resulted in over 400 deaths. The rapid succession of these developments convinced the governments of Belgium, Britain, France, Holland, and Italy—U.S. allies who earlier had rejected Washington's request for concerted action in clearing the Persian Gulf of mines—to dispatch warships to the region to help protect commercial ship traffic.[33]

In an effort to counter these negative international trends, Iran's leaders invited Perez de Cuellar to Tehran in September 1987 for substantive talks on how their country could comply with Resolution 598. Specifically, they told Perez de Cuellar that Iran would be willing to abide by a cease-fire (step one of the resolution) if simultaneously there was established an official commission of inquiry to determine which country had started the war (step six). Iraq subsequently refused to consider any modifications to the order in which the resolution's eight steps were to be implemented. Before Perez de Cuellar's arrival in Tehran, President Khamene'i had decided to attend the U.N. General Assembly meeting and personally plead Iran's case. What should have been a historic occasion, however, was transformed into diplomatic embarrassment when, on the eve of Khamene'i's address, the U.S. Navy apprehended an Iranian patrol boat laying mines in the Persian Gulf. Khamene'i's efforts to deny the mission of the mine-laden *Iran Ajr* completely overshadowed his conciliatory remarks and severely damaged his credibility. American and European leaders consequently were disinclined to take the Iranian president seriously. Thus, when Khamene'i announced at a New York press conference that Iran considered Saddam Hussein's removal from power a desirable objective rather than a necessary precondition to peace negotiations, most people failed to appreciate that he was signalling Iran's willingness to de-escalate tensions in the Gulf and negotiate modalities for implementing Resolution 598.[34]

Although the United States remained suspicious of Iran and tried to get the Security Council to impose sanctions, by October 1987 the fact that Tehran had not, as widely expected, rejected Resolution 598 persuaded some governments, notably those of China, France, the Soviet Union, and West Germany, that the Islamic Republic might be genuinely interested in a negotiated settlement of the war. The first three of these countries were permanent members of the Security Council. They discreetly informed Washington that as long as Iran was discussing Resolution 598 with the Secretary-General, they would consider exercising their veto privileges on any U.S.-sponsored motion pertaining to sanctions. Since the Soviet Union and France were the principal arms suppliers to Iraq, their willingness to accommodate Iran's temporizing diplomacy influenced other European governments gradually to distance themselves from the United States' strong anti-Iran position.

As 1987 ended, the United States naturally felt frustrated by its failure to convince other members of the Security Council of the need for sanctions against Iran, but the disappointment in Baghdad was much greater. The Iraqis' expectation that Resolution 598 would bring an end to the fighting had dissipated and was replaced by fears that Iran was successfully reestablishing a diplomatic offensive. This concern was a major factor in prompting Iraq to launch a renewed war of the cities at the end of February 1988.[35] Unlike the earlier aerial raids on Iranian urban centers, Iraq had now acquired from the Soviet Union long-range missiles that could be fired from Iraqi bases at targets over 300 miles away, deep inside Iran. For the next six weeks Tehran and more than 30 other major cities and towns were targets of intense missile attacks. Iraq fired more than 200 missiles at the Iranian capital, an average of five per day, all of which fell randomly, causing great consternation and the flight of nearly half the city's six million residents to refuge in more distant areas.[36]

During this same period Iraq also renewed the use of chemical weapons on the battlefronts, but on a significantly more intensive scale than in earlier years. The Iraqi town of Halabja in the mountains near the Iranian border became an infamous victim of toxic chemicals in March 1988 when Baghdad, suspecting Halabja's Kurdish population of collaborating with Iran, ordered the air force to saturate the town with mustard and nerve gases. Iranian forces, who entered Halabja after the attack, found at least 5,000 civilians who had died of chemical poisoning. The media in Iran featured stories and ghastly photos of Halabja for weeks after the incident. The sad fate of this town probably contributed more than any other single event to the rapid demoralization of the Iranian people and armed forces. After Halabja both the army and the Revolutionary Guards seemed to have lost their will to fight.[37] Indeed, when Iraq launched ground offensives a few weeks later, the Iranians uncharacteristically abandoned their positions en masse.

During the winter and spring of 1988 the United States still maintained a naval presence in the Persian Gulf and continued to criticize Iran for the continuation of the war. The leaders in Tehran, who yet rankled over the American intervention, blamed U.S. silence for Iraq's intensified use of chemical weapons and its missile attacks on Iran's civilian population centers. In their rhetoric they accused Washington of complicity in Baghdad's "crimes against humanity." Anti-American feeling was particularly high among personnel stationed in the Persian Gulf and

Gulf of Oman. Inevitably, some Revolutionary Guards units, with or without prior authorization from Tehran, directly engaged U.S. ships in minor clashes that left several Iranians dead. The most serious of these incidents occurred on July 3, 1988, when the USS *Vincennes*, following a battle with Iranian gunboats, shot down an Iran Air civilian passenger plane, which it mistook for an attacking jet; all 290 on board were killed.

The Iran Air disaster occurred at the time Iran's leaders were debating seriously their country's final response to Resolution 598. As the first anniversary of the resolution's passage approached, the pragmatists realized that further procrastination would be diplomatically untenable. Although the pragmatists' influence over foreign policy had enabled Iran to achieve some notable reverses to the setbacks experienced during the summer of 1987—relations with France, for example, had greatly improved, and the United States had failed to gain support for U.N.-imposed sanctions—they reluctantly concluded that the Security Council would not modify the order of implementation of Resolution 598's provisions as Iran desired. The pragmatists were even more concerned about the country's internal situation. During this same year popular exhaustion with the war and its attendant privations had increased dramatically and had begun to impact on the performance of conscripts at the front. Discussions with their hardline colleagues during early 1988 focused increasingly on the domestic implications of the war. The unexpected military reverses in the spring caused further anxiety about the war's potential political fallout. By June a majority of top leaders, including President Khamene'i, Prime Minister Mir Hussein Musavi, and Speaker of the Majlis Ali Akbar Hashemi Rafsanjani, subscribed to the pragmatist view that the continuation of the war posed a serious threat to the stability and even to the survival of the Islamic Republic. More hardline leaders, including Khomeini, did not agree that the situation was so grave, although they too were concerned about declining morale, especially among the troops on the front.

The Iran Air shootdown provided a dramatic incident that pragmatists seized upon to argue the case for accepting Resolution 598. Warning of the unpredictability of future developments if U.S. involvement in the war expanded and Iraq continued to use chemical weapons with impunity, they convinced the hardliners that a U.N.-supervised cessation of hostilities was the best course to follow so that Iran could put aside the war and get moving again on its internal revolutionary agenda.[38] On July 18, 1988, a few days short of Resolution 598's first anniversary, Tehran notified Perez de Cuellar that it accepted the Security Council's document without reservations. Khomeini himself subsequently ratified Iran's acceptance. The Iranian embrace of Resolution 598 was unexpected. Initially Iraq tried to take advantage of the new situation by setting preconditions to its own previous acceptance and by launching offensives against Iranian border towns. Nevertheless, the Secretary-General proceeded to recruit a special international team, the U.N. Iran-Iraq Military Observer Group (UNIIMOG), to station along the 750–mile border. Under pressure from Security Council members and its Arab allies, Iraq finally agreed to a cessation of hostilities, and on August 20 the cease-fire went into effect.[39]

THE FIFTH PHASE

The cease-fire inaugurated the fifth phase of the war. According to the terms of Resolution 598, the cease-fire should be followed by a withdrawal of all Iranian and Iraqi armed forces to their own territories and by negotiations leading to a permanent peace treaty. Iran again surprised diplomats by agreeing to participate in U.N.-mediated, face-to-face negotiations with the Iraqis. The first round of negotiations actually opened in Geneva, Switzerland, only five days after the cease-fire had gone into effect. Subsequent sessions were held at the United Nations in New York and again in Geneva. The Shatt al-Arab, the river that forms the common southern boundary between Iran and Iraq, immediately emerged as the major issue dividing the two countries. Other issues, however, proved to be equally intractable: withdrawal of Iraqi forces from some 400 square miles of occupied Iranian mountainous territory; an exchange of more than 70,000 prisoners of war; the fate of more than 30,000 Iraqi Kurds who fled to Iran following the bombing of their villages with toxic chemicals after the cease-fire had come into effect; a resolution of the status of some 200,000 Iraqi nationals of Iranian ancestry who had been expelled into Iran in 1980; reparations; and Iran's insistence on the right to search for contraband on vessels bound to and from Iraq.

During the first year of the cease-fire, no substantive progress toward peace was achieved in the four separate negotiating sessions that were held because Iraq insisted that its control of the Shatt al-Arab be recognized before consideration of other issues. Iran insisted that there must be shared sovereignty over the Shatt according to the terms of a prewar treaty. Control of the river actually has been a source of intermittent tension ever since Iraq was established as an independent country in 1932. At that time Britain, which had exercised influence in the Persian Gulf for a century and ruled over Iraq, set the Shatt al-Arab's international boundary along the Iranian shoreline rather than down the middle of the waterway, as was the more customary practice. This was an irritant to the Iranians, who found it necessary to pass through Iraqi territorial waters in order to reach their two principal ports of Abadan and Khorramshahr. Finally, in 1975 Iran and Iraq signed a treaty in Algiers recognizing the middle channel of the river as the international border.[40] Saddam Hussein had unilaterally abrogated the Algiers accord in September 1980, a few days before launching the invasion of Iran. Eight years later, during the first session of peace negotiations, Iraq's foreign minister reiterated the Iraqi position that the Algiers accord was null and void. Iran, in contrast, has insisted that the Algiers accord is a permanently and legally binding treaty.

Despite the lack of any progress in the peace negotiations—the only achievement has been the exchange of several hundred seriously ill and wounded prisoners, less than 3 percent of total prisoners of war—the cease-fire actually has held for one year. From the Iranian perspective the fighting is over. Both the pragmatists and the hardliners are in agreement on this point. There is less consensus, however, regarding the most appropriate strategy for securing genuine peace with an Iraqi regime that is deeply distrusted. Pragmatists tend to regard international pressure on Baghdad as the most effective means of keeping the peace process on track. Although they share with their hardline colleagues a belief in the righteousness of Iran's cause, most pragmatists recognize that international sympathy for the Islamic Republic's position has been lacking. Pragmatists consequently have advocated initiatives to normalize foreign relations, especially with those Arab and European countries that were friendly toward Iraq during the war. They maintain, for example, that if Iran's political and economic ties with Britain and France are based on mutual respect and interests, these countries will be more inclined to understand Iran's position on such critical issues as the Shatt boundary and reparations.

The hardliners generally do not support efforts to woo international support. They believe that Americans and Europeans are naturally antagonistic toward Iran because their country successfully demonstrated how a commitment to revolutionary Islam can liberate Third World countries from imperialist control. As evidence for their convictions, the hardliners cite the failure of Western countries to take action against Iraq in September 1988 after it was revealed that Baghdad had attacked its own Kurdish citizens with chemical weapons, causing more than 60,000 of them to flee into Turkey; the continued U.S. naval presence in the Persian Gulf; and Western criticisms of Khomeini's condemnation of an Indian-born British writer whose novel defamed the Prophet Mohammad and ridiculed Islamic tenets. Furthermore, the hardliners are convinced that Saddam Hussein's regime in Iraq has always served Western imperialist interests and therefore will continue to receive American and European diplomatic support no matter how unjust or inhumane its policies are.

During the initial six months following the cease-fire, the pragmatists generally dominated the formulation of foreign policy pertaining to peace negotiations and relations with Western countries because they had Khomeini's backing. The pragmatists' failure to line up international support for implementation of the other provisions of Resolution 598, however, undermined confidence in their conciliatory approach and enabled the hardliners to reassert their influence. Since Khomeini often served as an arbiter between the pragmatic and hardline visions of how foreign policy should be conducted, his unexpected death in June 1989 cast a shadow of uncertainty over the future course of diplomatic relations. In the post-Khomeini era Iran's attitude toward the peace process, including the extent and nature of relations with Western countries considered pro-Iraqi, will be determined by which of these alternative views controls foreign policy: the pragmatic view that it is possible to maintain relations with all countries, except the ideologically unacceptable regimes in Israel and South Africa, based on mutual respect; or the hardline view that perceives the West in general, and the United States in particular, as ineluctably anti-Iran and anti-Islamic.

NOTES

1. For an earlier attempt to divide the Iran-Iraq War into distinct phases, see my article "The Islamic Republic at War and Peace," *Middle East Report*, no. 156 (January–February 1989): 5–6.

2. For an excellent account of the political struggle between Bani-Sadr and the Islamic Republican party, see Shaul Bakhash, *The Reign of the Ayatollahs: Iran and the Islamic Revolution* (New York: Basic Books, 1984), pp. 92–165.

3. For a detailed analysis of the Mojahedin's developing conflict with the clergy after August 1979, see Ervand Abrahamian, *The Iranian Mojahedin* (New Haven and London: Yale University Press, 1989), pp. 186–218.

4. For a good overview of the attitudes of ethnic and religious minorities toward the revolution and the Islamic Republic, see Nikki Keddie, "The Minorities Question in Iran," in Shirin Tahir-Kheli and Shaheen Ayubi, eds., *The Iran-Iraq War: New Weapons, Old Conflicts* (New York: Praeger, 1983), pp. 85–108.

5. For more detail on the postrevolutionary purges of the military, see Nikola Schahgaldian, *The Iranian Military under the Islamic Republic* (Santa Monica, Calif.: Rand Corporation, 1987), pp. 17–23; and William Hickman, *Ravaged and Reborn: The Iranian Army, 1982* (Washington, D.C.: Brookings Institution, 1982), pp. 8–18.

6. U.S. efforts to marshal international diplomatic opinion against Iran during the hostage crisis are described in Warren Christopher et al., eds., *American Hostages in Iran: The Conduct of a Crisis* (New Haven: Yale University Press, 1985).

7. For a detailed descriptive account of the Iraqi invasion and Iran's offensive in 1981–82, see Edgar O'Ballance, *The Gulf War* (London: Brassey's, 1988), pp. 30–92.

8. Ralph King, *The United Nations and the Iran-Iraq War* (New York: Ford Foundation, 1987), pp. 15–17.

9. For the complete text of Saddam Hussein's statement and examples of

the Iranian reaction, see Foreign Broadcast Information Service, *Daily Report—Middle East and Africa*, FBIS-MEA-V-190, September 29, 1980, pp. E1-E14.

10. Excerpts of Khomeini's speech are in *New York Times*, September 30, 1980.

11. Rajai's address before the Security Council and Palme's mediation efforts in 1980–81 are summarized in Majid Khadduri, *The Gulf War: The Origins and Implications of the Iraq-Iran Conflict* (New York and Oxford: Oxford University Press, 1988), pp. 90–91, 99–100.

12. For a discussion of the virtual reign of terror from June 1981 to December 1982, see Bakhash, *Reign of the Ayatollahs*, pp. 217–32.

13. For more details on Iran's offensives between September 1981 and May 1982, see O'Ballance, *Gulf War*, pp. 67–72, 78–86.

14. Khadduri, *Gulf War*, p. 100.

15. In February 1987 a captured Iraqi pilot identified a fellow pilot whom he said had shot down the Algerian plane with a Soviet air-to-air missile; for details, see Gary Sick, "Trial by Error: Reflections on the Iran-Iraq War," *Middle East Journal* 43, no. 2 (Spring 1989): 236.

16. Iran's victories in May and June 1982 are summarized in O'Ballance, *Gulf War*, pp. 82–86.

17. Ibid., pp. 93–102, 114–20.

18. *Washington Post*, November 9, 1982.

19. Velayati's press conference is reproduced in FBIS-MEA-83-013, January 19, 1983, p. 3; for a detailed analysis of the differences over war policy among Iran's leaders, see *Washington Post*, May 18, 1985.

20. The initiation of the tanker war phase of the Iran-Iraq War is examined in Dilip Hiro, "Chronicle of the Gulf War," *MERIP Reports* 125/126 (July–September 1984): 12–13.

21. For a summary of all military activity during 1984–87 and its impact on Iran's oil exports, see O'Ballance, *Gulf War*, pp. 142–48, 153–56, 160–85, 189–98.

22. Sick, "Trial by Error," p. 237.

23. For more detail about Iran's relations with the Arab states of the GCC, see Eric Hooglund, "Iran and the Gulf War," *MERIP Middle East Report* 148 (September–October 1987): 17–18.

24. R. K. Ramazani, "Iran: Burying the Hatchet," *Foreign Policy* no. 60 (Fall 1985): 62–63.

25. For an analysis of Iran's role in the arms-for-hostages deals with the United States, see Eric Hooglund, "The Search for Iran's 'Moderates,'" *MERIP Middle East Report* 144 (January–February 1987): 5–6.

26. Hooglund, "Islamic Republic at War and Peace," p. 6.

27. See *Washington Post*, May 14, 1987.

28. Eric Hooglund, "Reagan's Iran: Factions behind US Policy in the Gulf," *Middle East Report* 151 (March–April 1988): 31.

29. Sick, "Trial by Error," p. 240.

30. Hooglund, "Islamic Republic at War and Peace," p. 7.

31. Ibid.

32. Ibid.

33. Anthony Parsons, "Iran and Western Europe," *Middle East Journal* 43, no. 2 (Spring 1989): 227.

34. Khamene'i's speeches and press conferences in New York are summarized in *Iran Times*, September 25, 1987, and October 2, 1987.

35. Sick, "Trial by Error," p. 241.

36. Hooglund, "Islamic Republic at War and Peace," p. 10.

37. For the impact of the chemical attack on Halabja, see *Iran Times*, March 25, 1988, and April 1 and 8, 1988.

38. Hooglund, "Islamic Republic at War and Peace," p. 8.

39. Sick, "Trial by Error," p. 243.

40. For a history of the Shatt al-Arab dispute, see Kaiyan Homi Kaikobad, *The Shatt al-Arab Boundary Question: A Legal Reappraisal* (Oxford: Clarendon Press, 1988), pp. 5–67.

4

The Iran-Iraq War

The View from Iraq

Phebe Marr

The eight-year Persian Gulf War has left permanent effects on Iraq, decisively changing its regional orientation and the thrust of its foreign policy. Part of this change has been an accelerated transition, under way before the war, from a state driven by revolutionary ideology to one based more on pragmatism and a rational calculation of its national interest.[1] The war has also proven the dominance of geostrategic factors for Iraq. In the postwar era, as in the prewar, Iraq faces the hard realities of its demographic structure, its geographic position, and the legacy of artificial and inadequate boundaries drawn by a former imperial power.[2] Although military victory has left it the strongest military power in the Gulf, Iraq's leadership may find it difficult to translate this victory into permanent solutions to long-standing problems or even to achieve some of its strategic and political objectives. This chapter analyzes Iraq's objectives in pursuing the war, the degree of success its government had in achieving them, and what permanent effects the war has left on Iraq's strategic posture in the region.

IRAQ'S WAR OBJECTIVES

Much ink has been spilled on Iraq's strategic and political objectives in the war.[3] Although Iraq's initial war aims have never been satisfactorily explained, they probably consisted of a mixture of goals—domestic, strategic, and instrumental. While not all deserve equal weight, at least four can be identified.

Regardless of the means chosen or the wisdom of the strategy applied, the first—and, in the Iraqi view, the chief—objective of the war was defensive: protection of the regime and the Iraqi state from the spread of the Iranian Revolution. The first and most immediate threat from Iran was maintenance of the regime, directly challenged by Ayatollah Khomeini's call for the overthrow of Saddam Hussein and the Baath Party and their replacement by an Islamic government similar to the one taking shape in Tehran.[4] It has often been claimed that the threat to regime and state in Iraq was more ephemeral than real and, in any event, could have been contained by means other than war. Perhaps this was so. But Saddam Hussein, a leader who has held power for over twenty years by taking few chances on internal security, felt otherwise. He had just assumed the presidency of the state in July 1979 in a transition marked by serious internal dissent in the leadership. Several years of increasing Shi'i unrest had been greatly exacerbated by the Iranian Revolution. In the face of verbal incitements to the Shi'i community, assassination attempts against Iraqi ministers, and attacks from Iran,[5] Hussein was not willing to take the risk.

A second potential threat concerned cohesion of the state. This threat rested on Iraq's demographic structure, a population mix of ethnic and sectarian groups that are sometimes scrambled (as in Baghdad) but more often concentrated in geographic regions. As is well known, Kurds, constituting about 15 to 20 percent of the population, inhabit the mountains and valleys of northeast Iraq. Arab Shi'a, comprising just over half the population, live in the densely populated river valleys from Baghdad south to Basra. Both Kurds and Shi'a inhabit the areas bordering Iran. Sunni Arabs, about 20 to 25 percent of the population, live in the area from Baghdad north to Mosul and along the Euphrates Valley to the borders of neighboring Syria and Jordan. Minorities of Christians and of Turkish and Persian speakers form the remainder of the population.[6] Dissolving traditional ethnic and sectarian loyalties and creating a sense of Iraqi identity have posed delicate problems for Iraq since its inception as a state in 1921. The problem has been exacerbated by the presence of the same ethnic and sectarian groups across frontiers in neighboring states. In times of conflict, these states have manipulated ambiguous cultural and political loyalties among Iraq's inhabitants to create unrest and to destabilize the central government in Baghdad. The most serious example, very fresh in Iraqi consciousness, was the Shah's support for a Kurdish rebellion in 1974 and 1975. Iran's support for a Shi'i revolution in the south, as well as its support for a Kurdish separatist rebellion in the north, had the potential for civil war or gradual political disintegration of the Iraqi state.[7]

A second, albeit distinctly subordinate, objective was to secure reversal of the 1975 decision on the Shatt al-Arab boundary.[8] Iraq wanted to regain the total control of the Shatt that it had lost under the 1975 Algiers agreement. Both Iraq's regime and much of its population resented the shift of the frontier from the mean low tide on the Iranian shore to the *thalweg*, or midchannel boundary, that gave Iran ownership over half of the river. In the Iraqi view its government had been compelled to accept this border revision to end Iran's support for a Kurdish rebellion that was gradually wresting control of the northern portion of the country from the central government in Baghdad.[9]

Iraq's obsession with total control of the Shatt al-Arab can only be understood in the context of its long history of border problems with Iran and its own limited access to the Gulf. In Iraq's view the 1975 agreement was simply the most recent example of Iranian expansion into Arab (mainly Iraqi) territory, preceded by Iran's incorporation of Muhammarah (Khuzistan) in 1925, the waters around Abadan (1937), and the islands of Abu Musa and the two Tunbs at the foot of the Gulf in 1971.[10] More important to Iraq is its limited Gulf shore. Geographically, Iraq may be likened to a man with huge lungs and a very tiny windpipe.[11] A country with substantial resources (oil, water, and a sizable educated population), Iraq is virtually landlocked, having a Gulf shoreline of only 26 miles. On the eastern boundary of that shore, Iran controls half of the Shatt, Iraq's main deep-water outlet to the Gulf; on its western boundary, Kuwait owns two islands, Warba and Bubiyan, that dominate the entrance to the Khor Abdallah estuary leading to Umm Qasr, Iraq's second port.

Secure access to the Gulf has always been important to Iraq. In the 1960s, however, it became a vital interest, spurred by several events. One was the development of new oil fields and an industrial complex near the head of the Gulf. Beginning in the 1960s, Iraq gradually decoupled its oil industry from the British-controlled Iraq Petroleum Company (IPC), centered on the Kirkuk oil fields in the north, which it nationalized in 1972.[12] Simultaneously, Iraq developed its rich Rumailah oil field near Basra. Along with new oil installations, Iraq constructed a major industrial complex in the Basra area consisting of iron, steel, petrochemical, and fertilizer plants. Even more important, in 1975, after repeated problems with Syria over its pipeline to the Mediterranean, Iraq constructed a "strategic pipeline" to take oil from Kirkuk to the Gulf, thus reducing the importance of the Mediterranean outlet and increasing the significance of the Gulf.[13] At the same time, Iraq's increased dependence on oil revenues for economic development and budgetary outlays, particularly after the oil price rise of 1973, reinforced the need for a secure and independent export outlet on the Gulf.

These developments coincided with an increasingly uncertain political environment for Iraq in the Gulf. In 1968 Britain announced its intention to withdraw from the Gulf, which it did in 1971. Iraq's traditional adversary, the Shah of Iran, made it clear that he would assume Britain's former role as Gulf hegemon, guaranteeing the region's stability. Thereafter, Iran increased its military arsenal to assure a balance of power in its favor. The Shah also contributed to Iraq's concern over Gulf access by challenging its authority in the Shatt and by calling into question the 1937 border agreement.[14] This concern was exacerbated in 1971 when the Shah incorporated three islands (Abu Musa and the two Tunbs) at the foot of the Gulf. For obvious reasons, unfettered passage through the Strait of Hormuz is as important to Iraq as its access to the Gulf in the north.

Iraq's modus vivendi with the Shah under the Algiers agreement was uncomfortable but stable, and it did allow Iraq access to and egress from the Gulf. Iran's new revolutionary regime not only refused to acknowledge the validity of the agreement but injected an element of revolutionary unpredictability into the equation, not only at the head, but also at the foot of the Gulf. While revision of the Shatt al-Arab border would not have been sufficient, in and of itself, to propel Iraq into a war, once the opportunity had been presented, it became an additional inducement.

Beyond these war aims, there may have been more intangible objectives—both political and ideological—that went beyond Iraq's vital interests. Like most intangibles, they are difficult to pin down, but through Hussein's speeches and actions we can catch more than a glimpse. Saddam Hussein desired to play a leading role in the Arab world, a role given impetus by the Camp David agreement. In November 1978, shortly after the Israeli-Egyptian peace agreement, Iraq took the initiative in convening a conference of Arab heads of state. The main outcome of this meeting was removal of Egypt from the Arab League and other institutions. Once Egypt had been isolated, Iraq's role was magnified; indeed, Iraq's only competitor remained Syria, which soon—and not surprisingly—took the opposing side in the war. Not long after this assembly, in February 1980, Saddam Hussein set forth an "Arab Charter" containing a new vision of inter-Arab relations in which Iraq could now play a leading role.[15] The Charter banned the use of force among Arab states, called for Arab solidarity against foreign (that is, non-Arab) aggression, and posed a new order based not on integral Arab unity, but on cooperation among Arab states. Hussein also had pretensions of playing a wider leadership role in the Third World through hosting the Non-Aligned Conference scheduled to convene in

Baghdad in 1982 and by assuming the presidency of that movement for the next four years. But it must be emphasized that the focus of this leadership role, and its raison d'être, was opposition to the Camp David agreement and to Israel, a position entirely compatible with Baath ideology.[16]

The Iranian Revolution interrupted these developments by focusing Iraq's attention on its eastern front. Gradually, Iraq's defensive objectives vis-à-vis Iran and its vision of an Arab leadership role fused; the Arab world was threatened, not only from expansionist Israel in the West, but also by a revolutionary Iran in the east. Iraq would be the guardian of the eastern front.[17] This is not to say that Hussein's vision of securing the Arab leadership role figured directly into his preemptive strike against Iran. Rather, it constituted the context in which the strike was made. The clash between Khomeini and Hussein was one of different, incompatible worldviews, that of Islamic internationalism on the one hand and secular Arab nationalism on the other. Continued propaganda and subversion from Iran could have undermined Hussein's position not only at home, but in the Arab world as well, while also undercutting the legitimacy of other Arab regimes in the region. A preemptive strike into Iran, if successful, would bolster Hussein's position, weaken the Islamic Republic, and consolidate a favorable balance of power for Iraq in the Arab world. These assumptions and perceptions—along with the opportunity to succeed—were not a *casus belli* in themselves; rather, they provided still another inducement and may have affected Hussein's choice of strategy.

Fourth, Iraq may also have entertained hopes of "liberating" Khuzistan, the province in southwest Iran containing vast oil resources and a majority of ethnic Arabs. Baathists have always considered this province part of the Arab homeland. However, articulation of this goal remained obscure and was probably more instrumental than serious. After Iran's attempts to stir up Iraq's Shi'a and Kurds, Iraq retaliated by reviving previously dormant calls for opposition to the Tehran regime among its ethnic minorities, including the Kurds and the Arabs of Khuzistan.[18] Nonetheless, establishment of an independent "Arabistan" in southwest Iran was never a clear, let alone serious, war objective of Iraq.

As the conflict accelerated and Iran's aggravated military and political weaknesses became more apparent, Iraq was presented with an opportunity to achieve all of these goals through the possible collapse of the Khomeini regime and its replacement with a leadership more amenable to Iraq's securing its vital interests. We cannot know what assessments went into Iraq's decision to cross the Iranian frontier in September 1980, but we do know that rather than adopt a strategy of containment as it had appeared to do earlier, Iraq elected to launch an offensive strike. Iraq may have reasoned that it had to prevent consolidation of a hostile regime in Iran by acting while the balance of political and military power was still in its favor. Or Baghdad may have hoped to create a shock sufficient to chasten the Iranian regime and compel Khomeini to accept Iraqi terms. Or Iraq may have become convinced that one bold military stroke might be sufficient to bring about a change of regimes—or at least personnel; revision of the Shatt agreement and adherence to the border security provisions of the Algiers agreement, and, as a corollary, greatly enhanced prestige on the Arab front all might be won at once. Whatever its intent toward the Iranian regime, Iraq made clear in a statement issued eight days after the invasion that it had no territorial designs on Iran beyond the Shatt border, to which Iraqi troops intended to withdraw once the issue of noninterference in its internal affairs was settled.[19] Thus collapse of the Iranian regime, desirable though that might have been, was apparently viewed by Baghdad as a means to an end rather than an end in itself.

THE STAGES OF WAR AND THE SHIFT OF PRIORITIES

For Iraq, the war went through three fairly well defined stages.[20] The first consisted of Iraq's offensive, lasting roughly from September 22, 1980, when Iraqi troops crossed into Iranian territory, until June 1982, when they were forced to withdraw to the international frontier.[21] The second, lasting six long years, was a grueling war of attrition in which Iraq lost the initiative to Iran in the ground war but was able to use the opportunity to build up its forces and develop their operational capacity. The third was Iraq's final offensive, which recaptured Iraqi territory held by Iran, destroyed Iran's military cohesiveness, captured massive amounts of Iranian equipment, and finally brought Iranian acceptance of a cease-fire.[22] As Iraq's fortunes shifted in the war, so too did its priorities; gradually Baghdad's aims became less visionary and more realistic. In the end, Iraq may have achieved more prestige and potential for Arab leadership than realization of its vital interests. But the war produced profound changes in Iraq and for its role in the region.

The first phase of the Gulf War was a disaster for Iraq and generated a serious domestic backlash against the regime. Conventional wisdom claims that Iraq overestimated its power and underestimated Iran's resources and its will to resist.[23] A more recent study takes issue with this view.[24] It claims that Iraq planned a limited war for more general purposes—to destroy Iranian forces and to compel Iranian compliance with its wishes—but that Baghdad did not adjust its means to its ends. Rather than having underestimated its foe, Iraq failed to use its superior military power to advantage to defeat the Iranian army. For the ends desired, nothing short of total war would have sufficed. For total war, the Iraqi leadership would have needed the complete support of its populace, and this it did not have.[25] The limited war strategy was incompatible with these larger objectives and it failed. Instead of ending up with a short war, Iraq was forced into a protracted, grueling war of attrition.

Whatever the strategy, this initial phase of the war quickly revealed Iraq's vulnerabilities. From the opening days of the war, its Gulf ports were closed by Iranian bombardment, making Iraq a truly landlocked country and reducing its oil exports from over 3 million barrels per day (b/d) in 1979 to 1 million b/d in 1980.[26] Precisely because it had anticipated a brief war, Iraq followed an economic strategy designed to provide its people with both guns and butter. As a result, Iraq was forced to draw down its substantial financial resources and rapidly acquired a sizable debt to finance the war. This phase ended when Iran, suffering substantial human sacrifices, managed to push Iraqi forces back to the international frontier. In June 1982 Saddam Hussein called for a negotiated settlement on the basis of the 1975 accord.[27]

These realities and Iraq's humiliating defeat stripped Baghdad's war aims down to its vital interests—maintenance of the regime (soon equated almost wholly with survival of the state), preservation of the 1975 boundaries, and survival of the nation in its present form. A definitive end was put to the myth that Khuzistan was Arab and could be "liberated," and little has been heard since of this goal. Hussein's aspirations to Third World leadership were severely set back. The Non-Aligned Conference had to be shifted from Baghdad to New Delhi to avoid war casualties, and Iraq came under some opprobrium for having started a war that it could not end. The Iraqi claim to Arab world leadership appeared equally hollow. As Iraq fought for its life, support had to be enlisted from other Arab countries, rather than the reverse. Most significant of all, Iraq's failure to unseat the Islamic regime in Tehran or to compel a change in its behavior ended any hopes of a united Arab front against Camp David by refocusing the attention of the entire Arab world on the war with Iran, rather than on Israel and Egypt. However, in the course of the long war of attrition, Iraq learned a number of lessons—strategic, political, and economic—and finally developed a coherent set of strategies to deal with its problems. Both the lessons learned and their results will have lasting effects on postwar Iraq and its regional policies.

LESSONS LEARNED IN THE WAR

The first lesson learned by Iraq was the need to secure regional allies. During the conflict Iraq focused on measures to compensate for its lack of strategic depth and forged ties with Arab allies in the region, notably Jordan and Egypt.[28] Both states, for their own reasons, came to Iraq's aid with political and other means of support. Egypt provided spare parts for Soviet equipment and over a million workers to supplant Iraqis fighting at the front; Jordan gave Iraq an outlet to the sea at Aqaba to help circumvent the closure of Iraq's Gulf ports. In the Gulf some members of the newly formed Gulf Cooperation Council (GCC) gradually came to Iraq's aid by providing funds for war equipment and overland routes to Gulf ports and in most, though not all, cases by imposing an economic boycott of Iran.[29] These steps gave Iraq the strategic depth it lacked on its own; in return, however, Iraq became more closely tied to pro-Western states in the area, a decided policy reorientation. The postwar period also has seen the formation of the Arab Cooperation Council (ACC), consisting of Egypt, Jordan, North Yemen, and Iraq, which has formalized Iraq's adhesion to a centrist bloc in the Arab world.

The extent of this shift became evident as early as January 1983, when Iraq published a statement that Saddam Hussein had given earlier to U.S. Representative Stephen Solarz. In it the Iraqi president indicated that he would acquiesce in any solution to the Arab-Israeli conflict agreed upon by the frontline states and the Palestine Liberation Organization (PLO) and, further, that a secure environment for Israel was needed.[30] This remarkable statement represented a substantial shift in Iraqi policy on the Arab-Israeli conflict and virtually brought Iraq into the Arab mainstream on this issue. Not coincidentally, it also isolated Syria, Iran's Arab ally.

Second, to overcome its manpower gap with Iran, Iraq became determined at all costs to maintain and increase a technological edge over Iran, particularly in the military arena. The consequence was a rise in the lethality of Gulf warfare to a level hitherto unseen in the Middle East. Eventually, Iraq developed and used intermediate range missiles in attacks on civilian populations[31] and chemical weapons at the front and, on occasion, against civilians.[32] The situation also raised the specter of a future arms race, not only in these fields, but possibly in nuclear weapons as well.[33] As the war continued, Iraq not only built up the size of its armed forces but also improved their training, organization, and military command structure, the results of which were evidenced in the final phase of the war. The Iraqi air force arm also greatly increased its reach and proficiency. By 1986 Iraq was able to conduct midair refueling and to strike Sirri and Larak Islands at the foot of the Gulf, about 400 miles from Iraq's border.[34] To help accomplish these ends, Iraq diversified its supply sources by reducing dependence on the Soviet Union and increasing purchases of equipment from France, Brazil, and other countries.[35] Iraq also developed a domestic arms industry. These steps have given Iraq not only an edge in military proficiency and experience but also superiority in equipment and technology—an advantage that has shifted the military balance in the Gulf in Baghdad's favor. Iraq can be expected to hold on to that favorable military balance for much of the decade of the 1990s.

As a third lesson, Iraq recognized the need for economic reform and in 1983 introduced austerity measures. These policies reduced current expenditures, but not enough to alleviate the deficit caused by the war. More significant, Iraq undertook modest reform of its economic structure by privatizing portions of the economy, notably agriculture, medicine, and light industry. This effort was aimed at efficiency and also at capturing capital and foreign-exchange resources in the private sector. Whatever the motive, Iraq's market orientation will outlast the war and promises to become a growing feature of the Iraqi economy.

Fourth, to overcome closure of its ports, Iraq developed a network of petroleum pipelines designed to give it flexibility. This became a matter of dire necessity when Syria, once allied with Iran, closed down the Iraqi pipeline passing through its territory in April 1982. Iraq initially expanded its pipeline through Turkey to the Mediterranean in 1984 and in 1987 built a second Turkish leg. Then Iraq constructed a spur to the Saudi pipeline to Yanbu, thereby creating an outlet to the Red Sea. (This has been replaced by a new, Iraqi-owned, 1.6 million b/d pipeline to a port south of Yanbu on the Red Sea completed in 1989.) From a low point of 650,000 b/d in 1982, this pipeline network, together with oil trucked across Jordan to Aqaba, increased Iraq's exports to 2.5 million b/d by the end of 1987.[36] These pipelines have also given Iraq a variety of export outlets that should provide flexibility and a degree of economic independence since they will prevent any one country from controlling Iraq's oil lifeline in the future. In the postwar period Iraq has commenced reconstruction of its offshore oil terminals in the Gulf that will eventually add several million barrels per day of export capacity as well. In addition, Iraq was able to garner financial support from the GCC said to have totaled at least $35 billion by the war's end.[37] Although nominally loans, these monies are not expected to be repaid. Cumulatively, these efforts gradually enabled Iraq to increase its income in the oil sector and to withstand the economic impact of a long war.

Fifth, Iraq brought the war to the rest of the Gulf. Tied down on land along a 750–mile frontier by Iran's superiority in manpower, Iraq used its air power to attack Iran's Kharg Island oil terminal and its shipping at sea in what became known as the "tanker war." These measures were only partially successful. Despite periodic bombing, Kharg Island continued to operate, although Iraq forced Iran to institute a shuttle service that ferried crude oil from Kharg to the islands of Sirri in the southern Gulf and Larak at the entrance to the Gulf, where Iraq's military reach seldom extended. Iraq's main purpose in the tanker war was to reduce Iran's source of revenue—oil exports. After 1986 these attacks became more effective, destroying a major part of the Kharg Island terminal and later the floating replacement terminals at Sirri and Lavan islands at the foot of the Gulf. Iran's oil exports were cut back from about 2.2 million b/d in mid–1986 to below 1.5 million b/d by 1988.[38] However, market factors, the fall of the dollar and Iranian oil production problems probably played as much of a role in placing economic restraints on Iran's ability to conduct the war. Saudi pressure may also have placed limits on Iraq's bombing missions. One lesson Iraq may have learned from the tanker war is the limitation of its power in the Gulf. Despite greatly improved bombing missions after 1986 and successful raids on Kharg, on Sirri and Larak, and on Gulf tanker traffic, Iraq could not reduce Iran's oil exports sufficiently to take it out of the war.

In another respect, however, Iraq's strategy in carrying the war to the Gulf paid handsome dividends. Eventually, it brought a large U.S. military presence into the Gulf. Early in 1987, after several months of Iranian targeting of shipping headed for Kuwait, that state sought protection from the five permanent members of the Security Council (but in reality from the two superpowers). The Soviet Union responded immediately by allowing Kuwait to charter four Soviet tankers, a low-key operation that attracted little local attention. The United States reflagged eleven Kuwaiti ships and then undertook a major escort operation that brought into the Gulf not only U.S. naval and air assets, but also those of five other European countries as well. In April 1988, in response to damage done by mines to a U.S. vessel, the United States attacked Iranian offshore installations and a number of Iranian naval vessels.[39] Meanwhile, Iraq continued to attack Iranian shipping with impunity. These actions further served to isolate Iran and put pressure on the Khomeini regime to accept the cease-fire.

For Iraq, the last stage in the war began after the critical battles for Basra in December 1986 and again early in 1987, which proved to be the turning point of the war. Iran failed to breach Iraqi defenses around Basra, although bombardment drove out many of its inhabitants. In the course of the battle, Iran's human losses were massive, finally outstripping its absorptive capacity and making subsequent recruitment for any new offensives extremely difficult.

Iraq correctly assessed Iran's weakness. In April 1988 Iraq went on the offensive once again using brutal but effective tactics to bring about the final cease-fire. Intensive missile and air attacks on Iran's cities, especially Tehran, wore down morale. Well-planned and coordinated attacks drove Iranians out of al-Faw, Majnun, and Iraqi territory east of Basra. In some attacks chemical weapons were used. Finally, the Iraqi army drove into Iranian territory, where it destroyed the cohesion of Iranian forces and carried back to Iraq massive amounts of Iranian equipment. In this offensive Iraq also took additional Iranian prisoners of war partially to offset Iraqi POWs held in Iran; Iraq also retained pockets of Iranian territory that could be used as bargaining chips in future negotiations. This last campaign not only delivered a devastating blow to Iranian military forces; it also left Iraq the strongest military power in the Gulf. Nevertheless, the April offensive gave Iraq's leadership an unsavory international reputation for the means by which its victory had been attained—a negative image that went far toward eliminating gains Baghdad had gradually made in improving its international image.

THE BALANCE SHEET

What, on balance, did Iraq achieve of its original objectives after eight long years of war? Iraq succeeded in its defensive goals. The regime, whether in the person of Saddam Hussein or the institution of the Baath Party, remains intact and more solidly based than in 1979 when it faced a mounting Shi'i rebellion. In fact, the war has placed unprecedented power in the hands of Saddam Hussein and the central government.

Iraq was also successful in protecting the cohesion and integrity of the state. Indeed, among the Arab population, the war and defense of the country generated a far greater sense of Iraqi patriotism than had existed before. The overwhelming majority of Shi'a, who comprised the majority of foot soldiers, proved that their Iraqi identity was stronger than their sectarian loyalty. This new Iraqi nationalism (admittedly only partially shared by the Kurds) may be the most positive, although intangible, achievement of the war.

Iraq's victory has even enabled the country to recoup some of its potential for leadership in the Arab world. Iraq's armed forces are now the largest, best equipped, and most experienced in the Arab world. Moreover, most Arab leaders are impressed with Iraq's ability to withstand a punishing eight-year ordeal and emerge triumphant at the end. Iraq's oil reserves—officially cited as 100 billion barrels—are second only to Saudi Arabia's; they provide an economic base for its military power. Iraq's pipelines give the country flexibility to export from a number of sources and reduce its dependence on any one outlet. Increased production facilities will make Iraq a major producer before the end of the next decade. All of these factors add up to considerable power.

Notwithstanding these gains, Iraq failed to achieve the more ambitious goals of its original offensive. The demise of the Islamic regime in Tehran remains as elusive as it was in 1980, although Iraq's effort certainly did much to weaken that regime and to blunt the spread of the revolution. While the death of Ayatollah Khomeini in June 1989 may have tempered radical Islamic fundamentalism in Iran, the revolution remains alive. The attempt to revise the 1975 agreement on the Shatt al-Arab boundary has thus far proved futile. Meanwhile, the river goes unused and will likely remain unusable absent an agreement with Iran—a development that will not be achieved easily. Far from gaining more secure access to the Gulf, Iraq now finds its postwar access even more limited. Greater access to the Gulf will only come gradually as Iraq develops offshore oil terminals and alternative ports at Umm Qasr and Khor al-Zubair.

Against these gains must be matched the enormous cost of the war. Although figures are notoriously unreliable, estimates place Iraq's casualties at about 400,000, of whom 150,000—about 4 to 5 percent of its military-age population—were killed.[40] An entire generation has lost a decade of its life, and the country has only begun to face the social costs it will have to pay. Iraq's booming prewar economy and rapid economic development have probably been set back two decades (one for the war years and one for postwar reconstruction). A large non-Arab debt will slow economic recovery. A revived Kurdish rebellion in the north has led to draconian measures to end the "Kurdish problem" once and for all, including resettlement of some 500,000 Kurds from border towns, creating upheaval in Kurdish areas and inciting international disapproval. Iraq is meanwhile engaged in a lethal arms race that may well prove to be an economic burden and possibly even a security risk as the international community, including the Soviet Union, eyes Iraq's buildup with concern and dismay. Closer to home, worries in Israel about the shift in the military balance of power may come to threaten Iraq's future far more than Iran.

Furthermore, it remains to be seen whether sheer military power can be translated into political influence. Recent attempts by Iraq to pressure Kuwait for lease of the two islands at the entrance to the Khor Abdallah channel indicate otherwise. Perhaps the most important lesson for Iraq in the Gulf War is that its reach cannot exceed its grasp. Iraq has been most successful in defending its own soil and in taking steps designed to strengthen Iraqi "nationhood"; Iraq has been least successful in attempting to project its power throughout the region, especially into Iran. When all is said and done, Iraq's geography and demographic structure put serious limitations on its future foreign policy. In the Gulf Iraq is limited by minimal access, by a long Iranian shore stretching down to the Strait of Hormuz, and now by the formation of an independent GCC on the Arab side of the Gulf, an organization that likely will act as a balancing agent between Iran and Iraq. Internally, domestic tranquility and national cohesion depend not only on protection of an extensive border with Iran, but on finding ways to satisfy legitimate concerns of ethnic and sectarian groups and on their integration into the state. These are major challenges that confront the Baghdad regime on the road to reconstruction after its protracted and costly war with Iran.

NOTES

The views and findings in this article are those of the author and should not be construed as representing the policy or position of the National Defense University, the Department of Defense, or the U.S. government.

1. For an exposition of these changes and their limitations, see Fred Axelgard, *A New Iraq? The Gulf War and Implications for U.S. Policy* (New York: Praeger, 1988).

2. These realities are clearly outlined in Christine Moss Helms, "Iraq," in Samuel F. Wells, Jr., and Mark Bruzonsky, eds., *Security in the Middle East* (Boulder, Colo.: Westview Press, 1987).

3. Iraq's motives have been sharply debated, with strikingly different assessments given by Iran, Iraq, and various scholars. For a variety of views, see Efraim Karsh, *The Iran-Iraq War: A Military Analysis*, Adelphi Papers 220 (London: International Institute for Strategic Studies [IISS], 1987); Efraim Karsh, "Military Power and Foreign Policy Goals: The Iran-Iraq War Revisited," *International Affairs* 64 (Winter 1987/88): 83–95; Ralph King, *The Iran-Iraq War: The Political Implications*, Adelphi Papers 219 (London: IISS, 1987); William O. Staudenmaier, "A Strategic Analysis," in Shirin Tahir-Kheli and Shaheen Ayubi, eds., *The Iran-Iraq War* (New York: Praeger, 1983); and Shahram Chubin and Charles Tripp, *Iran and Iraq at War* (Boulder, Colo.: Westview Press, 1988), chaps. 2 and 4.

4. Majid Khadduri, *The Gulf War* (New York: Oxford University Press, 1988), pp. 111–12.

5. Cross-border fire between both countries escalated toward the end of 1979 and during 1980. Baghdad cited more than 15 intensive Iranian bombardments of Iraqi territory between August 1979 and June 1980, and on September 4 and 7, 1980, Iran shelled the cities of Khanaqin and Mandali, despite repeated Iraqi protests. See the statement of Sa'dun Hammadi, Iraqi minister of foreign affairs, to the Security Council, October 15, 1980, in Tareq Ismael, *Iran and Iraq: Roots of Conflict* (Syracuse: Syracuse University Press, 1982), pp. 203–12. For an excellent analysis of Iraq's defensive posture, see Karsh, *Iran-Iraq War*.

6. Richard F. Nyrop, *Iraq: A Country Study*, Foreign Area Studies Handbook (Washington, D.C.: Government Printing Office, 1979), p. 67.

7. Khomeini's call for revolution was theoretically ecumenical and was meant to appeal to all Muslims. However, given his emphasis on the unique role of the *faqih* (chief jurist) and other distinctly Shi'i doctrines, as well as Iran's position as the leading Shi'i state, his "call" appealed mainly to Shi'a. Iranian support for Iraqi Kurdish dissidents became apparent in July 1979 when the Barzani brothers, exiled leaders of the Kurdish Democratic party, were permitted to return to Iraq in contravention of the 1975 agreement with the Shah.

8. For the Iraqi view of this long and tortuous dispute, see Khalid al-Izzi, *The Shatt al-Arab Dispute: A Legal Study* (London: Third World Center for Research and Publishing, 1981). For an Iranian perspective, see S. H. Amin, "The Iran-Iraq Conflict: Legal Implications," *International and Comparative Law Quarterly* 31 (January 1982): 167–68.

9. The Algiers agreement had two main components. One was a shift of the

Shatt al-Arab boundary to the *thalweg*; the other provided for the inviolability of the frontier. The text of the agreement is to be found in Ismael, *Iran and Iraq*, pp. 62–68.

10. A good summary of this historical legacy is given in Jasim Abdulghani, *Iraq and Iran: The Years of Crisis* (Baltimore: Johns Hopkins University Press, 1984), chap. 1.

11. I am indebted to Amatzia Baram for this graphic illustration.

12. On the petroleum nationalization, see Edith Penrose and E. F. Penrose, *Iraq: International Relations and National Development* (Boulder, Colo.: Westview Press, 1978), chaps. 16 and 17.

13. In 1966 Syria stopped throughput in the pipeline in a dispute over transit fees. In 1972 Syria again demanded an upward revision of transit fees that virtually eliminated all Iraq's profits from nationalization.

14. This concern was expressed in several confrontations between the two countries. In 1969, soon after the Baath Party came to power, the Shah demanded a revision of the Shatt boundary, and when Iraq refused, Iran publicly abrogated the treaty of 1937. In 1971 Iraq broke diplomatic relations with Iran after the Shah occupied the three islands at the foot of the Gulf. By the mid-1970s the Shah was supporting a Kurdish rebellion in the north (along with Israel and the United States) ultimately leading to the 1975 agreement, in which Iraq was forced to recognize Iran's de facto dominance in the Gulf. For the U.S. role, see *Village Voice*, February 16, 1976, Special Supplement, p. 85; John Prados, *Presidents' Secret Wars*, 2d ed. (New York: Quill, 1986), pp. 313–15.

15. Phebe Marr, *The Modern History of Iraq* (Boulder, Colo.: Westview Press, 1985), p. 245.

16. Baath ideology is founded on the notion of an Arab renaissance (*baath*) based on a secular, progressive nationalism and on pan-Arab unity, anti-imperialism, anti-Zionism, and a modified socialism. Since the war all of the last four items have been modified, some substantially, and the ideological component of the regime has been reduced.

17. The fact that Iraq saw collusion between Israel and Iran during the war (substantiated by "Irangate" revelations) reinforced this view. In Iraq the war was known as Hussein's "Qadisiyyah," referring to the seventh-century battle in which Arab Muslims defeated Persian Zoroastrians.

18. In 1981 Tariq Aziz suggested that he might be willing to see the disintegration of the Iranian state. King, *Iran-Iraq War*, p. 10. After 1982 nothing more was heard of the idea.

19. King, *Iran-Iraq War*, p. 5.

20. For a detailed exposition of the war in its various stages, see Anthony H. Cordesman, *The Iran-Iraq War and Western Security, 1984–1987* (London: Jane's, 1987).

21. Iraq dates the war from the shelling by Iran of Iraqi towns in early September 1980.

22. Insufficient attention has been given to this third phase of the war, which revealed Iraq's organizational and material strength compared to that of Iran.

23. For this view, see Staudenmaier, "Strategic Analysis," pp. 36–37.

24. Karsh, "Military Power and Foreign Policy Goals."

25. For an in-depth analysis of the strategic role played by Hussein's concern over lack of support in the war, see Chubin and Tripp, *Iran and Iraq at War*, chap. 2. In Tripp's view the causes of the war, as well as the strategy followed, stem largely from the authoritarian nature of the regime.

26. Iraq's oil exports were further reduced to 650,000 b/d in 1982 when Syria shut down the pipeline to the Mediterranean; this was the low point of oil exports for Iraq during the war.

27. King, *Iran-Iraq War*, p. 11.

28. Jordan supported Iraq from the first days of the war. Egypt's ties with Iraq, designed to foster its return to the Arab League, developed more slowly.

29. Formed in 1981, the Gulf Cooperation Council (GCC) was established in part as a defensive alliance to deal with the war, but it did not admit Iraq, nor is it likely to do so. Not all GCC states supported Iraq with enthusiasm. The United Arab Emirates traded openly with Iran throughout the war, and Oman maintained relatively close relations with Iran as well. For the GCC role in the war, see King, *Iran-Iraq War*, chap. 3; Wayne White, "The Iran-Iraq War: A Challenge to the Arab Gulf States," in H. Richard Sindelar III and John Peterson, eds., *Crosscurrents in the Gulf* (London: Routledge, 1988).

30. Fred Axelgard, *U.S.-Arab Relations: The Iraqi Dimension* (Jacksonville, Ill.: National Council on U.S.-Arab Relations, 1985), pp. 8–9.

31. Joseph Yager, *Nuclear Nonproliferation Strategy in the Middle East and North Africa*, (McLean, Va.: Center for National Security Negotiations, 1989), p. 15. The Iraqis used Soviet Scuds that were modified by reducing their weight and probably by strapping on additional booster rockets in order to reach Tehran.

32. Few issues have generated as much public concern—and aversion—for Iraq as its use of chemical weapons in the war and the controversy over their use after the war on Kurdish rebels. The Iraqis have admitted using chemical weapons during the war but deny their use on Kurds after the cease-fire. While no firm physical proof of such use has been found, independent verification has not been permitted by Iraq. The case for their use has been based mainly on extensive circumstantial evidence gathered through interviews with Kurds who fled to Turkey and elsewhere.

33. For a discussion of Iraq's nuclear aims, see Yager, *Nuclear Nonproliferation Strategy*, pp. 7–9, 10–14.

34. Cordesman, *Iran-Iraq War*, pp. 106–8.

35. Ibid., pp. 25–27. Iraq's major supplier of military equipment remained the Soviet Union (55 percent), but it received about 20–25 percent of its supplies from France, mainly Mirage planes.

36. U.S. Department of Commerce, *Foreign Economic Trends, Iraq* (Washington, D.C.: Government Printing Office, 1989), p. 3.

37. This figure is an estimate. Some sources place the amount as high as $50 billion. See, for example, Cordesman, *Iran-Iraq War*, p. 3.

38. George Joffe, "The Gulf War," in *The Middle East and North Africa, 1989* (London: Europa Publications, 1989), p. 114.

39. Ibid., pp. 116–17; Jochen Hippler, "NATO Goes to the Persian Gulf," *Middle East Report* 18, no. 6 (1988): 18–19.

40. Amatzia Baram, "After the Iran-Iraq War—What?" *The Jerusalem Quarterly* 49 (Winter 1989): 85.

5

Israel and the Iran-Iraq War

Bernard Reich

The interrelationship of the Arab-Israeli and Persian Gulf zones of the Middle East, and the effect on politics and strategy of each on the other, has long generated a tendency to see the two sectors as separate and distinct, although the links between them are many and complex. The Iran-Iraq War hostilities and the subsequent cease-fire provide an opportunity to reassess the interrelationship.

BEFORE THE IRAN-IRAQ WAR

During the period before the Iran-Iraq War, Iraq participated in several wars against Israel (in 1948–49, in 1967, and in 1973) and remained in a state of war with it. Iraq was among those Arab states that took the lead against Egyptian President Anwar Sadat's peace overtures to Israel in 1977 and 1978, it opposed the Egypt-Israel Peace Treaty of 1979, and it harbored and supported anti-Israel Palestinian terrorist groups. Nevertheless, Iraq's Arab world role was circumscribed by a significant disagreement with Syria over the leadership of the Baath movement, among other issues, and some of its neighbors in the Persian Gulf/Arabian Peninsula zone regarded Iraq as a potential threat to their security and stability.

Before the Iranian Revolution Iran was a relatively minor actor in the Arab-Israeli sector, and the Shah's regime had an ambivalent relationship with Arab states and Israel. Links with Israel varied from close to cool, depending on the subject area and the time frame. With the ouster of the Shah and the coming to power of the Ayatollah Ruhollah Khomeini, the relationship between Israel and Iran became marked by strong hostility.

The Shah's regime differed with the Arab states on numerous issues, and while Iran was seen as a threat to some states, it played a positive role in the survival of others (for example, Oman). With the Iranian Revolution, these relationships also changed and, in the case of Iraq, led to the Iran-Iraq War.

Prerevolutionary Iranian policy in the Arab-Israeli zone was based on a number of interrelated factors. Iran's historical fear of its northern border enemy, the Soviet Union (previously Russia), was enhanced by a dread of encirclement by states linked to that power. The Shah feared Arab radicalism that might spread from states such as Egypt and Iraq to its Gulf neighbors and to Iran itself, thereby threatening its sea link through the Strait of Hormuz to the Indian Ocean and the rest of the world. The traditional enmity with Iraq was based on religion (Iranian affinity with the Shi'a minority in Iraq), territory (the demarcation of the Shatt al-Arab boundary), and Arab irredentism (Iraqi support for the Arab population of Iran's Khuzistan province), as well as on political rivalries that focused on Gulf-zone dominance. There was also a desire, shared with other monarchies such as Saudi Arabia, Jordan, and Morocco, to maintain a conservative (moderate) stability in the region. And there was a multifaceted relationship with Israel based on strategic-political concerns (especially about radical Arab intentions) and economic interests.

Iran's policies were somewhat contradictory. The Shah's close bilateral ties with Israel and an often-negative bilateral relationship with many Arab states were not reflected in his approach to the Arab-Israeli conflict, where Iran tended to support the Arab position. Hostile relations with Egypt and Syria and the discreet friendship with Israel were not consonant with Iran's pronouncements concerning the Arab-Israeli conflict. In 1947 Iran opposed the Palestine Partition Plan that led to the creation of Israel and supported the proposal for a federal state in Palestine that was endorsed by the Arab states. From 1948 onward, Iran endorsed the rights of the Palestinians and voted for U.N. resolutions supporting the Palestinian refugees' choice of repatriation or compensation. Nevertheless, Iran established diplomatic relations with Israel in 1950.

In the Suez crisis of 1956, Iran supported Egypt's right to nationalize the canal and opposed the use of force against Egypt but was deeply concerned with ensuring freedom of navigation in the canal, through which some 75 percent of Iran's imports and exports passed. As a member of the executive committee of the Canal Users' Association, Iran was among those calling for Egypt to end restrictions on free passage through the waterway. Yet in November 1956 Iran joined the United States and the Soviet Union in calling for an emergency session of the U.N. General Assembly to condemn the Israeli-French-British invasion of Egypt.

Iranian policy became more supportive of the Arab position after the June 1967 war. The Red Lion and Sun, the Iranian version of the Red Cross, dispatched medical aid to Jordan and Iraq. Afterward, the Shah called for Israeli withdrawal from occupied territory and stated that control of the Muslim holy places in Jerusalem, which had come under Israeli control, must not be in the hands of non-Muslims.

During the October War of 1973 Iran offered transport pilots and planes to Saudi Arabia and allowed the Soviet Union to overfly Iran to deliver military supplies to its Arab clients, in addition to medical assistance provided to the Arab states. At the same time, Iran refused to permit volunteers traveling to Israel from Australia to use Tehran as a transfer point. Although Iran did not participate in the Arab oil-production reductions and the embargo imposed on the United States and other states friendly to Israel, it took the lead in increasing oil prices, which multiplied the effect of the Arab oil weapon. Despite some differences over optimal pricing and over the use of oil as a political weapon, Iran and the Arab oil producers cooperated within OPEC to the joint benefit of both. Nevertheless, Iran remained a supplier of oil to Israel during and after the conflict.

After the termination of hostilities, the Shah visited Egypt and Jordan and endorsed their perspectives of the Arab-Israeli conflict. The Iranian government announced its agreement with the 1974 decision of the Arab summit at Rabat endorsing self-determination for the Palestinians and recognizing the Palestine Liberation Organization (PLO) as their "sole legitimate representative." Iran's delegation voted for similar resolutions in the United Nations. Nevertheless, the Shah was uncomfortable with the radical character and terrorist methods of some of the Palestinians. For this reason, despite Iran's diplomatic support for the PLO in international forums, the Shah did not maintain formal contact with the organization and was careful to distinguish between the Palestinians in general and such factions as George Habash's Popular Front for the Liberation of Palestine (PFLP), which openly associated with Iranian dissidents. Various Palestinian factions, including the mainstream groups under Yasser Arafat's leadership, provided training and other support for Iranian revolutionaries beginning in the early 1970s, although this was not acknowledged until after the success of the Iranian Revolution. The Shah supported the Sadat initiative of November 1977.

Prerevolutionary Iran maintained positive and extensive bilateral relations with Israel and relations of a less substantial nature with many of the Arab states, but generally in public pronouncements it supported the Arab position in the conflict.[1] Iran endorsed the view that Israel should withdraw from occupied territories and supported the rights of the Palestinians, although it opposed terrorism as a means of attaining Arab goals. Iran's role in the October War, its subsequent military efforts in support of moderate Arab regimes elsewhere (such as Oman), and its improved bilateral relations with Sadat's Egypt and other Arab states led to some speculation that its role in the future might be more active. The Iranian ambivalence changed with the revolution.

THE PERIOD OF HOSTILITIES (1980–1988)

The size and capability of the opposing military forces,[2] as well as the lack of constraints imposed on their activities by civilian authorities or by more general rules of warfare and ethical considerations, generated substantial concern throughout the Middle East during the period of hostilities. The dominant public reaction of the Arab states came in the creation of the Gulf Cooperation Council (GCC) in 1981. The Saudi-initiated GCC linked six Arab states (Saudi Arabia, Kuwait, Oman, Bahrain, Qatar, and the United Arab Emirates), although the dominant force was and remains Saudi Arabia, in an effort to achieve closer cooperation and to enhance their defense capabilities. Its original and continuing concern was a perceived threat from Iran that combined military and subversive capabilities with a political-ideological component based on a fundamentalist Islamic approach. But there was and is some uneasiness about Iraq and its regional ambitions.

For Israel, the Iran-Iraq War had a number of significant strategic and tactical implications, given the centrality of the Arab threat and Israel's focus on security and resolution of the Arab-Israeli conflict. Arab world divisions were emphasized as the war polarized the Arab states into two camps—the more radical group (Syria, Libya, and South Yemen) tended to favor Iran, while the others (including Jordan, the Gulf states, and Egypt) supported Iraq, although the level of support varied from state to state and over time. The Arab world divisions helped to prevent the formation of a united war front against Israel, thus relieving much of the pressure on Israel's eastern front and substantially reducing the danger of a major Arab-Israeli war. Partly as a consequence of these war-necessitated alignments, there was a moderation in Iraqi pronouncements concerning the Arab-Israeli conflict. In contrast with Iraq's previous strong opposition to Egypt's peace treaty with Israel, Iraq and Egypt cooperated closely during the war effort, and Iraqi criticism of Egypt abated.

Israel's principal gain from the war was that two major regional powers, both regarded as hostile, were occupied in a struggle with each other that gave Israel a respite. Midhat al-Zahid of Egypt's Al-Ahram Center has emphasized this point:

The outbreak of the Gulf War was tantamount to a golden opportunity for Israel, which found itself in an unenviable position after the Iranian Revolution. This is because a regional power, which could join the ranks of its enemies, had emerged from that war. And that was dangerous for Israel. The war gave Israel the opportunity not only to neutralize this potential danger, but also to distract Iraq with a secondary conflict that would keep it out of a confrontation with it. The Gulf war would weaken the possibilities of reviving the northeastern front.[3]

Israel's approach had been to establish cooperative and friendly relations with Iran on the eastern flank of the Arab world. The utility of burdening Iran and Iraq with a war was clear since it rendered them unable to become involved in other conflicts. Providing arms to Iran was a means of continuing the war to the advantage of Israel; Israel sought to maintain a balance of power as a means of prolonging the conflict by denying victory to either party.[4]

Israel's role in Irangate suggests some of these calculations, but other factors, especially the nature of the U.S.-Israel relationship, were crucial. U.S. policy concerning the Iran-Iraq War derived from a number of considerations, including the need to protect and advance its interests. A protracted conflict between Iran and Iraq was not seen as detrimental to those interests unless it expanded to involve other states or posed a threat to freedom of navigation and/or the flow of oil from the Gulf or unless the Soviet Union and its allies could exploit the situation to their benefit. Some argued that the continuation of hostilities might even have derivative benefits for U.S. policy.

The Carter administration sought to prevent a victory for either combatant, to ensure freedom of navigation and the flow of oil through the Strait of Hormuz, and to ensure the security of the Gulf states against possible threats that might derive from the expansion of the war. The Reagan administration seemed to continue, and in some respects to expand, these policy elements. However, while the United States maintained a declaratory posture of neutrality in the Gulf War, the Reagan administration not only took practical steps to prevent an Iraqi economic and military collapse, but also became involved in military supply to Iran—an approach that came to be known as Irangate.[5] Shipments of arms in support of the Reagan initiative with Iran began in the summer of 1985 and continued until the fall of 1986. Some of the early shipments in 1985 were made by Israel acting on behalf of the United States, which apparently replenished Israeli stocks. On January 17, 1986, President Reagan signed an intelligence "finding" authorizing direct sales of arms by the United States to Iran, which led to a number of shipments in 1986. Israel played a key role in facilitating U.S. deliveries and, some believe, continued its own supply of arms to Iran.

Israel saw itself primarily as supporting U.S. policy, although there were derivative effects of a continued conflict between Iraq and Iran. Then Foreign Minister Shimon Peres elaborated on this theme: "There was a limited arms deal [between Israel and Iran] because of our desire to help the United States free its hostages. It was never more than $10–$20 million. . . . We never provided arms to Iran out of a desire to see it win."[6]

THE CEASE-FIRE AND SUBSEQUENT DEVELOPMENTS

The surprise Iranian acceptance of the cease-fire in July 1988 led to substantial speculation in Israel concerning both the reasons for the decision and the implications of the cease-fire for the region and beyond. Shimon Peres provided Israel's reaction:

It immediately raises the question of the status of Iran and Iraq in the region. Iraq has built up a very large army with over 50 divisions, with a strong Air Force and missile setup, but it also suffered a large number of human losses. The question is whether it will now direct itself toward rehabilitating the country or whether it will be enticed into seeking hegemony in the Arab world. We will not be able to know that immediately. . . . I believe that neither of the two countries [Iran and Iraq] at this stage has yet decided which way it will turn with its power and war weariness.[7]

The Iran-Iraq War gave Israel a "breathing spell." For eight years Israel had a respite from the prospects of a major war with the Arab states, especially one that might emanate from Iraq or have Iraqi involvement, or include a substantial threat from Iran. Further, during the war in Lebanon in 1982, Israel could act with relative impunity without having to seriously consider possible Iraqi or Iranian intervention. The continuation of the Iran-Iraq War thus proved beneficial to Israel in that negative sense. At the same time, however, Israel was not able to capitalize on the hostilities or on Arab preoccupation with that conflict to gain movement of consequence in its quest for peace and security.

The cease-fire initially was welcomed in Israel, but this reaction soon was replaced by a more complex assessment of the long- and short-term implications of the end of hostilities. After its initial surprise the immediate question and concern for Israel was whether Iraq and Iran would concentrate their energies and resources on internal reconstruction or on redeployment and alternate use of the military, perhaps against Israel. Lt. Gen. Dan Shomron, the Israel Defense Forces (IDF) chief of staff, disclosed in early August 1988 that Israel had already conducted exercises in preparation for the winding down of the Persian Gulf War. Shomron noted that even prior to the cease-fire the troops "completed a maneuver based on the presumption that the war had ended and [Iraqi] forces are free."[8]

Various schools of thought have emerged in Israel about the future roles of Iraq and Iran in the region. Israel's concerns about the prospects for war were expressed by Prime Minister Yitzhak Shamir several months before the acceptance of the cease-fire:

It is strange and most disturbing that while the two superpowers have agreed to limit and destroy medium-range missiles, countries in our region are in the process of acquiring the same missiles in growing quantities. Even more alarming are the reports of the development of poison gas and chemical weapons by Arab governments. The use of such terrible tools of death in the Iran-Iraq war should have triggered an international outcry and prompted a determined action by the civilized world. Governments that use these weapons, in contravention of international conventions and basic human morality, should be universally condemned.[9]

During the hostilities Iraq built up a very large army and a strong air force and missile capability, although it also suffered substantial destruction of its infrastructure, requiring major reconstruction and rehabilitation. It also might be tempted to seek a major leadership role in the Gulf or in the Arab world. Two alternative trends were identified: (1) a radical, bellicose, outward-looking regime, seeking overseas adventure to divert concern from domestic miseries and failures, and (2) an inward-oriented regime dedicated to domestic rehabilitation in an effort to restore the system.

Iraq's answer to the question of priorities in the wake of the cease-fire was supplied by Taha Yasin Ramadhan, who holds a number of senior positions in the government and in the Baath party. In March 1989 he asserted that "our priority is on reconstruction. We have initiated this at Basra. . . . Then we will move to Faw. We have made enormous progress."[10]

Iraq's traditional role in the Arab-Israeli conflict has been as a participant, though not as a central actor. Iraq fought in the 1948, 1967, and 1973 wars, albeit in the latter two conflicts with relatively minor forces. Its participation in 1973 was by an expeditionary force of relatively small size. Iraq now has a much larger and better-equipped force with substantial battlefield experience and is a far more substantial factor in the eastern front facing Israel. Iraq's improved situation is not simply a matter of improved and increased ground forces; it also has a more able air force and expanded missile forces, both with enhanced capability and experience.

Iraq has acquired, and has shown an ability and willingness to use, chemical weapons, as demonstrated in part by their utilization against Iraqi Kurdish populations.[11] Israel's concern about chemical warfare has not been restricted to Iraq, and Israel has been active in training its troops to deal with the potential use of such weapons.[12]

At the same time, Iraq also has acquired and used ballistic missiles. They have been employed against civilian populations in the so-called "war of the cities" with Iran.[13] Israel's minister of defense, Yitzhak Rabin, noted that "Iraq's improved Scuds, whose range was extended to approximately 650 km at the expense of mounting a smaller, 200 to 300–kg warhead on it, constitutes a threat in that it can be launched from Iraqi territory against almost any Israeli target. For the first time ever, an Arab country that is not a confrontation state has the capability of attacking Israel with a surface-to-surface missile without dispatching expeditionary units to one of the confrontation states."[14] In an editorial entitled "The Missile Threat" published on March 23, 1988, the *Jerusalem Post* observed:

The originally tactical Soviet Scud-B's upgraded and boosted-up by the Iraqis are accurate and have a range of over 600 kilometres. Turned west, as they could be one day, these same missiles would cover the entire face of Israel, including the territories, without a single Iraqi soldier crossing his country's border with Jordan. It is not too difficult to imagine the impact these Iraqi missiles might have if they were equipped with chemical, let alone, nuclear, warheads, and if the enemy were not deterred, or for that matter subdued in time by Israel's superior might.

The matter of gas warfare and missile use by Iraq (and possibly by Iran as well) has an additional dimension that concerns Israel. This is the fact that the international response to the use of these weapons has been timid and tepid. Rabin has said: "One of our fears is that the Arab world and its leaders might be deluded to believe that the lack of international reaction to the use of missiles and gases [in the Iran-Iraq War] gives them some kind of legitimization to use them." He added: "They know they should not be deluded to believe that, because it is a whole different ball game when it comes to us. If they are, God forbid, they should know we will hit them back 100 times harder."[15]

Added to other military concerns in the case of Iraq is the matter of a potential nuclear capability. In an editorial entitled "The New Iraqi Nuclear Threat," the *Jerusalem Post* on April 3, 1989, stated that "Iraq is now back on the trail of a nuclear capability. . . . Iraq being what it is, and having proved that again in the last stage of the war with Iran, and in the campaign against the helpless Kurds, it would be foolish, indeed suicidal, of Israel's leaders to count on the rulers of Baghdad to confine the use of the bomb, once they have acquired it, to genuine self-defence."

The *Washington Post* reported on March 31, 1989, that Iraq was engaged in a program to build nuclear warheads for use with a strategic missile.[16] On April 3 Iraq denounced the *Washington Post* report. Israel has previously shown itself willing and able to respond to a potential nuclear threat. On June 7, 1981, Israel announced the successful destruction of the Iraqi Osirak nuclear reactor. In response to speculation that Israel might be willing to utilize a similar tactic should Iraq acquire a nuclear capability, it has been suggested that Israel would face significant obstacles if it attempted to carry out a preemptive strike against the new Iraqi nuclear reactor.[17]

Domestic rehabilitation seems to be the likely alternative for Iraq in the short run. The Saddam Hussein regime had been reassuring its population that with the end of the war it would turn to domestic reconstruction to help alleviate the suffering of the population, to reward it for its support and sacrifices during the war, and to provide a "safety valve" as a way of preventing future antiregime reactions. The relative well-being of the population before the war and the promises and pledges during the hostilities suggest the need to concentrate, at least in the short run, on the domestic front. Restoring Iraq to its former economic levels and regaining its standard of living are important considerations in the regime's calculations. There are other factors.

In recent years the Iraqi regime has been increasingly supportive of the more moderate Arab camp on matters related to the Arab-Israeli conflict. Despite its earlier leadership of the opposition to President Anwar Sadat of Egypt, the Camp David Accords, and the Egypt-Israel Peace Treaty, Iraq has supported peace negotiations between Israel and a Jordanian-Palestinian delegation. Nevertheless, Iraq does not yet appear to have reconciled itself to the existence of Israel, nor has it relinquished its anti-Israel stance and ideology. There is an ambivalence, if not a contradiction, in Baghdad's approach. The Iraqi regime has also made it clear that the PLO is free to arrive at any solution to the Palestinian issue with Israel that it prefers.[18] This is in line with its apparent perspective that the Palestine problem appears to be of diminished priority and that it no longer sees itself as a confrontation state in the Palestinian battle against Israel.

The competition, if not conflict, with Syria adds to this policy trend. Iraq has not suggested its willingness to support Syria in the event of conflict with Israel or other antagonists and remains at odds with Syria over the latter's support for Iran during the Iran-Iraq War. To the traditional animosity and rivalry one must add the alignment during the Iran-Iraq War and the recent clashes by proxy in the Lebanese civil war.[19]

Is Iraq "serious" about the relative priority of reconstruction versus potential war with Israel? Iraq has made statements regarding no war with Israel, and an obvious need for rehabilitation exists in the short run. Nevertheless, the ideological commitment to the destruction of Israel appears to remain intact.

At the same time, it is possible that Saddam Hussein might alter his priorities or reassess Iraq's perceived needs in a manner that might generate external adventure. It is possible that in the wake of Iraq's failure to achieve a victory in the war and to reconstruct its economic and social systems, an alternative Shi'ite-oriented regime might emerge in Iraq, and it could be linked to Iran. Liberating Jerusalem and over-throwing heretical regimes (perhaps Saudi Arabia and its GCC sup-porters) might take precedence in foreign policy. A military-led overthrow might install a regime seeking closer links with Syria and perhaps with the Soviet Union. Such a regime might refocus on the Palestine issue and enlarge Iraq's role as a supporter of anti-Israel forces. Such a regime would be responsive to the criticisms of Saddam Hussein alleging that by attacking Iran, he had forgotten the true Arab and Baathist enemy (that is, Israel) and had betrayed the Palestinian cause. These or similar changes could lead to more involvement of Iraq in external political machinations, could increase the potential threat to Israel, and could raise the prospects for destabilizing efforts directed at the more moderate Arab states.

Given these various factors, the short-term focus of Iraq is likely to be on internal reconstruction, with a consequent reduction in military size and revamping of force structure. At the same time, Iraq will have to maintain a sizable standing army even during "peacetime" to meet its regional and internal security needs. It is unlikely that Iraq would reduce its forces to prewar levels. With a sizable standing army, Iraq could, if it chose to, easily participate in a war with Israel—even one not of its own design or initiation. Despite its probable short-term pref-erence to avoid conflict, Iraq is desirous of avoiding isolation within the Arab world. It needs to retain its links with and support from the more conservative Arab states. The Arab states, especially the oil-rich ones of the Gulf and the Arabian Peninsula, but also Jordan, were especially important for resources and logistical support for Iraq during the Gulf War. Given the likely persistence of tensions with Iran despite the cease-fire of 1988, support from these states will remain crucial for Iraq. If Iraq continues to harbor desires for a greater and more prominent, perhaps even leadership, role in the Arab world, then it must retain positive relations with the GCC states and Jordan, as well as other Arab states. There is also the possibility that the rivalry between Iraq and Egypt might reemerge with the end of the Gulf War.[20] If the Arab world were to get involved in a large-scale conflict with Israel, Iraq could not remain aloof. An additional consideration must be that a major loss in a war with Israel would have significant repercussions in the Gulf sector and would make Iraq and others more vulnerable to potential Iranian machinations.

Among these calculations is the centrality of the Palestine question for the Gulf Arab states. References to Palestine and the Arab-Israeli conflict appear often in the public statements of Gulf leaders. There is a popular perception of a link between the Palestine question and the Gulf, since both Palestine and the Gulf region are Arab lands and both are viewed as having felt the imprint of Western imperialism, of which Israel is identified as a regional manifestation. The Palestinian issue is a popular one, and Arab rulers have been highly visible in welcoming and entertaining visiting Palestinian leaders and in providing verbal and financial support to the PLO and other Palestinian organizations. There are sizable Palestinian communities in the Gulf states, and their members often occupy important positions and contribute to the local economies. The Palestinian communities sustain a heightened sensitivity to the Arab-Israeli conflict. They exert considerable influence, enhanced by their prominent role in education, the media, the oil industry, and government service. There is a dual concern that a new Arab-Israeli war could compel adoption of potentially problematic policies, some of which might have devastating effects on their economies. At the same time, a stalemate on the Palestinian issue might prompt Palestinian militants to engage in sabotage, especially against the highly important and extremely vulnerable oil sector.

One Israeli assessment of the role Iraq might play in a future war against Israel has been offered by retired IDF Brigadier General Aharon Levran. He has said that it will be difficult for the Arabs to forge a war coalition and an eastern front against Israel in the near term. His argument is based on the emergence of an Iranian threat to the GCC states, as well as to Jordan and Egypt. As a consequence, "It is doubtful whether the deep-rooted enmity between Iran and Iraq would permit Iraq and the other Arabs to be sanguine about the threat from the east for many years to come."[21] However, this does not mean that Iraq would be incapable of dispatching an expeditionary force in the event of a serious confrontation between Israel and its neighbors. "Iraq would probably be unable or unwilling to take part in an Arab-Israel military confrontation to a degree that would seriously endanger Israel."[22] Nonetheless, Iraq will be a factor in a future war.

The Iranian equation is similarly complex, but the main lines are clear. Iran's revolutionary regime has been unremittingly hostile to Israel since its inauguration. Despite the arms transfers and other links during Irangate, Iran and Israel have had no positive dealings since the ouster of the Shah. Iran has made clear its opposition to Israeli control of Muslim holy places in Jerusalem, and liberation of that city figured prominently as a theme of the late Ayatollah's regime. During the hostilities Iranians were constantly reminded that "Baghdad is on the road to Jerusalem." Despite the rhetoric and close links with the PLO, the Hezbollah, and other anti-Israel terrorists in Lebanon, Iran's conflict with Iraq prevented any substantial participation in the conflict against Israel during the 1980s, and the postwar Iranian situation clearly precludes any such actions in the near term. Nevertheless, Iran's possession of, and willingness to use, a chemical warfare capability and a ballistic missile capacity must be included in Israel's assessment of the potential threats from the east.[23] Continued limited support for the PLO and Hezbollah is a likely course.

The issue of Israel's relations with Iran is, however, not a simple one. As Shimon Peres pointed out, "How could Israel live with Iran under Khomeini? Everything we stand for historically and ideologically runs counter to what Khomeini wants to do in the Middle East, from his crusade against any expression of progress in the region to his crusade, which he refers to day and night, to make his way to Jerusalem. We represent two different worlds, two different approaches."[24]

Despite the record of Iranian hostility, Israelis seem eager to identify potential positive developments. Recognizing the value of the pre-revolution relationship with Iran and understanding the geostrategic nature of that state, Israelis often think in terms of potential improvement in links and reassess factors that may contribute to such an improvement. There is a school of thought in Israel that focuses on the significance of Iran and the necessity of a positive Iran-Israel relationship.

Shmuel Segev, columnist for *Maariv*, has argued that Israel's approach to Iran during the course of the war was appropriate. One of the main lessons was that "The war and the way it ended justified the policy conducted by the United States and Israel toward Iran. . . . The cease-fire in the Persian Gulf opens new horizons for Israel's diplomacy. A wise, open-minded, and imaginative leadership could now modestly try to open new bridges to Tehran without closing the door on a dialogue with Iraq and other Arab countries."[25]

In a similar vein, Ya'acov Nimrodi, a former Israeli military attaché to Iran and a figure in the Israeli-U.S.-Iranian connection during Irangate, has argued:

Israel's policy should be based on the wish to achieve understanding and closeness with Iranian people, in the hope that the regime, too, will see the advantages of ties with Israel. . . . I am convinced that an Iranian-Israeli connection is likely to be of benefit to both sides. . . . Even if an "Iraqi option" existed (and I believe this was never the case), it no longer exists today. Iran's decision to accept the cease-fire created a new situation in the Persian Gulf: Iran, which in the past appeared to be strong and secure, has been compelled to admit its weakness. The geo-strategic reality that constituted the basis for its turning to the West in 1985 is fruitful ground for Iran's return to the West today, and it is likely to lead to further developments that will bring it closer to Israel as well.[26]

The death of the Ayatollah Khomeini in June 1989 raised again the question of the Israeli relationship with Iran. The initial reaction was cautious, suggesting that it was too early to reach a definitive assessment, but reflected an optimism that conditions might change for the better. In responding to a question whether this might lead to a new dialogue with Iran, Foreign Minister Moshe Arens opined, "We do know that Khomeini was a fanatic, a man responsible for the death of hundreds of thousands; an outspoken enemy of Israel. And so I suppose things cannot get any worse, and hopefully they will get better."[27]

PROSPECTS

In assessing and evaluating the interrelationship of the Persian Gulf sector and the Arab-Israeli conflict, Israelis examine both the past record and the existing potential. A major question facing Israel is whether it could have taken better advantage of the "breathing spell" to make progress toward peace and security. Some observers argue that major opportunities were lost, but little specific evidence is provided to suggest how the situation might have been improved. An interesting assessment argument in a somewhat different vein was offered by Rabin: "Nevertheless, I believe that we failed to fully exploit this situation [the Iran-Iraq War] until the end of 1984. When the national unity government was formed we did the right thing in cutting back our defense budget. We did this in view of the peace with Egypt and the Iraq-Iran war, and thereby salvaged the state economy. We also extricated the IDF from the Lebanese quagmire."[28] Others look wistfully at the period of relative reprieve, given the dramatic growth in Iraqi and Iranian military capability (both equipment and experience) that was a consequence of the conflict.[29] Vast amounts of new and deadly weapons systems, including ballistic missiles and chemical warfare capabilities, available to the large and battle-hardened forces of Iran and Iraq and the cessation of hostilities have made both states figure more prominently in the Arab-Israeli sector and in Israel's foreign- and security-policy calculations.

Israelis recognize that the period of the Iran-Iraq War was unique, and that with the cease-fire they now confront a new regional situation. While hoping for an improvement in the prospects for peace and for improved relations (especially with Iran), Israelis also recognize that a rapid, major, and positive improvement in their situation is unlikely. They evince concern over the prospects that Iraq and/or Iran might join in a war against them, but that concern is cast into a broader perspective that suggests that there are but limited prospects of such an occurrence.[30] Israelis continue to debate the best course to follow in seeking a more positive relationship with the Gulf's major powers.

NOTES

Another verision of this work has appeared in *Middle East Focus* (Winter/Spring 1990).

1. For further details see Bernard Reich, David E. Pollock, and Sally Ann Baynard, "The Iranian Revolution and Its Effects on the Middle East," in U.S. Congress, Joint Economic Committee, *Economic Consequences of the Revolution in Iran* (Washington, D.C.: Government Printing Office, 1980), pp. 179–207.

2. See, for example, the data in the annual editions of *The Military Balance* issued by the International Institute for Strategic Studies (IISS), London.

3. Midhat al-Zahid, "Israel and the Iraq-Iran War," *Al-Siyash al-Duwaliyah*, July 1986.

4. The argument asserts: "It is also easy to understand the reasons for Israel's strategy of blocking an Iraqi victory. From Israel's point of view Iraq is still straddling the fence: it has not severed all its relations with the rejection front, and it has not totally aligned itself with the moderates' camp. Seen from that perspective, victory for Iraq could strengthen its regional position, particularly in the Gulf. It may induce the coastal areas of the Gulf to unite under the Iraqi flag either in a limited regional plan or a comprehensive Arab one. But Israel is also focusing on another extremely important angle because an Iraqi victory would give the Iraqi army moral stature as well as military experience, combat efficiency and more armaments. And that could constitute a threat to Israel's security." Ibid.

5. See John Tower, Edmund Muskie, and Brent Scowcroft, *The Tower Commission Report* (New York: Bantam Books and Times Books, 1987).

6. "Peres Cited on Effects," Foreign Broadcast Information Service, *Daily Report*-Near East & South Asia (hereinafter FBIS-NES), FBIS-NES-88–132, July 11, 1988, p. 26 (interview on IDF Radio, July 11, 1988).

7. "Peres on Decisions," FBIS-NES-88–138, July 19, 1988, p. 32 (Israel Radio, July 18, 1988). Other senior officials expressed similar concerns.

8. *Washington Post*, August 12, 1988.

9. "Shamir on 'Alarming' Arab Acquisitions," FBIS-NES-88–096, May 18, 1988, pp. 27, 28 (speech by Shamir on May 17, 1988, as broadcast on Israel Radio).

10. Cited in Christine Helms, "Taha Yasin Ramadhan: The Future of Iraq and the Ruling Party," *Middle East Insight* 6:5 (Spring 1989): 20.

11. See, for example, Philip A. G. Sabin and Efraim Karsh, "Escalation in the Iran-Iraq War," *Survival* 31, no. 3 (May/June 1989): 241–54.

12. IDF Chief Engineering Officer Tat Aluf Yosef Ayal said in August 1988 that "we're preparing ourselves for all possibilities, including having to fight in areas contaminated by chemical agents." Quoted in *Jerusalem Post* International Edition, Week ending August 27, 1988, p. 5.

13. For details of Iraq's (and Iran's) missile capability, see Martin S. Navias, "Ballistic Missile Proliferation in the Middle East," *Survival* 31, no. 3 (May/June 1989): 225–39.

14. "Defense Minister on Military Threats, Balance," FBIS-NES–88–064, April 4, 1988, pp. 27, 28 (interview with Rabin published in *Maariv*, April 1, 1988). The missile threat acquired by Israel's enemies during the course of the Iran-Iraq War seemed to be of particular strategic concern to Rabin: "I believe that basically Israel is threatened by any Arab country that is in possession of ground-to-ground missiles that can be fired from their own soil and hit Israel. You have to bear in mind that since 1948 the Arab countries' air forces could not penetrate the air space of Israel in a meaningful way to drop any meaningful pay load of bombs on our centers of population. The air defense of Israel, the Israeli Air Force, proved that any attempt would be and will be foiled. Therefore, the push to acquiring ground-to-ground missiles was based on the Arab countries' perception that this is a kind of armament that once you push the button it reaches the target within the technological limitation of the ground-to-ground missile." "Rabin Comments on U.S. Talks on Missile Threat," FBIS-NES–99–128, July 5, 1988, p. 23 (Israel Radio, July 2, 1988).

15. "Rabin Warns Arabs against Use of Chemical Weapons," FBIS-NES-88–140, July 21, 1988, pp. 28, 29 (on Israel Radio, July 20, 1988).

16. G. Frankel, "Iraq Said Developing A-Weapons," *Washington Post*, March 31, 1989, p. A1; also see "An Iraqi Bomb?" (editorial), *Washington Post*, April 3, 1989.

17. See D. Ottaway, "Strike on Iraq No Longer Easy Option for Israel, Analysts Say," *Washington Post*, March 31, 1989, p. A32.

18. Taha Yasin Ramadhan has observed: "Our attitude has been stable and consistent since 1978. We stand beside the PLO because it is regarded as the sole representative of the Palestinian people. There are differences of opinion. However, we only advise, but don't oppose their position. We appreciate their practical attitude and what they declared in Algeria. This decision is in accord with international realities now developing about the PLO." Helms, "Taha Yasin Ramadhan," p. 18.

19. In March 1989 Taha Yasin Ramadhan noted: "As for Syria, during the last eight years, they sided with Iran. This is not the attitude of the Syrian people, but the ruler and his ruling clique. We believe it will not last long. It is not a secret. If we had established relations now through the mediation of other Arab countries, it would not have been natural since this traitorous enemy has placed wounds upon the Iraqi people. Relations with Syria cannot be like those with Jordan or Yemen. [As long as] this ruling clique stands with Iran, we can have no relations with them." Ibid., p. 19.

20. A foreign-policy expert for Egypt's Wafd party has suggested that "Egypt and Iraq are friends on the surface but they are also potent rivals. Egypt is going to be the first country to suffer from the war's end." *Wall Street Journal*, September 9, 1988.

21. Aharon Levran, "The Iraq-Iran War: The Military Balance, Major Developments, and Repercussions," *Global Affairs* 1 (Summer 1986): 87.

22. Ibid.

23. See Sabin and Karsh, "Escalation in the Iran-Iraq War," and Navias, "Ballistic Missile Proliferation."

24. "Peres Cited on Effects," FBIS-NES-88–132, July 11, 1988, pp. 26, 27 (interview on IDF Radio, July 11, 1988).

25. "Gulf Cease-Fire Said to Open 'New Horizons,'" FBIS-NES-88–144, July 27, 1988 (*Maariv*, July 20, 1988).

26. Ya'acov Nimrodi, "Iran: The Logic behind the Fanaticism," *Jerusalem Post* International Edition, Week ending August 27, 1988, p. 7.

27. "Arens on U.S.-PLO Dialogue," FBIS-NES-89–107, p. 19 (radio interview, June 5, 1989). Similar perspectives were offered by Prime Minister Shamir and Defense Minister Rabin.

28. "Rabin Cited," FBIS-NES-88–139, July 20, 1988, p. 26 (Rabin interview on Tel Aviv Educational Television, July 19, 1988).

29. For a post–cease-fire Israeli assessment of the military balance, see Dore Gold, "Assessing the Buildup along Israel's Eastern Front," *IDF Journal*, no. 17 (Summer 1989): 34–38.

30. In assessing future prospects, Rabin offered the following observations: "In the immediate future, namely the next year or 2, even if the war ends, a political solution is found, and mutual suspicions are allayed, I cannot anticipate Iraq gleefully rushing into another war adventure at once. . . . Iran also falls within this category. . . . In order for Iran to march toward Jerusalem . . . it must pass through Iraq. I cannot envision an Iranian-Iraqi partnership against any common enemy." "Rabin Cited," FBIS-NES-88–139, July 20, 1988, p. 26 (Interview on Tel Aviv Educational Television, July 19, 1988).

6

The Gulf Cooperation Council and the Gulf War

Joseph A. Kechichian

For nearly a decade the conservative Arab Gulf monarchies of Bahrain, Kuwait, Oman, Qatar, Saudi Arabia, and the United Arab Emirates (UAE) were preoccupied with the Iran-Iraq War. Vulnerable to both internal and external convulsions, and partly in response to the war, the six governments on May 25, 1981, established the Cooperation Council of the Arab Gulf States (CCAGS), or as it is generally known, the Gulf Cooperation Council (GCC).[1]

The preponderant Iranian military power in the Persian Gulf greatly influenced the GCC states' early evaluations of the conflict's outcome. Iraqi claims of rapid and total victory notwithstanding, GCC leaders expected Iran to engage in a war of attrition. Seasoned Gulf rulers understood that the war would act as a legitimizing factor for Tehran to support the fledgling revolution. Yet despite ominous forecasts of imminent internal revolts in most GCC states, conservative Gulf rulers turned the war between Iran and Iraq into an opportunity to strengthen their resolve, psychologically and physically, to withstand Iraqi and/or Iranian threats to their security and stability. The war became the catalyst that permitted GCC states to streamline differences, adopt joint policies, coordinate military efforts, cooperate with outside powers, and forge a sense of political union.

THE THREATENING WAR

Between 1981 and 1988 the Iran-Iraq War remained the top agenda item for GCC states. The primary fear was the potential spreading of a war that would engulf the six states in internal revolts. GCC officials called on both belligerents to accept a cease-fire and resolve time-tested differences, but their very limited influence on Iran and Iraq did not produce contemplated results. The GCC states' chief concern was to prevent the conflict from spilling over into their territories. The war persuaded them that joint defense policies were long overdue. Despite this realization, the conservative monarchies were faced with two troubling facts. First, since threat perceptions differed considerably among the six in 1981, individual states' policies toward Iran and Iraq differed from the council's unified position. Second, the GCC's unified position evolved slowly during the eight years, an indication of the council's decision-making process when confronted with rapidly changing developments.

GCC Member States and the War

During the conflict Saudi Arabia and Kuwait adopted very controversial policies in the region by extending generous financial assistance to Iraq. While disagreements may exist over the amounts—estimates range from $25 to $65 billion—both Riyadh and Kuwait acted in their perceived national interests by assisting Iraq.[2] Riyadh and Kuwait viewed their support to Baghdad—and not just to Saddam Hussein's regime, as some detractors have posited—as the lesser of two evils. The eruption of the Iranian Revolution and the resultant Khomeini government's plan to export the "Islamic Revolution" to the lower Gulf caused jitters in Saudi Arabia and Kuwait over this potential but real threat to their stability. Arab support to Iraq reflected this basic concern. Equally important, Baghdad's war was also publicly viewed by all GCC states as Iraq's attempt to challenge the Iranian revolutionary regime. In private, of course, GCC leaders were no less concerned over potential Iraqi hegemony in the Gulf region. Ironically, Baghdad's reaction to Saudi and Kuwaiti assistance was not that of a grateful recipient. Rather, time and again, Iraqi officials hinted that "expected" Arab support was not adequately forthcoming, thus compelling Baghdad to turn to France and the Soviet Union for military and financial assistance.[3] Presumably it was this limitation that forced Baghdad to increase its barter deals with France, providing Paris with petroleum in exchange for advanced weapons.

By 1988 the Iraqi debt had grown so large that it was doubtful whether it could ever be repaid in full. Iraq's foreign debt in 1985 stood at $65 billion, with perhaps half owed to GCC states; by early 1988 borrowings had reportedly reached the $100 billion figure.[4] Debtor and creditor expectations remained very low, for GCC states did not extend "commercial" loans to Iraq. Rather, they chose to provide financial assistance purely for political reasons. Obviously Iraq could repay its debts through increased oil sales. At a time when the world oil glut had lowered prices considerably, however, no GCC state wanted to jeopardize its financial stability by insisting that Iraq meet its debt schedule in that fashion. GCC states therefore enjoyed a certain advantage in dealing with Iraq. Baghdad's indebtedness considerably moderated Iraq's adventurism, especially in the Gulf region. Consequently, by forgiving Iraqi debts, the GCC may have partially softened one of its primary sources of threat.

The willingness by Saudi Arabia and Kuwait to provide financial assistance to Iraq must be contrasted with their reluctance to provide military support. Despite claims to the contrary, of the Arab states, only Jordan, Egypt, and the Sudan sent troops and military hardware to Iraq. GCC states did not provide Baghdad with armaments from their own small arsenals, although Saudi Arabia probably financed some Iraqi arms purchases from France. In light of the perceived Iranian threat to their security, why did the GCC states not provide military support to Iraq? A number of explanations are apparent.

First, the military capacity of the strongest GCC state, Saudi Arabia, remained very limited and stretched thin throughout the 1980s. The Saudis needed to defend themselves—and a quarter of the world's proven reserves of petroleum—in a largely vulnerable land mass half the size of the United States from Iranian, Iraqi, Israeli, and Soviet threats. While Riyadh did embark on a systematic military buildup, the Saudis had little surplus materials to spare. The five smaller sheikhdoms, whose combined manpower in 1980 was less than 100,000, were in a similar situation. Compared with Iranian and Iraqi forces deployed on the battlefront, GCC troops could hardly tip the existing military balance in the Persian Gulf (see table 1). The only exception was the Royal Saudi Air Force, whose undisputed superiority by 1983 could have conceivably inflicted unacceptable damage on Iranian armed forces. Any decision to deploy advanced Saudi air power to the war front, however, would have meant expansion of the conflict to engulf the nonbelligerent Arab Gulf states, an option totally rejected by Riyadh. This was a second reason why GCC states refused to provide military support to Iraq. None of the six conservative monarchies wished to be dragged into a war with an outcome that appeared dangerously unpredictable and with an initial Iraqi-articulated purpose—to foster Arab hegemony in the Persian Gulf—that remained uninspiring.

All GCC member states shared these views, with certain variations. The UAE, for example, opted to pursue its special relationship with Iran,

Table 1
Comparative Military Forces: GCC States, Iran, Iraq, and Israel, 1988–1989

Description	GCC	Iran	Iraq	Israel
Population:	19,064,000	52,800,000	16,278,000	4,466,000
Citizens:	11,414,000			
Expatriates:	7,650,000			
Armed Forces:				
Total	160,950	650,500	1,000,000	141,000[1]
Army	122,300	305,000[2]	955,000	104,000
Navy	14,950	14,500	5,000	9,000
Air Force	23,700	35,000	40,000	28,000
Paramilitary	62,950	1,000,000	4,800	4,500
Revolutionary Guards	-	250,000	-	-
Reserves	-	350,000	650,000	504,000
Forces Abroad	-	2,000	-	1,500
Opposition forces	-	25,500	62,500	-
Military Equipment:				
Tanks	1,084	1,000	4,500	3,850
Naval Crafts	83	42[3]	43	59
Combat Aircrafts	382	50[3]	500	577

Source: Institute for International Strategic Studies, *The Military Balance, 1988–1989* (London: IISS, 1988).

Note: Data for Iran and Iraq are very tentative given the lack of reliable figures on losses.

[1] Israeli armed forces include 110,000 conscripts and at mobilization stands at 645,000, of whom 100,000 can be mobilized in about 24 hours. The army at mobilization stands at 598,000, the navy at 10,000, and the air force at 37,000.

[2] Regular army of 305,000 includes 250,000 conscripts.

[3] Iran's prewar inventory of naval crafts was 63. Losses and problems with servicing reduced the number of operational crafts to a handful. For the air force, prewar inventory stood at 316.

fully blessed by the GCC Secretariat to maintain an open and friendly line of communication with Tehran. Nevertheless, the continued Iranian occupation of three small islands (Abu Musa, Greater Tunb, and Little Tunb) continued to hover over that relationship. This reality limited the extent to which the UAE and Iran could bridge their differences and actually cooperate. Iraqi intelligence sources often rekindled the thorny debate to widen the gulf between Iran and the GCC. The disputes were real enough, and the islands occupied enough, but no efforts were spared to reawaken dormant factors.

Equally important, the Kuwaiti islands of Bubiyan and Warba came to occupy significant roles in Iraqi-GCC relations. Throughout the 1980s Baghdad reminded Kuwait, and all Arab states for that matter, that this was an Arab war against Persian "hegemony" and, as a result, that Iraq should receive all the aid the Arab world could muster. For strategic reasons, Bubiyan and Warba were critical to the Iraqis, and the Kuwaitis were pressured to accommodate. Only Iranian counterpressures, demonstrated by bombing selected petroleum facilities and by encouraging sympathetic Kuwaiti Shi'as to engage in antistate activities (including but not limited to terrorism), persuaded Kuwait not to concede to Iraq. Thus both Iraq and Iran interfered in the internal affairs of GCC states in order to steer the course that the Gulf states would follow during the conflict.

GCC Diplomacy

Following its first summit meeting in May 1981 in Abu Dhabi, the GCC Supreme Council declared that the Persian Gulf should remain free of international conflicts. Furthermore, the statement of the heads of state called for an end to the war, indicating that "it is one of the problems that threaten the region's security and increases the possibility of foreign intervention in the region."[5] This position was reiterated after the GCC's second summit meeting held in Riyadh in November 1981, when the Supreme Council "expressed the hope that the efforts stemming from the Islamic Conference and the efforts of the non-aligned and the United Nations, would be successful."[6] When Iran gained the upper hand over Iraq and was increasing its verbal threats against Arab Gulf states, the GCC turned to the Islamic Conference Organization (ICO) and the United Nations to accomplish what it could not achieve by itself. Consequently, the GCC's unified position came to emphasize the role of the ICO as a mediator between the two warring states. The first concrete evidence of this emphasis was revealed in the GCC Ministerial Council's statement issued after its second emergency meeting, held in Riyadh on April 20, 1982. The council declared its support for all efforts being made to end the war between Iraq and Iran, especially to stop the "shedding of Islamic blood and protect the region's security and stability."[7]

No official communiqué was issued by the foreign ministers after their third emergency meeting in Kuwait on May 15, 1982, but Saudi foreign minister Prince Saud al-Faysal revealed that the meeting was adjourned until May 30, 1982, to permit key Arab states to complete negotiations on behalf of the council. Informal contacts were established by Algeria and Syria to ascertain whether Iranian and Iraqi military advances had altered the political balance in the region. Algerian and Syrian representatives were expected to brief GCC foreign ministers on the results of their exploratory talks before the council would agree on a unified position. In reality, the adjournment was a tactical move by the GCC to appraise day-to-day developments on the ground, as the battle for Khorramshahr was in full rage. The texture of the war changed dramatically after this battle when Iran recaptured Khorramshahr in May 1982 and went on the offensive, apparently with considerable success.[8] Following the second session of the foreign ministers' third emergency meeting, which had shifted to Riyadh on May 30, 1982, the final communiqué reiterated the council's established position on ending the bloodshed between two Muslim states. It also lauded the efforts of the ICO's "good offices committee" to embark on a fresh mediation round. But in a break with past policy, the council issued a specific call to the "Islamic Republic of Iran" to respond positively to Iraq's peace initiatives and achieve "this objective at this historic and decisive turning point in which the Islamic nation is the target of a fierce Zionist onslaught aimed at the entire Islamic entity."[9] For the first time since the outbreak of hostilities, the GCC identified Iran as the intransigent party rejecting all mediation efforts and, presumably, a peaceful settlement of the conflict. This call was repeated in July 1982, when the Ministerial Council "appreciated" Iraq's posture in withdrawing its forces from Iranian territory to international borders and its readiness to settle the conflict through diplomatic negotiations so as to ensure the rights of both sides. The foreign ministers also hoped that "Iran w[ould] respond to this initiative in a fraternal Islamic spirit to spare the region any escalation of the conflict or to expose it to division, disorder and instability which w[ould] only benefit outside forces who [we]re concerned with neither the well-being of the states of the region nor their security or stability."[10]

Significantly, these GCC diplomatic overtures attempted to achieve two specific goals. First, the Arab Gulf states' newly found boldness permitted them to call on both sides to seize existing opportunities and end their dispute on an equitable basis. This stood in sharp contrast to the timid statements issued in 1981. Second, by 1982 GCC states had decided to "share" the responsibility for resolving a regional conflict with the larger Islamic community, thus broadening the peace parameters when their influence on both Iraq and Iran was rapidly waning. Such a major change in policy also indicated that GCC states perceived their role in a more restricted "space," illustrating perhaps their reserved foreign policy style. However, 1982 also marked the awakening of the GCC in shouldering its security responsibilities more forcefully. GCC defense ministers authorized comprehensive cooperation in security affairs to complement the organization's diplomatic initiatives.

By November 1982, when the GCC heads of state gathered in Bahrain for their third summit meeting, the council's attention was clearly focused on Iran's persistent intransigence in the war. Yet in Manama the Supreme Council was also confronted with the repercussions of Iran's involvement in the December 1981 Bahrain coup attempt. More than any other event, the Bahrain coup plot molded the GCC's view on how to react toward Iran. In fact, although the Saudis failed to convince other GCC states to provide additional financial assistance to Iraq, they succeeded in "identifying" the Islamic Revolution as a threat to the GCC. The organization's subsequent actions clarified this joint perception. Immediately after the 1982 summit meeting, GCC defense ministers, chiefs of staff, and interior ministers gathered to coordinate their contingency plans for containing the Gulf War to preclude its spillover into their territories. The six states declared that the Iranian invasion of Iraq was "dangerous" and affirmed support for Iraq's effort to end the war peacefully. They also criticized Iran for "crossing its international border with Iraq" and noted how these developments posed a threat "to the safety and security of the Arab nation and the violation of its sovereignty."[11] They again asked Iran to respond to the peace missions sponsored by the ICO, the Non-Aligned Movement (NAM), and the United Nations. These initiatives brought no response from Tehran.

Another prominent consideration may have prompted the GCC's new joint strategy. According to the Saudi magazine *Al-Majallah*, the GCC Supreme Council was briefed on UAE President Zayid's consultations with Iranian leaders who apparently rejected Abu Dhabi's mediation efforts.[12] Given the repeated Iranian rejections of all mediation efforts, the council decided that it could no longer postpone its response and hence chose officially to support Iraq.

Following the 1983 fourth summit meeting held in Qatar, the GCC heads of state endorsed U.N. Security Council Resolution 540 (October 31, 1983), which "call[ed] for an end to all military activities in the Gulf and for refraining from attacking cities, economic installations and ports, and for an immediate end to all hostilities in the Gulf area, including all sea routes and waterways."[13] Throughout 1983 similar calls for peace had been issued by all six states, as well as the GCC Secretariat. A unified position on the war explicitly identifying freedom of navigation in the Persian Gulf was finally approved in late 1983. Importantly, no significant deviations from it have occurred since then. Iran's refusal to accept the mediation efforts of Syria, Algeria, the UAE, the ICO, the NAM, and the United Nations contributed to solidifying this unified position, which was reinforced by the GCC decision to appoint Algeria as the go-between with Iran on this issue.[14] Yet divisions within the Arab world further polarized members of the League of Arab States (LAS) into two camps. Syria and Libya supported Iran in what was perhaps the most controversial decision in modern Middle Eastern affairs. In fact, Syria, Libya, and Iran issued a joint "Damascus Communiqué" following their January 23, 1983, tripartite meeting that condemned the Iraqi regime of Saddam Hussein and expressed support for Iran in the war.[15] The letter and spirit of the "Damascus Communiqué" led GCC foreign ministers to administer a strong rebuke to the three countries. Speaking for the GCC, Bahrain's foreign minister stated after the Ministerial Council's sixth ordinary meeting that the "tripartite agreement d[id] not serve the unity of Arab ranks and w[ould] not help to end the Iran-Iraq war." He further advocated the unification of the Arab position around the LAS Fez decisions, a new agenda for the upcoming New Delhi NAM summit, and coordination of the respective GCC states' positions to isolate Iran in the less developed world's premier forum.[16]

The New Delhi summit in 1983 called on both belligerents to accept a cease-fire and withdraw to their respective international borders. Noting the long-term needs of both Iran and Iraq in war reparations, leaders at the NAM summit appealed to the United Nations to consider deploying a peacekeeping force on the Iran-Iraq border, to facilitate a cease-fire, and to initiate negotiations. This marked the first time that the notion of U.N. peacekeeping operations for the Iran-Iraq War was discussed at an international forum. Tehran rejected the NAM resolution, while Baghdad, increasingly feeling the burden of a costly conflict, expressed a desire to negotiate a peaceful settlement.

In early 1984 the Gulf War intensified. This escalation prompted concern that exacerbated fighting might erupt in the spring, thus further threatening petroleum exports from the region. Both belligerent states were at a critical juncture as Iran prepared for a massive attack on Iraq. Two large-scale Iranian offensives were launched in February 1984 with little success. This escalation in the conflict, coupled with the Iraqi decision to bomb Iranian oil facilities at Kharg Island, noticeably altered the conduct of the war and may have affected its outcome. To stop repeated Iranian "human-wave" offensives, Iraq resorted to using chemical weapons and massive bombings of civilian targets, with devastating consequences. Iraq renewed its threat to hit any vessels approaching Iran's main oil export terminal at Kharg with its newly acquired French-made Super Etendard and Mirage F–1 warplanes, raising fears that in retaliation Iran would attempt to blockade the strategic Strait of Hormuz. Added to this heightened level of violence, any threat to the Strait of Hormuz would have sharply reduced the quantity of petroleum available in the world markets, thus inviting energy-dependent Western countries to protect their perceived interests by deploying naval armadas in the Persian Gulf.

Iraq's attempts to threaten Iran's oil exports were not lightly dismissed in Tehran. In reaction, Iran capped off about 100 offshore wells in its Nowruz and Ardeshir fields in December 1983, using concrete at the seabed—a process that required redrilling. Having protected these facilities, Iran began moving large numbers of troops to the southern front to launch a "final" offensive. As many as 500,000 troops were transferred, setting the stage "for a war of attrition—since Iran c[ould] sustain much higher casualty and replacement rates than Iraq."[17] In response to these tactical deployments and fearing a probable defeat, Iraq once again resorted to using chemical weapons.

Iraq used banned chemical weapons against human-wave attacks in clear violation of the 1925 Geneva Protocol, which Baghdad had signed in 1931. The speaker of the Iranian parliament, Hojatolislam Hashemi Rafsanjani, declared that 400 Iranian soldiers alone were killed in early March 1984 near Basra by Iraqi chemical attacks. Citing "available evidence" that Iraq had indeed used mustard gas and possibly other chemical weapons, the U.S. Department of State confirmed the Iranian reports and expressed support for a U.N. investigation. Despite Iraqi denials that such weapons were employed, hospitalized Iranian soldiers in Austria and Sweden supplied unequivocal human evidence. Their skin rashes could only be traced to the effects of toxins. Citing "substantial evidence" gathered by independent observers, U.N. Secretary-General Javier Perez de Cuellar "deplored" the use of chemical weapons and condemned Iran for these actions. GCC states were numbed by these revelations. Their public silence notwithstanding, the GCC states were manifestly concerned over the potential consequences of chemical warfare for their security.

The Tanker War and the GCC

In the wake of the gruesome events at Basra, and while the Iranian representative at the United Nations, Rajai Khorassani, boasted that Tehran was also capable of manufacturing chemical weapons, GCC states failed to react. Before the impact of chemical warfare had fully registered, the war intensified. In a fierce battle, code-named "Operation Before Dawn–5," Iran captured one of the two Majnun islands on the marshes north of Basra. The importance of this position, only six miles from the Baghdad-Basra highway, did not elude strategists mapping

Tehran's military progress. In response to this significant setback, Iraq unleashed its potent air force. The war consequently entered a new phase with frequent air attacks on ships in the Gulf. But on May 14, 1984, two Kuwaiti oil tankers came under attack, followed by a Saudi tanker on May 17. These air raids directly threatened GCC members. While the identity of the attackers was not immediately known, there was little doubt that both Iraq and Iran were involved. The Saudi tanker struck in its own territorial waters dramatically increased the regional stakes of the war.

The international community's main interest was to guarantee the flow of oil, whereas the concern of GCC states was to contain this most recent escalation. On May 17, 1984, GCC foreign ministers convened an emergency session, "decided to raise the question of Iranian attacks on Kuwaiti and Saudi oil tankers at an emergency meeting of the Arab League, in order to take a unified Arab stand on the attacks," and denounced Iran for its attacks.[18] Initiated as a tactical step, this move was intended to delay or even avoid a public GCC pronouncement on the war; the preferred option was a joint Arab statement. As expected, the LAS on May 20 accused Iran of aggression in the war, "specifically in connection with attacks against Arab shipping in the Persian Gulf."[19] Saudi Foreign Minister Saud al-Faysal declared that the LAS would have "to take action" to end the crisis in the Gulf, though he provided no specific proposals.

A few days after the LAS Tunis meeting, both Iran and Iraq launched new attacks on tankers and cargo ships. In response, GCC countries increased their diplomatic activities. They also acknowledged that their military surveillance efforts were enhanced to "ward off aggression."[20] On the diplomatic front, GCC states sought U.N. condemnation of the attacks on oil tankers and sent an Arab League diplomatic mission to Tokyo asking Japan to reduce its economic ties with Iran. The Japanese rejected the LAS plea, however, insisting on maintaining "neutrality" in the conflict.[21] Once again, the United Nations issued a "balanced" resolution without mentioning either belligerent in its preamble, despite U.S. backing for strong condemnation of Iran in these attacks. Citing "grave concern with the growing escalation in the Gulf," the United States announced that it was supplying Saudi Arabia with "400 Stinger antiaircraft missiles," as well as a U.S. Air Force KC-10 aerial tanker to refuel Saudi air force jets.[22] These shipments may not have significantly altered the balance of power in the region, but they did emphasize an important new military reality: The Saudis would be responsible for the defense of GCC states.

In addition to the Stingers, the United States agreed to accelerate the delivery of extra-capacity fuel tanks ordered by the Saudis in 1981 for their F-15s. The new equipment presumably would permit Riyadh to increase its surveillance in the Gulf and thwart any future attacks against GCC states. On June 5, 1984, a Royal Saudi Air Force jet, guided by AWACS sentry aircraft, intercepted intruding Iranian warplanes and destroyed one F-4 Phantom fighter-bomber. This military action removed all doubts as to where the GCC states stood. Despite GCC Secretary-General Abdallah Bisharah's 1982 statement that member states had become a "party" to the war, the June 5, 1984, Saudi action against an Iranian aircraft marked the first military involvement by a GCC member state against a belligerent in the war.[23] If the GCC was not a party to the war and was indeed seeking to end the conflict peacefully, it would have to pursue new policies to achieve such a goal after June 1984.

Riyadh's military actions severely weakened the GCC's diplomatic position as a neutral party seeking to mediate an end to the war, but they simultaneously raised the organization's military confidence. Measured against regional threats, one GCC member had conclusively demonstrated its resolve to defend GCC states' territorial integrity and perceived interests.

At the conclusion of their November 1984 fifth summit meeting, the GCC heads of state reiterated their call for a peaceful resolution of the war and stressed the need for dialogue and negotiations. Once again the council linked the war to the safety of navigation in Gulf waters and called on Iran to "participate in the efforts which aim at finding a solution based on attaining the rights of both parties."[24]

The GCC states' repeated calls for dialogue were muffled by the escalation of hostilities. In early 1985 Baghdad increased its attacks on Iranian oil-exporting facilities, and Tehran reciprocated by threatening to close the Strait of Hormuz to all shipping. The annual Iranian spring offensive was repulsed by Iraq, but also reintroduced were the devastating attacks on cities and towns, where thousands of civilians perished. In response, Iran launched long-range missiles against Baghdad and Basra, and Iraq retaliated by unleashing its air force to strafe-bomb Tehran, Isfahan, Tabriz, and other urban centers.[25]

The GCC states' fourteenth foreign ministers meeting expressed "sorrow and pain for the sufferings of innocent civilians and for the destruction caused by this war to the peoples of the two neighboring countries which are linked together by faith and neighborliness."[26] Yet the foreign ministers called on Tehran "to respond to the international efforts" aimed at ending the war and affirmed their "full solidarity with Iraq in preserving the sovereignty, safety and integrity of its territory." They also "demanded" that Iran "should not cross Iraqi territory and should respect the international borders between the two countries." At the same time, GCC states were equally concerned over Iraqi intransigence in escalating the conflict. The tanker war was slowly but surely eroding the GCC states' diplomatic successes.

THE MENACING WAR

Although over 300 ships were hit in the Persian Gulf between 1984 and 1988, human casualties were limited. Mostly nationals from Asian countries, especially Filipinos and Bangladeshis, paid the ultimate price to haul oil and goods to and from the Gulf region. Ironically, the tanker war proved beneficial to GCC states, where salvage operations created an economic miniboom. Bahrain and the UAE emirate of Dubai were particularly well suited to profit because of their dry-dock repair facilities. Nevertheless, the tanker war became very menacing. GCC states were losing important customers as insurance rates for ships sailing in the Persian Gulf skyrocketed. The order of the day was to avoid sailing through the Persian Gulf if at all possible.

One GCC response to this economic threat was to revive dormant pipeline projects to divert petroleum exports passing through the Strait of Hormuz. But no matter how innovative these schemes were, GCC states remained "locked" in and around the Arabian Peninsula. Simply stated, pipeline outlets bypassing the Strait of Hormuz were still very much dependent on the Strait of Bab al-Mandeb in the Horn of Africa and the Suez Canal in Egypt, neither of which was entirely secure. The ideal pipeline outlet for the GCC would go through Oman directly to the Arabian Sea, but despite active consideration in 1984, projected high costs postponed its construction. No less important, the GCC pipeline was left on paper because abundant oil continued to pass through the Hormuz chokepoint.

The GCC states' internal security dilemmas were rekindled in 1985. Two terrorist acts in Kuwait—an assassination attempt on the ruler on May 25 and a series of explosions on July 11—solidified their resolve to adopt a joint unified internal security agreement. The lone dissenting voice in the council, Kuwait, now became the prime target of subversion. To their credit, Kuwaiti authorities arrested several culprits and, after lengthy legal proceedings, sentenced 17 individuals to prison terms. The fate of these 17 prisoners threatened to alter Kuwait's policies in the area. Their supporters, mainly disenfranchised Shi'as in Iraq and Iran, carried out reprisals against GCC nationals and American and French interests through hijackings and bombings. Kuwait maintained its steadfastness but also increased internal security contacts with its more conservative neighbors.

The al-Faw Occupation

For GCC states, the year 1986 threatened to be cataclysmic. The February 10 Iranian attack on al-Faw Peninsula and its subsequent occupation meant that the war was inching southward. Close to 30,000

Iranian troops, mostly ideologically motivated members of the Revolutionary Guards, were poised on a strategic piece of territory only a few miles from Kuwait. GCC states were shaken. When Iraqi military efforts to dislodge entrenched Iranians failed repeatedly throughout 1986, the GCC states decided to increase ongoing defense cooperation efforts, thus reverting from their more cautious diplomatic agenda. The latter course was especially significant because the GCC states, having singled out Iran as the intransigent party in all their official statements since 1981, had opted for a more conciliatory posture in 1985. The Muscat Summit communiqué on November 6, 1985, for example, conspicuously failed to cite Iran as the procrastinating party in the war.[27] This political softening was designed to appease Iran, decrease the level of violence in the region—especially internal acts of subversion—and goad both belligerent governments to the negotiating table. The al-Faw occupation jolted GCC states into a new reality. Appeasing Iran and cajoling Iraq would not eliminate the threat of war. In fact, both Iran and Iraq escalated the conflict throughout 1986.

The Iraqis seized Mehran in May (only to lose it in June), isolated the Kurdish north with devastating results for the local inhabitants, continued to bomb towns and cities, and upped the "tanker war" tempo. Iran retaliated helter-skelter, despite its critical manpower problems and an acute internal economic crisis. GCC states cringed as Tehran launched successive offensives. The year ended with mixed results. Baghdad triumphed in its efforts to stop Iranian attacks, and Tehran attempted to justify its continued "human-wave" assaults to an increasingly skeptical population. GCC states ordered additional sophisticated weapons and increased their joint military training programs.[28]

The Reality of 1987

GCC states were numbed by the revelations of the Iran-Contra scandal in late 1986. Although the Saudi government had provided financial support to the Nicaraguan contras, the American arms-for-hostages deal shocked indignant Gulf rulers, many of whom felt betrayed by the United States. At no other time was American credibility this low in the region. Washington's exercise in strategic diplomacy, limited both in initiative and substance, was not lost to seasoned rulers. GCC leaders braced for the inevitable backlash from displeased citizens angry at their own governments' overt pro-American penchants. Unable to reconcile their anti-Iranian rhetoric with actual policies, GCC leaders rattled the sword of Islam by authorizing anti-Khomeini demonstrations. In private, however, they correctly assessed the Iran-Contra scandal as a significant change in Iranian foreign policy. It was soon apparent that Hashemi Rafsanjani, speaker of the Iranian parliament, was instrumental in the arms-for-hostages deal. For the conservative monarchies, this revived pragmatism meant that the Islamic Revolution was entering a new phase. Tehran was charting its postwar political agenda and, to no one's surprise, decided to end its self-imposed isolation from the international community. But at the same time, the 2,000 American-made TOW antitank weapons and the unspecified number of HAWK antiaircraft missiles transferred to Iran via Israel proved to be quite effective on the battlefield.

Cooperation between Tehran and Moscow was also in full swing in 1987. The Soviets provided an estimated 200 Scud-B missiles to Iran in exchange for two ELINT (electronic-intelligence) monitoring stations on their soil.[29] Emboldened by the victory of the Karbala–5 offensive, Ayatollah Khomeini exhorted volunteers gathered to commemorate the anniversary of the Islamic Revolution to continue the war until victory.[30]

Iranian battlefield victories alarmed GCC leaders. In response to significant military gains and partly to appease anxious Gulf rulers, Iraq renewed its attack on oil tankers, targeting the Iranian shuttle between Kharg and Sirri Islands for heavy aerial pounding. These attacks prompted Iran to deploy Chinese-made Silkworm missiles on Qeshm Island and the coastal town of Kuhestak on the Strait of Hormuz. The Silkworm emplacements confirmed extensive Chinese arms supplies to Iran. In the end, dozens of neutral ships were hit by missiles. Kuwait was singled out by Iran as a favorite target, allegedly for providing financial and logistical aid to Iraq. Against a rash of Iranian and Iraqi attacks on Kuwaiti ships, the vulnerable sheikhdom approached Washington and Moscow for protection.

Internationalization of the War

The often-promised Iranian "final victory" did not materialize in early 1987, though Speaker Rafsanjani declared that Iran would defeat Iraq "during the current Iranian year."[31] Operations Karbala-8 and Karbala-9 proved inconclusive, save for very large casualties because Iranian forces fell into numerous traps. Baghdad received detailed plans for the Karbala-9 offensive from Iranian military sources, "who simply demanded that the Iraqis should stop bombing Iranian cities in return."[32] One can assume that Iraqi morale rose after these land operations. But the war moved to the Gulf itself, where both combatants unleashed repeated attacks by aircraft and speedboats against tankers. During 1987, 274 vessels were hit in the Gulf and 64 sailors were killed, including 37 Americans when the USS *Stark* was hit by an Iraqi Exocet missile on May 17.

Although Washington queried Baghdad on the causes of the "accident," GCC states forcefully embarked on the American roller coaster by blaming Iran for the attack. Indeed, the *Stark* was hit in an area where Iranian vessels had launched previous attacks on GCC shipping. But Iraq probably staged this attack to internationalize the war by dragging the United States and the GCC states along. The rationale for such an action implied that Baghdad would finally force the international community to impose its long-sought-after cease-fire. Though Washington had conclusively established the real identity of the attacker (by relying on data from its AWACS sentry aircraft), blaming Iran proved more politically expedient. Ironically, the United States appeared compelled to follow this misguided course largely to salvage its much-tarnished credibility in the Arab Gulf following the scandalous revelations of its Israeli-brokered arms-for-hostages deal with Iran. To his credit, Iraqi president Saddam Hussein proved quite prescient by quickly accepting responsibility for the incident, notwithstanding his having successfully internationalized the war. The *Stark* incident signified that the war would lose its momentum simply because the United States and GCC states would not stay the course and absorb high casualty rates. "Free navigation" in the Persian Gulf, which had never been impugned since the outbreak of hostilities in 1980, turned into a buzzword in Western political circles. A formidable Western armada was deployed to the region, and Washington even agreed to reflag eleven Kuwaiti oil tankers, partially in response to Moscow's leasing of three Soviet tankers to the sheikhdom.

The introduction of escorted convoys created new dilemmas as the world watched on television supertankers acting as mine-clearing vessels for vulnerable frigates. Iran refrained from attacking the U.S. naval force directly but resorted to various forms of harassment, including laying mines, hit-and-run attacks by small patrol boats, and periodic stop-and-search actions on tanker traffic. When in October 1987 Tehran fired Silkworm missiles from the occupied al-Faw Peninsula and damaged the reflagged tanker *Sea Isle City* inside Kuwaiti waters, Washington retaliated by destroying an oil platform in the Rostam field and, using the U.S. Navy's Sea Air and Land (SEAL) commandos, blew up a second one nearby. Within a few weeks of the *Stark* incident, Iraq resumed its raids on tankers but moved its attacks south, near the Strait of Hormuz. Washington, in consultation with GCC states, played a central role in framing U.N. Security Council Resolution 598, which passed unanimously on July 20. Tehran rejected the resolution on grounds that it did not meet its requirement that Iraq be punished for initiating the conflict. In due course, mine-clearing ships were also dispatched to the Gulf.

The year ended in anxiety as Iran and Iraq continued their military posturing. GCC states welcomed the Western military presence. Emboldened by this protection, they challenged Iran to accept the reality that an outright Iraqi defeat was not in the cards. Saudi Arabia in particular resorted to force when, on July 31, 1987, close to 400 Iranian pilgrims were gunned down in Mecca. Riyadh broke its diplomatic relations with Tehran and acquired long-range missiles from the People's Republic of China, thus posing further threats to Iran. At the end of the 1987 eighth summit meeting held in Riyadh, the GCC heads of state repeated their calls on the international community to take decisive measures to end the Gulf War. Yet the tone of the final statement suggested that a compromise was reached only after considerable debate. Saudi Arabia and Kuwait had urged that the council adopt a strong anti-Iranian resolution, whereas Oman and the UAE counseled for a continued dialogue with Tehran. In the end, the "Council noted with great regret Iran's procrastination regarding accepting [U.N.] resolution [598]."[33] It did not mention either Iraq or the latter's attack on the USS *Stark*. In a postsummit news conference the Saudi foreign minister, Prince Saud al-Faysal, stated that "the door of dialogue with Iran [was] not closed," because "the aim of the GCC countries [was] to halt the war and to put an end to Iranian attacks against the GCC states."[34] By early 1988 the stage was set for rapid changes bringing the conflict to a halt. For the first time since the outbreak of hostilities, GCC states were in a relatively strong position to influence its political outcome.

STALEMATE IN THE GULF

Early in 1988 Iraq accelerated the use of medium-range missiles against Tehran and other Iranian cities. The daily bombardments proved particularly effective as a demoralizing factor, as half of Tehran's 8 million inhabitants were forced to flee the capital. Thousands of civilians perished in the "war of the cities." No other belligerents had ever systematically hammered each other's capitals with missiles in the history of warfare. This first was added to Iraq's resort to chemical weapons, with gruesome results. The fact that few members of the international community protested in outrage at the use of chemical weapons or the bombings of civilian targets probably enhanced the Iraqi resolve to act decisively. Iraq went on the offensive by recapturing al-Faw Peninsula in a surprise attack on April 19, 1988. Yet despite material shortages and poor training, Iranian forces led by the ideologically motivated Revolutionary Guards were determined to stay the course. It seems safe to suggest, nonetheless, that Iran's military capability was severely impaired by parallel command structures between the army and the Revolutionary Guards. Throughout the war's eight years repeated friction and organizational overlap between the two forces frequently hampered Iranian planning, coordination, and tactics. That Iran fought for so long with so little indicated that sheer resolve could postpone the inevitable. It could not be a match for firepower, however.

By the summer of 1988 the regional and international environments were well set to stop the bloodshed on terms acceptable to both revolutionary hierarchies. The brutality of both belligerents aside, the presence of foreign forces clearly persuaded Iran that the end was near. Although Iran had proven that mines scattered throughout the Persian Gulf could be effective—be they modern ones or 80–year-old "Russian"-made contact devices—it could not oppose the entire West. Absent the Western armada in the Gulf, the outcome of the war might have been quite different. But the U.S. Navy disposed of its Iranian counterpart in a few hours on April 19 after the USS *Samuel Roberts* struck a mine east of Bahrain. Washington ordered the destruction of two Iranian oil platforms, and when Tehran retaliated, U.S. Navy ships sank or crippled six armed Iranian vessels. Unfortunately, well-equipped navies, capable of massive retaliation, could still make errors.

On July 3, 1988, the Aegis missile cruiser USS *Vincennes*, firing at Iranian gunboats, mistook an Iran Air Airbus A-300 airliner for an attacking Iranian F-14 fighter plane and shot it down, killing all 290 people aboard. Ayatollah Khomeini figuratively swallowed his "poison pill," agreed to a cease-fire, and probably saved his revolution. The GCC states, while no doubt elated that the war had ended, remained clearly nervous, as Saddam Hussein's victory statements were quick in presenting Iraq (and himself) as the champion of all Arabs.

Iran accepted a cease-fire but did not abandon its revolutionary principles. Under the circumstances, revolutionary Iran and republican Iraq offered scant solace to the conservative Arab Gulf monarchies. The GCC states also realized that their security expectations could only be assured if cooperation and coordination among them continued.

CONCLUSION: GCC DEFENSE COOPERATION

GCC leaders concluded in 1981 that cooperation in all fields, including defense, would be unrealizable so long as they remained militarily weak. Even on paper their military strength was unimpressive, despite several major purchases of sophisticated weapons systems in the late 1970s. Consequently, they decided to allocate some $50 billion per year for defense expenditures. By 1988 the GCC's military strength stood at 160,950 men. More importantly, 382 modern combat aircraft were available as a first line of defense.

As the largest GCC state, Saudi Arabia slowly built an impressive military machine. With Iran and Iraq decimating each other, Saudi forces gradually came to dominate the skies over the Persian Gulf. Riyadh upgraded its F-15 interceptors and in 1987 placed an order with Britain for 72 Tornado fighter-bombers, thus giving it an almost insurmountable edge in the area. Further, the Saudis not only welcomed 4 U.S. Air Force

AWACS sentry aircraft in 1980 but purchased 5 of their own, deploying the first in 1986. The AWACS in tandem with the F-15s clearly gave Saudi Arabia, and presumably the GCC, a credible deterrent capability.

Security concerns in the Gulf prompted GCC leaders to seek closer military cooperation at the organizational level as well. On January 25, 1982, GCC defense ministers agreed to create a joint command establishment and appoint military officers for specific GCC duties.[35] An effort was also made to create military academies open to citizens from all six states. During their October 1982 meeting the defense ministers authorized the formation of a joint air defense network and a Gulf arms industry within the context of an overall military buildup. These issues were further discussed at the third Bahrain summit, where it was decided to initiate joint military exercises.[36]

These milestone decisions led to the first joint exercises, code-named Peninsula Shield, on October 7, 1983, in the UAE. A modest affair by modern military standards, this military gathering was followed by the larger Peninsula Shield II in October 1984 (held near Hafr al-Batin in Saudi Arabia) and Peninsula Shield III in 1987. For the first time in this century, forces from all six states participated in cooperative military activities aimed at defending their territories. Secretary-General Bisharah declared in November 1983 that GCC states were strong enough to defend themselves and warned that any attempt to block the Strait of Hormuz would introduce foreign forces into the region. Between 1984 and 1987 repeated Iranian and Iraqi threats to block the strait, efforts to internationalize the Gulf War, and direct attacks on GCC states brought a massive Western military presence to the area. As a result, GCC states established their cherished security principle: Each conservative Arab Gulf monarchy shared an identical security preoccupation. As the Gulf War entered a political hiatus in 1989, the GCC had crossed yet another hurdle. It had shed the fear of the Iranian Revolution and successfully checked the Iran-Iraq War. Whereas the Gulf War had initially posed a threat to the GCC states, the end result was a stronger, more unified military structure.

NOTES

1. Abdallah al-Ishal, *Al-Itar al-Qanuni wal-Siyasi li-Majlis al-Taawun al-Khaliji* (The legal and political framework of the Gulf Cooperation Council) (Riyadh, Saudi Arabia: n.p., 1983); Abdallah Fahd al-Nafisi, *Majlis al-Taawun al-Khaliji: At-Itar al-Siyasi wal-Istratiji* (The Gulf Cooperation Council: The political and strategic framework) (London: Ta-Ha Publishers, 1982); Emile A. Nakhleh, *The Gulf Cooperation Council: Policies, Problems, and Prospects* (New York: Praeger, 1986); Erik R. Peterson, *The Gulf Cooperation Council: Search for Unity in a Dynamic Region* (Boulder, Colo.: Westview Press, 1988); R. K. Ramazani with Joseph A.

Kechichian, *The Gulf Cooperation Council: Record and Analysis* (Charlottesville: University Press of Virginia, 1988).

2. It is difficult to ascertain with any degree of certainty the extent of GCC financial assistance to Iraq. An early estimate of $16 billion was subsequently raised to $30 billion and, more recently, to around $40 billion. See David B. Ottaway, "Gulf Arabs Place Reins on Iraq While Filling War Chest," *Washington Post*, December 21, 1987, p. A22; Edmund Ghareeb, "The Forgotten War," *American-Arab Affairs* 5 (Summer 1983): 69; *The Military Balance, 1987–1988* (London: International Institute for Strategic Studies, 1987), p. 93.

3. John Vinocur, "Iraq Reports France Will Buy More Oil and Continue Its Aid," *New York Times*, January 8, 1983, p. 4.

4. Robin Mannock, "The Gulf War: When Money Is No Object," *An-Nahar Arab Report and Memo* 11 (January 16, 1987): 2–3.

5. "Gulf Cooperation Council Issues Final Statement," Foreign Broadcast Information Service, *Daily Report*-Middle East, and Africa (hereafter FBIS-MEA), 81–101, May 27, 1981, p. A2.

6. "GCC Issues Statement," FBIS-MEA-V–81–218, November 12, 1981, p. C4.

7. "Gulf Cooperation Council Meeting Opens in Riyadh," FBIS-MEA-V–82–077, April 21, 1982, p. C2.

8. Edgar O'Ballance, *The Gulf War* (London: Brassey's Defence Publishers, 1988), pp. 78–92.

9. "GCC Foreign Ministers Meet in Riyadh 30–31 May," FBIS-MEA-V–82–105, June 1, 1982, p. C3.

10. "Text of GCC Ministerial Council Statement," FBIS-MEA-V–82–135, July 14, 1982, pp. C1–C2.

11. "Third GCC Summit Concludes in Bahrain, 11 November," FBIS-MEA-V–82–219, November 12, 1982, p. C2.

12. *Al-Majallah*, November 12, 1982, p. 2.

13. "GCC Summit Winds Up Activities in Qatar," FBIS-MEA-V–83–218, November 9, 1984, p. C4; "Iran and Iraq Urged Again to End Conflict," *UN Chronicle* 20 (December 1983): 25.

14. *Al-Sharq al-Awsat*, February 18, 1983, p. 3; "Fes Summit: Gulf War Resolution," FBIS-MEA-V–82–176, September 10, 1982, p. A19.

15. "Syrian, Iranian, Libyan Foreign Ministers Meet," FBIS-MEA-V-83-016, January 24, 1983, pp. H1–H3.

16. "GCC Ministerial Council Meetings Begin in Riyadh," FBIS-MEA-V–83–036, February 22, 1983, p. C3.

17. Anthony H. Cordesman, "The Iran-Iraq War in 1984: An Escalating Threat to the Gulf and the West," *Armed Forces Journal*, 122 (March 1984): 23.

18. "Ministers Arrive in Riyadh for GCC Meeting," FBIS-MEA-V–84–097, May 17, 1984, p. C1; *Al-Jazirah* 4250 (May 18, 1984): 1.

19. "Arab League Calls Iran an Aggressor for Moves in Gulf," *New York Times*, May 21, 1984, p. A1.

20. "Gulf States Boost Military and Diplomatic Activity," *Wall Street Journal*, May 21, 1984, p. 35.

21. William Chapman, "Japan Rebuffs Arab League Appeal," *Washington Post*, May 23, 1984, p. A28.

22. Don Oberdorfer and Rick Atkinson, "U.S. Cites 'Concern' over Persian Gulf in Sending Missiles," *Washington Post*, May 30, 1984, p. A1.

23. Bisharah was quoted in the Sharjah, UAE, newspaper *al-Khalij*: "How can [the GCC states] be mediators in an issue in which we are a major party?" *Al-Khalij*, January 16, 1982, p. 1. The GCC secretary-general denied the statement, but to no avail. The newspaper stood by its story and called on the council states to "pause and define a clearer stand on Mr. Bisharah's statement." "Daily Quotes Bisharah Remarks on Gulf Problems," FBIS-MEA-V–82–013, January 20, 1982, pp. C1–C4.

24. "Further Reportage on GCC Meeting: Closing Statement Issued," FBIS-MEA-V–84–231, November 29, 1984, p. C2.

25. Initial attacks on Baghdad were not acknowledged by the Iraqi government, which termed the bombings as "car bombs" planted by enemies of the state. Elaine Sciolino, "Bank in Baghdad Ripped by Blast; Cause in Dispute," *New York Times*, March 15, 1985, pp. A1, A11; "Iraq Says It Bombed Teheran," *New York Times*, March 19, 1985, p. A4; Herbert H. Denton, "4th Blast Rocks Baghdad; Iranian Missiles Suspected," *Washington Post*, March 20, 1985, pp. A1, A16; Herbert H. Denton, "Baghdad Steps Up Air War on Iran," *Washington Post*, March 22, 1985, pp. A25, A31; Judith Miller, "Iraqis Announce Attacks on Iran After Explosion Shakes Baghdad," *New York Times*, April 1, 1985, p. A8.

26. "Further Reportage on GCC Foreign Ministers Meeting," FBIS-MEA-V–85–053, March 19, 1985, p. C1.

27. "Sixth GCC Summit Issues Final Communiqué," FBIS-MEA-V–85–215, November 6, 1985, pp. C1–C2.

28. O'Ballance, *Gulf War*, pp. 173–92.

29. Ibid., p. 199.

30. "Khomeini Speech on Revolution Anniversary," Foreign Broadcast Information Service *Daily Report*—South Asia (hereafter FBIS-SAS VIII) 87–028, February 11, 1987, pp. I1–I2.

31. "Majlis Speaker Comments on War, Economic Resources," FBIS-SAS-VIII–87–065, April 6, 1987, p. I1.

32. O'Ballance, *Gulf War*, p. 201.

33. "GCC Summit in Riyadh: Final Statement Issued," Foreign Broadcast Information Service *Daily Report*—Near East and South Asia (hereafter FBIS-NES), FBIS-NES–87–250, December 30, 1987, p. I2.

34. "Al-Faysal Holds News Conference," FBIS-NES–87–250, December 30, 1987, p. I7.

35. Abdallah Khawaja Nakih, "Ta'ziz al-Taawun al-Askari bayna dual al-Majlis," *Al-Bilad* 6946 (January 25, 1982): 1.

36. "Summit to Study Eco-military Cooperation," *Emirates News* 11 (October 27, 1982): 1.

7

U.S. Policy and the Gulf War

A Question of Means

Thomas L. McNaugher

It would have been hard to find a less potent superpower than the United States as it faced the Persian Gulf at the outset of the Iran-Iraq War. Unwilling or unable to save the Shah of Iran, U.S. policymakers stood idly by as revolution convulsed the country that had throughout the previous decade been the principal guardian of U.S. interests in the Gulf. Nearly a year later, revolutionary Iranian students seized the American embassy in Tehran, taking 54 U.S. diplomats hostage; over the next fourteen months the hostage crisis became both symptom and symbol of U.S. powerlessness. The Shah's fall was a net gain for the Soviet Union, and the superpower balance in the region seemed to shift still further toward Moscow in December 1979, when Soviet troops invaded Afghanistan. With its hostages still imprisoned in Iran, its relations with Iraq long since severed, and its military forces without firm footing in the region, the United States could do little more than watch as Iraqi troops invaded Iran on September 22, 1980.

The war only increased the concern with which most Americans viewed events in the Gulf. Twice in the 1970s events in the region had sent major shocks through the world's oil market. The market slackened over the course of 1980. But the fact that Iran and Iraq attacked each other's oil facilities within days after the war began, combined with Iran's dominant position along the vital Strait of Hormuz, still raised the prospect of yet another painful increase in the price of oil. Meanwhile, having assumed that the Soviet invasion of Afghanistan was a step in Moscow's efforts to extend its influence into the Gulf, many Americans concluded that the war offered yet another opportunity for Soviet intrigue.

Yet there was little the United States could do to avert such prospects. President Carter had announced his doctrine in January 1980, making clear the nation's interest in the region's oil and its fear of Soviet advances. But the military "teeth" in that policy—the so-called Rapid Deployment Joint Task Force (RDJTF)—was not formally created until March of that year and even then lacked the size and transportation needed to make it a serious instrument of policy. Besides, U.S. diplomats had been largely stymied in their efforts to find bases or points of entry in the region for U.S. forces. Although the oil sheikhdoms of the Arabian Peninsula depended, in the end, on U.S. security guarantees, none was as willing as the Shah to host a U.S. presence.

With the region in general and the war zone in particular beyond their reach, U.S. diplomats fell back on multilateral approaches. They joined other members of the United Nations Security Council in calling for an end to the war. They vowed to keep the Strait of Hormuz open, but when pressed, they asserted that they would prefer a multilateral naval force to unilateral U.S. military action.[1] As a show of support to Saudi Arabia, two AWACS aircraft were stationed there within weeks after the war began—a move that culminated in the sale of five such aircraft to the Saudis the next year. In each case, save perhaps the last, U.S. actions represented the absence of policy—indeed, the absence of policy instruments.

Despite its unilateralist rhetoric and occasional military activism, the Reagan administration did little to alter its predecessor's approach to the Gulf and particularly to the Gulf War. While Reagan-era defense budgets fueled growth in the readiness of the RDJTF (which became Central Command, or CENTCOM, in January 1983), the administration made no effort to project these forces to the Gulf, partly because the oil sheikhdoms remained less than anxious for the help. As the balance in the war shifted toward Iran after 1982, the United States tilted toward Iraq, reestablishing diplomatic relations in November 1985. In 1984 it inaugurated "Operation Staunch" to curtail the flow of arms to Iran, a policy staff members of the National Security Council violated in 1985 and 1986 when they traded arms to Iran for the release of U.S. hostages in Lebanon. Fortunately, U.S. capabilities and intentions went untested; although the war produced its share of surprises and crises, it never departed from the bloody stalemate that set in midway through 1982. Reagan administration policymakers thus were able to look elsewhere for challenges.

In 1987, however, they found their challenge in the Gulf. In July of that year U.S. warships began to convoy U.S. flagships, eleven of which were Kuwaiti oil tankers, through the Gulf to Kuwait. Over the next year U.S. military forces tracked and captured an Iranian minelayer, destroyed several of Iran's offshore oil platforms, sank or badly damaged two Iranian frigates, and, in a tragic accident, shot down an Iranian commercial airliner, killing 290 passengers. In the background, U.S. diplomats worked within the United Nations to forge a resolution "with teeth in it," meaning one that would actually do something to end the war. Others worked bilaterally to curtail the flow of arms to Iran. These policies succeeded; in July of 1988, shortly after its airliner had been downed, Iran agreed to sign the U.N. cease-fire resolution.

This looked like a major policy success along the forceful, unilateralist lines the Reagan administration had espoused all along. Successful it was, both in helping to bring the war to a cease-fire and in reestablishing the nation's credibility in the region. But the United States was less the unilateral participant than the lead player among many players, in New York as well as the Gulf, whose influence it helped bring to bear on Iran in what proved to be a successful exercise of multilateral power. Given the reluctance of local states to host a large U.S. military presence and the Soviet Union's emergence as a more formidable diplomatic player in regional affairs, it is in the role of conductor, rather than soloist, that the United States is likely to exercise influence in the future.

WADING IN

Because U.S. activism in the Gulf followed closely on the heels of revelations about U.S. arms sales to Iran, reflagging in particular has often been seen as a reaction to the Iranscam debacle. No doubt national embarrassment and a felt need to restore U.S. credibility played a role in shaping U.S. Gulf policy, but the origins of U.S. military policy and diplomacy were substantially more complex and subtle than this suggests.

Reflagging was Kuwait's idea, after all. It may be that news of U.S. arms sales to Iran tweaked Kuwait's insecurity and encouraged its rulers to seek reaffirmation of U.S. security commitments. But Iran had already found ways of tweaking Kuwait's insecurities. Iran's victory at al-Faw in February 1986 raised fear throughout the Arab Gulf states that Iran might be on the verge of winning the ground war, and Iran's leaders skillfully exploited such fears by talking incessantly of an upcoming "offensive to end all offensives." That prospect held out special significance for Kuwait, which lay so close to the battlefield. Meanwhile, in September 1986 Iran stepped up its attacks on Gulf shipping, focusing particularly on ships doing business with Kuwait.[2]

Kuwait's call for help ultimately went out to virtually all members of the U.N. Security Council, but it went first to the Soviet Union, on grounds that the Soviets "could act more quickly than the Americans," and also because Iranscam made Kuwait uncertain of U.S. intentions.[3] Nonetheless, Kuwait approached the United States in January 1987, asking whether Kuwaiti tankers flying the U.S. flag would be given the same protection as other American flagships. Near the end of January U.S. policymakers responded positively to Kuwait's request. Significantly, although U.S. diplomats knew by that time that the Soviets were entertaining a similar request, they were unaware of any Soviet agreement to reflag. The U.S. response seems to have had less to do with guilt born of Iranscam or fear of a Soviet intrusion in the region than with the prevailing assumption that extending U.S. naval protection to a few more tankers would differ little from "business as usual" in the Gulf. Up to that point the U.S. Navy had found intermittent convoys an effective deterrent to Iranian action. Iran even refrained from harassing ships carrying other flags when they sailed in the vicinity of U.S. warships. Although the CIA assigned some risk to the operation, it suggested that the probable Iranian response to reflagging would be terrorism—hardly a new threat—rather than direct attacks on U.S. warships.[4] Initial briefings thus suggested that reflagging would require little if any increase in the size of the Middle East Force (MIDEASTFOR).[5] Furthermore, Defense Department military planners had little to do with the initial reflagging decision.[6]

The purpose, scope, and urgency attached to the operation expanded soon thereafter, however, for reasons unrelated to Iranscam. In formally asking for U.S. flags for six of its tankers late in February 1987, Kuwait let it be known that the Soviet Union had agreed to reflag five. U.S. officials vigorously urged Kuwait to give the Soviets a much smaller role in the operation and offered to compensate by providing U.S. flags for all eleven tankers. In the final Kuwaiti-Soviet agreement, the Soviets were reduced to chartering three of their own smaller tankers to Kuwait, a situation that fortuitously allowed them to soft-pedal their own naval role in Kuwait's support while seeking diplomatic openings in Tehran.[7] From the U.S. perspective, reflagging ceased to be a low-key move to reassure Kuwait and became in addition a vehicle for keeping the Soviets out of the Gulf.

Three months later, but still two months before U.S. warships first began protecting reflagged tankers, the operation's scope took a substantial jump thanks, ironically, to Iraq. On May 17 an Iraqi Mirage fired two Exocet missiles into the side of the USS *Stark*, killing 37 American sailors. At this point the U.S. naval presence in the Gulf, and with it ongoing plans to reflag Kuwaiti tankers, burst into public view. Faced with massive criticism from Capitol Hill that it had underestimated the operation's risks, the administration moved quickly to protect itself as well as Kuwait's tankers. Within three days of the *Stark* attack, the president approved a request to increase MIDEASTFOR's size from six ships to nine.[8] By the end of June the battleship *Missouri* and its escorts had been ordered into the Arabian Sea. By the time the first convoy of reflagged Kuwaiti tankers began the two-day journey up the Gulf on July 17, the U.S. fleet in or near the Gulf had grown to roughly 33 vessels, largely in response to domestic political pressure.

By raising the prospect of a bruising War Powers Resolution battle on Capitol Hill, the *Stark* incident also affected official definitions of the navy's mission. To President Reagan, for example, reflagging was a commitment to "freedom of navigation" and "preserving the free flow of oil through the Strait of Hormuz." But the tanker war had never seriously threatened the flow of oil from the Gulf, and other U.S. policy statements made clear that reflagging "was *not* . . . an open-ended unilateral American commitment to defend all non-belligerent shipping in the Persian Gulf."[9] Most likely, the president's statements were meant to reinforce the appearance of neutrality; the U.S. Navy always protected freedom of the seas, after all, whereas protecting Kuwaiti tankers sounded too much like taking sides with Iraq in the war. In practice, the president's insistence on U.S. neutrality, combined with increasingly effective consultations with key members of Congress, mooted the War Powers issue. But it did nothing to provide either the public or military planners with a realistic view of what was going on.

Official mission statements were only slightly more helpful in defining the navy's mission. Defense Secretary Caspar Weinberger was concise in asserting that "MIDEASTFOR is tasked with providing protection to U.S.-flagged vessels including the reflagged Kuwaiti vessels sailing within or transiting through the international waters of the Gulf of Oman, Strait of Hormuz, and the Persian Gulf." But he went on to give MIDEASTFOR the mission of "assisting friendly regional states"—whatever that meant. Further, he suggested that "the continued presence of U.S. forces in the Persian Gulf . . . acts as a moderating element with regard to the Iran-Iraq war." This was less a mission statement than an assumption, and an unwarranted one at that in view of the domestic debate shaping up in Iran as the outlines of U.S. policy emerged publicly.[10]

Notwithstanding these vague and rather gradiose statements, in practice the United States tended toward a minimalist approach to its new role in the Gulf. The U.S. Navy never protected the shipping of other Gulf Arab states or even non-U.S. flagships dealing with Kuwait. U.S. ship captains stood by as Iran's strikes on commercial Gulf shipping reached new highs in 1987 and early 1988, topping in frequency those of Iraq for the first time in the war.[11] At the start, at least, U.S. military strategy was sensitive to the risk of a counterproductive confrontation with Iran's Revolutionary Guards.

Such moderation paid dividends. On July 24, 1987, the USS *Bridgeton*, the first of Kuwait's tankers to be escorted north, struck a mine north of Bahrain. The world was then treated to the spectacle of U.S. warships meekly following the *Bridgeton*, now a "minesweeper," as it limped toward Kuwait's harbor. Seemingly adding to its embarrassment, the United States expressed uncertainty about just who laid the mines ("invisible hands," the Iranians retorted) and did not retaliate. Whether what followed was the result of deliberate choice in Tehran or sheer euphoria among Iran's Revolutionary Guards remains unclear, but over the next month mines appeared everywhere in the Gulf, as well as outside the Strait of Hormuz in the Gulf of Oman. Specifically in response to the latter threat, Great Britain and France expanded their Gulf naval operations, while by September Italy, Denmark, and Belgium agreed to introduce their own minesweeping flotillas into the Gulf. The U.S. Navy's mission did not change, but U.S. warships now became part of a larger international effort in the Gulf that reflected ongoing efforts in the United Nations to bring Iran to the negotiating table. Congressional pressure on the War Powers and burden-sharing issues subsided as the nation's allies took up positions in the Gulf, while Iran's ability to single out the United States declined commensurately.

The low-key U.S. approach continued into September, when U.S. helicopters followed the Iranian landing ship *Iran Ajr* as it began to lay mines in the northern Gulf. The ship was captured and boarded the next day, and shortly thereafter the world was treated to photographic proof, if any were needed, of Iran's mine-laying operations.[12] The operation was run with minimal force; 3 Iranians were killed and 2 were lost at sea, but the remaining 26 were returned to Iran soon thereafter. Thus the incident provided more embarrassment than provocation to Iran. That the crew was returned via Oman, which remained on friendly terms with Iran, suggested a laudable degree of political sensitivity in Washington.

Despite the seeming value of taking a low-key approach to reflagging, the scope of the operation slowly but steadily expanded over the last year of the war in response to pressures only partly related to events in the Gulf. One of the few precise elements among the mission statements proffered in the wake of the *Stark* incident came from Under Secretary of State Michael Armacost, who made clear that the "GCC states recognize their responsibility for protecting all shipping in their territorial waters."[13] In October Iran's ever-clever Revolutionary Guards probed Armacost's sincerity by firing a Silkworm missile from Iranian-occupied al-Faw into the *Sea Isle City*, one of Kuwait's eleven reflagged tankers, while the ship waited to unload its cargo in Kuwait's territorial waters.

Whatever the initial understanding, Kuwait's clear desire for a broader U.S. security umbrella and U.S. concern for its own credibility led the United States to retaliate by destroying the Rostum offshore oil platform, a nonproducing platform used by Iran as a communications center to coordinate strikes in the Gulf.[14] In the background, U.S. policymakers made clear that they were not anxious for an escalating confrontation with Iran.

This apparently suited the Iranians, who conspicuously avoided confronting the United States for the next six months. By this time Iran's domestic political and economic problems were overshadowing its dealings with the United States. Mobilization problems prevented Iran from mounting its usual winter offensive late in 1987, for example. There were increasing signs that Iran's economy was near collapse, mostly the result of war and Iraqi bombs. An avalanche of missiles fired from Iraq at most major Iranian cities starting late in February 1988 and continuing through mid-April—the so-called "war of the cities"—produced little physical damage but vast confusion and panic in the government as well as the public. By mid-April the morale and strength of Iran's border forces had sunk to the point where Iraqi forces were able to snap up al-Faw in a matter of a few days.

It may be that anger spawned by the war of the cities prompted Iran to strike out. Whatever the motivation, in April Iranian Revolutionary Guards once again began laying mines in the waters of the northern Gulf, one of which was hit by the destroyer USS *Roberts*. On April 18 U.S. warships destroyed two offshore oil platforms in the southern Gulf that served as Revolutionary Guards command centers. Because one of them (the Sirri platform) was responsible for roughly 8 percent of Iran's oil exports, U.S. retaliation in this case represented an escalation over the previous policy of either defending ships or striking military targets. Interviews suggest that the choice to escalate was driven at least partly by the sense that the U.S. public would stand for nothing less in the face of continuing Iranian provocation.

Over the next several hours two of Iran's frigates left their base at Bandar Abbas to challenge the U.S. Navy. The rude greeting these ships received from the U.S. Navy prompted Defense Secretary Frank Carlucci to call the Iranians "foolhardy."[15] But the Iranian move should not have been so surprising. The United States was now hitting the same targets Iraq had been hitting for some years. From an Iranian perspective the strike on the Sirri platform represented the emergence of a U.S.-Iraqi axis, a perception no doubt reinforced by the fact that Iraqi forces recaptured al-Faw on the very same day.[16] Iran's leaders, no less than those in Washington, had public opinion to contend with.

The incremental U.S. escalation continued. Two weeks after the Sirri strike, President Reagan gave U.S. ship captains permission to come to the aid of friendly nonbelligerent commercial vessels asking for help. The move was partly a response to requests from "Saudi Arabia and the United Arab Emirates, from U.S. oil shippers with hulls steaming in the Gulf under non-U.S. flags, and from frustrated U.S. Navy ship commanders in the Gulf, who believed they could do more with their forces."[17] Interviews suggest that at least some U.S. military planners sensed that Iran was vulnerable and should be subjected to increasing U.S. pressure. Whatever the motives behind the shift in policy, clearly the U.S. "tilt" toward Iraq had been replaced by a virtual embrace of Iraqi aims and tactics.

Things went smoothly until July 3, when the Airbus tragedy shocked Iranians and Americans alike. In the United States the tragedy reopened the controversies that had plagued reflagging at its start: What was the Navy's mission? Was the United States at war with Iran? How would the United States know when it had won? In Iran, by contrast, the tragedy seemed to be the last straw on a war-weary camel's back. Within two weeks of the Airbus incident, Iran agreed to sign the U.N. cease-fire resolution, citing the Airbus tragedy as one reason for doing so. The controversy in the United States was suddenly replaced by self-congratulations on a job well done.

THE COURSE OF U.N. DIPLOMACY

While American strategists negotiated with events in the Gulf, U.S. diplomats negotiated within the United Nations to create the political context for reflagging and to orchestrate additional pressure on Iran. There they sought with mixed results to forge U.N. Security Council Resolution 598, calling for a cease-fire, and the so-called "Second Resolution," which sought to embargo arms shipments to belligerents that refused to accept the cease-fire. In the end, Resolution 598 provided a vehicle for registering Iran's growing isolation and also for Iran's escape from the shooting war. Over the eighteen months leading up to that point, ongoing negotiations in the United Nations interacted continuously with politics in Tehran as well as political intercourse among international actors in ways that helped produce a cease-fire after eight years of bloody and indecisive conflict.

Arguably it was in the United Nations, rather than in the Gulf itself, that the United States sought most arduously to undo the damage caused by Iranscam. While dealing behind the scenes with Kuwait on reflagging, for example, President Reagan referred publicly in February 1987 to his interest in "an international effort to bring Iran into negotiations," suggesting that he was more interested in diplomatic than military approaches to ending the war.[18] Operation Staunch had begun life in 1984 as a unilateral U.S. effort to curb the flow of arms to Iran, and Iranscam raised obvious questions about the sincerity of that policy. With Resolution 598 the United States sought to lay those questions to rest, while with the Second Resolution it sought to internationalize Operation Staunch. Thus, although the decision to launch yet another U.N. resolution on the Gulf War came from Secretary-General Perez de Cuellar, U.S. diplomats worked aggressively in subsequent months to forge a "resolution with teeth in it."

Significantly, while reflagging was shaped importantly by the desire to "keep the Soviets out of the Gulf," at the United Nations U.S. diplomacy success inevitably required Soviet cooperation, not to mention the acquiescence, if not active support, of other Security Council members.[19] Indeed, at the core of the negotiations that produced Resolution 598 lay a bilateral negotiation between the superpowers. Although Britain and France, in particular, also played actively in shaping the resolution, interviews suggest that when the superpowers reached agreement on an issue, other members of the Security Council normally followed suit. As one U.S. observer put it, the Security Council provided "a multilateral setting for a bilateral negotiation."[20]

Perez de Cuellar called for a new resolution near the end of 1986; Resolution 598 was not signed until July 1987. The Security Council's deliberations stalled partly on the question of balance in the resolution's reference to the competing demands of the belligerents. As finally passed, Resolution 598 contained clauses clearly aimed at mollifying Iran. Its call for a commission of inquiry into responsibility for starting the war, for example, and its reference to the "need for reconstruction efforts, with appropriate international assistance, once the conflict is ended," both responded to long-standing Iranian demands. Its first paragraph, by contrast, was emphatically pro-Iraqi in demanding that "as a first step towards a negotiated settlement, Iran and Iraq observe an immediate cease-fire, discontinue all military actions on land, at sea and in the air, and withdraw all forces to the internationally recognized boundaries without delay."[21] U.S. diplomats insisted on this wording over the objections of European diplomats who found it unrealistic, perhaps because Iraqi diplomats, buoyed and confident after their military had successfully defeated Iran's "offensive to end all offensives" in January, made it plain that they would reject any resolution lacking the proper wording.[22] For some Americans, on the other hand, the resolution's wording was a way of bringing pressure to bear on Iran.[23]

The second major bone of contention in forging Resolution 598 was the U.S. insistence that the resolution impose sanctions on either belligerent should it fail to agree to a cease-fire. Given the resolution's wording, Iran was the obvious target. Interviews suggest that no other Security Council member was terribly comfortable with the idea of sanctions. With the British in particular balking at economic sanctions on grounds that they would not work, agreement was finally reached on an arms embargo. This sat well with U.S. officials, since it echoed their efforts to reinvigorate "Operation Staunch" in the wake of Iranscam. Still, enough debate remained on the issue to stall Security Council agreement until late June, when the sanctions portion of the original resolution was split off to become the "Second Resolution." Resolution 598 was passed unanimously on July 20, 1987, but the sanctions U.S. diplomats had sought became a matter of continuing diplomacy for some months to come.[24]

Both of these issues continued to provoke controversy in the months after Resolution 598 was passed. To no one's surprise, Iraq quickly signed the resolution, making much of its call for a simultaneous cease-fire and withdrawal. Iran refused to sign the resolution but, rather than rejecting it outright, called attention instead to the need for a commission to inquire into who started the war. After visiting Baghdad and Tehran in September, Perez de Cuellar publicly separated the cease-fire from the call for a withdrawal but dodged Iran's call for the creation of such a commission, apparently on grounds that the formulation of a commission in the absence of a cease-fire would force Iraq to reject Resolution 598 and scuttle the negotiating process.[25]

Arguably Iran's position became slightly more flexible in the months immediately after the Security Council passed Resolution 598. Iranian President Ali Khamene'i journeyed to the United States in mid-September to deliver a speech that contained much of the usual vituperation but notably lacked the long-standing Iranian call for the removal of Iraqi president Saddam Hussein. Whether this was a serious bargaining position or an Iranian attempt to buy time and stall implementation of the Second Resolution may never be known; probably different groups in Iran had different motives. Clearly the existence of Resolution 598, combined with the growing international naval presence in the Gulf, was having some effort on the internal debate in Iran.

President Reagan used the occasion of Khamene'i's visit to New York and Iran's rejection of Resolution 598 to launch a campaign to pass the Second Resolution. The effort failed some months later, however, as it became clear that the Soviet Union would not cooperate. Although U.S. diplomats made much of the refusal, Moscow was never as isolated on this issue as the United States sought to portray. China, which maintained a profitable and controversial arms trade with Iran, stated publicly that it would sign if the Soviets signed, but of course this was never tested. Even European states that agreed to sign were reluctant to push the Soviets on the issue. In the end, it is not clear that all U.S. diplomats involved felt strongly about passing the resolution. To some, the mere effort to pass the resolution and to stigmatize those who refused was itself useful in pressuring potential arms traffickers like Brazil or Argentina on a bilateral basis into forgoing sales to Iran while the war continued.

This approach seems to have worked reasonably well. By the end of 1987 the United States seems to have recovered from the stigma attached to its own efforts to sell arms to Iran to the point where "Operation Staunch" was once again in full swing. China's sale of Silkworm antiship missiles to Iran was a special problem for obvious reasons. Faced with the threat of an embargo on the sale of U.S. military technology to China, the Chinese finally agreed to stop doing what they had never publicly admitted to doing in the first place. In September 1987 the British finally ordered Iran to close its London weapons procurement office, said to have done "the paper work on an estimated 70 percent of Tehran's worldwide weapons purchases."[26]

Although Moscow and its East European allies never fully stopped shipping arms to Iran, the level of shipments was militarily insignificant.[27] Clearly Moscow was playing its own game with both belligerents even as it helped shape the U.N. approach to the war and, to a lesser extent, participated in reflagging. Moscow may also have been reluctant to isolate itself from Iran as it took grave risks in withdrawing its forces from Afghanistan. Both superpowers were engaged in a mixed-sum game; both were seeking unilateral advantage in the Gulf, yet both were cooperating at other levels to pressure Iran into signing the cease-fire.

Whatever the nature of Moscow's game, Iranians had little doubt about Moscow's priorities. Mutual suspicions prevented the development of a serious improvement in Soviet-Iranian economic ties, despite frequent references to the prospect. Meanwhile, Soviet arms flowed in huge quantities to Iraq, while Soviet ships plied the Gulf in defense of Kuwaiti ships. Whatever Moscow's position on the Second Resolution, it had signed the first and made clear to Iran its desire to see the war end. The last straw may have come in February 1988, when Soviet-made rockets began to rain down on Tehran, prompting demonstrations outside the Soviet embassy in Tehran and a temporary rift in Soviet-Iranian relations. From an Iranian perspective the Soviet Union was siding with much of the rest of the world in calling for an end to the war.

The extent of Iran's isolation became painfully clear to Iranian Prime Minister Mir Hussein Musavi, who journeyed to the United Nations in July 1988 to ask the United Nations to condemn the United States for downing his country's airliner. Instead, Musavi found diplomats telling him to end the war. Iran's isolation was nearly complete, and this, as much as the Western navies sailing the Gulf, must have pushed Iran toward accepting Resolution 598.

CONCLUSION

By playing a leading role in the Gulf as well as in the United Nations, the United States unquestionably helped bring Iran to the negotiating table in 1988. In addition, U.S. policy helped reestablish U.S. credibility among the Gulf Arab states by demonstrating that the United States could sustain a low-key, politically sensitive, and consistent military policy. Indeed, U.S. military planners were quite pleased with the degree of cooperation they enjoyed from Gulf states normally reluctant to be so forthcoming. Meanwhile, U.S. policy "kept the Soviets out of the Gulf" in any significant operational sense, while U.S. policymakers nonetheless worked successfully with the Soviets in the United Nations in forging Resolution 598. All these produced a certain sense of satisfaction among U.S. diplomats involved in the year's events.

Still, the United States shared credit for bringing the cease-fire into effect with a wide range of factors. Iraq's extended bombing campaign, of which the tanker war was but a minor part, slowly ground Iran's economy down to crisis levels by the end of 1987, and Iran's efforts to deal with its economy only exacerbated deep fissures among competing political factions in Tehran. Economic deprivation combined with battlefield stalemate to produce a remarkable degree of war weariness across Iran. Without denying Iraq credit for improving martial skills, for example, the fact remains that the Iranian soldiers Iraq encountered at al-Faw in 1988 were a shabby and demoralized lot in comparison to the Revolutionary Guards that had taken the town two years before. The "war of the cities" provoked confusion and fear out of all proportion to the relatively meager physical damage Iraq's missiles wreaked on cities like Tehran and Isfahan. In some sense, Iraq can be said to have won its war with Iran.

Nor can the role of luck be entirely overlooked. No one could have predicted when U.S. ships first began convoy operations that Iran would move rapidly toward economic and political crisis. To the contrary, Iranian rhetoric and harassment tactics in the summer of 1987 suggested that the real danger might lie in a resurgence of revolutionary radicalism and belligerence that, had it been sustained, might have dragged the United States into an escalating slugging match with Iran. Meanwhile, interviews suggest that few members of the Security Council held out much hope for Resolution 598 when it first began to take shape. Events in New York and the Gulf moved in ways that added to the resolution's force as time went on.

In this sense U.S. policy toward the war should be a source of humility as well as pride. Events need not always push in a positive direction; U.S. luck is not always good. The more important point is that policy was never entirely under control. Once U.S. forces were committed, for example, their precise mission was defined in response to regional concerns, perceptions of public support, congressional pressures, and an uncertain sense of Iran's capabilities and intentions. U.S. strategists found it hard to maintain the moderate tone with which they began reflagging. The limits of U.S. power were more obvious in New York, where Resolution 598 represented the outcome of tough bargaining among a wide range of actors, including the Soviet Union. In crises U.S. policy toward the Gulf is likely always to involve the multilateral qualities demonstrated over the last year of the Gulf war. Hopefully, events and other actors will conspire to grant success in the future as they did then.

NOTES

Grateful acknowledgment is given for permission to reprint this chapter from *The Iran-Iraq War: Impact and Implications*, ed. Efraim Karsh. London: The Macmillan Press Ltd., 1990.

1. See especially the statement of Secretary of State Edmund S. Muskie, made on September 25, 1980, and reprinted in *Department of State Bulletin*, November 1980, pp. 36–37.

2. On Iranian targeting of Kuwaiti and other GCC shipping, see U.S. Congress, House Committee on Armed Services, *National Security Policy Implications of United States Operations in the Persian Gulf*, Report of the Defense Policy Panel and the Investigations Subcommittee, 100th Cong., 1st sess., July 1987 (Washington, D.C.: Government Printing Office, 1987), p. 8, fig. 3.

3. See the interview with Abdul Fattah al-Badr, chairman of the Kuwait Oil Tanker Company, in Milton Viorst, "A Reporter at Large: Out of the Desert," *New Yorker*, May 16, 1988, p. 49.

4. Tim Carrington and Robert S. Greenberger, "CIA Says Terror by Iran Is Likely over Gulf Moves," *Wall Street Journal*, June 18, 1987, p. 5.

5. In April the U.S. Navy was ordered to increase the amount of time spent in the Gulf, while the Indian Ocean tour of the carrier USS *Kitty Hawk* and its task force was extended and the carrier was ordered to deploy nearer the Gulf. The latter move had more to do with Iran's Silkworm threat, however, than with military requirements for reflagging. For a chronology, see Robert J. Ciarrocchi, *U.S., Soviet, and Western European Naval Forces in the Persian Gulf Region*, Congressional Research Service Report 87–956F, (December 8, 1987), p. 6.

6. See Bernard E. Trainor, "U.S. Officers Troubled by Plan to Aid Gulf Shipping," *New York Times*, June 29, 1987, p. A6. Department of Defense (DOD) officials attended all key interagency meetings leading up to the decision, but operational planners were not consulted until the decision had been made.

7. Tensions in Soviet-Iranian relations concerning initial Soviet convoys in support of Kuwait's chartered tankers subsided almost as soon as Tehran became fully aware of the size and scope of the U.S. reflagging operation. Soviet Deputy Foreign Minister Yuliy Vorontsov visited Tehran several times over the summer of 1987 to discuss ways to improve Soviet-Iranian economic ties. The "heavy-handed" U.S. response to Kuwait's actions thus allowed Moscow not only to

"meet the Kuwaiti request for reflagging, but to use the opening as leverage to actually *improve* relations with Tehran at the same time." Francis Fukuyama, "Patterns of Soviet Third World Policy," *Problems of Communism*, September–October 1987, pp. 8–9 (emphasis in original).

8. Ciarrocchi, *U.S., Soviet, and Western European Naval Forces in the Persian Gulf Region*, p. 9.

9. Caspar W. Weinberger, *A Report to the Congress on Security Arrangements in the Persian Gulf*, June 15, 1987, p. i (emphasis in original).

10. The most precise public Defense Department mission statement is Weinberger, *Security Arrangements in the Persian Gulf*. The State Department equivalent is U.S. Department of State, *U.S. Policy in the Persian Gulf*, Special Report no. 166, July 1987.

11. Iran attacked 92 ships in 1987, more than Iraq attacked in that or any other year of the war. See Ronald O'Rourke, "Gulf Ops," *U.S. Naval Institute Proceedings* 115/5/1035 (Naval Review 1989), p. 43.

12. Richard Halloran, "U.S. Reports Firing on Iranian Vessel Seen Laying Mines," *New York Times*, September 22, 1987, p. A1, and Halloran, "Secret U.S. Army Unit Had Role in Raid in Gulf," *New York Times*, September 24, 1987, p. A12.

13. Department of State, *U.S. Policy in the Persian Gulf*, p. 12.

14. See Gerald F. Seib, "U.S. Must Decide If an Attack on Iran Is Worth Enormous, Long-term Risks," *Wall Street Journal*, October 19, 1987, p. 26.

15. George C. Wilson and Molly Moore, "U.S. Sinks or Cripples 6 Iranian Ships in Gulf Battles," *Washington Post*, April 19, 1988, p. 1.

16. For a chronology of the day's various battles, see "The Day in Detail: What Happened Where," *Washington Post*, April 19, 1988, p. A22.

17. O'Rourke, "Gulf Ops," p. 47.

18. For presidential statements during this period, see Department of State, *U.S. Policy in the Persian Gulf*, p. 8.

19. U.S. diplomats made no secret of clashing U.S. approaches to the Soviet Union. As Under Secretary of State Michael Armacost put it, the U.S. "preference would be for a Western protective regime [in the Gulf]. . . . The best way for the [superpowers] to collaborate in our stated common interest . . . is through the work currently being undertaken in the Security Council." Department of State, *U.S. Policy in the Persian Gulf*, p. 12.

20. Author's interview, U.S. Department of State, May 31, 1989.

21. For the resolution's full text, see *New York Times*, September 25, 1987, p. A8.

22. Author's interviews with Iraqi officials, Baghdad, December 1987.

23. In interviews U.S. diplomats suggested that Resolution 598's first clause was never meant to imply simultaneity; the words "immediately" and "without delay" actually referred to different schedules. It is not clear that the resolution was understood this way by the public or by the belligerents.

24. See Gary Sick, "The Internationalization of the Iran-Iraq War: The Events of 1987" (Unpublished paper written for the Center for International and Strategic Affairs, UCLA, April 22, 1988), p. 20.

25. Perez de Cuellar noted after a visit to Tehran early in September that "there was no reference on the part of the Iranian authorities to a rejection of

any part of the resolution." For the text of his statement, see Foreign Broadcast Information Service (FBIS), *Daily Report—South Asia*, FBIS-NES-87–183, September 22, 1987, pp. 45–47.

26. Karen DeYoung, "Iran's Arms Procurers Ordered out of London," *Washington Post*, September 24, 1987, p. A27. See also "Europeans Slow the Flow of Arms to Iran," *Wall Street Journal*, September 22, 1987, p. 28.

27. Interviews produced mixed assessments of the level of Soviet and East European arms transfers to Iran over this period, with some suggesting that such transfers declined even though Moscow never signed the Second Resolution while others contended that they remained constant throughout.

8

The Role of U.S. Military Force in the Gulf War

Maxwell Orme Johnson

The late Ayatollah Khomeini announced on July 20, 1988, that he was taking personal responsibility for the cease-fire "in the interest of the Islamic Republic, [and that] making this decision was deadlier than swallowing poison."[1] With a cease-fire in the Iran-Iraq War, a fascinating and turbulent chapter in the history of the use of American military force closed. The de facto end of the Iran-Iraq War did not, however, signal the conclusion of American military involvement in the Gulf, just as the crossing of the Shatt al-Arab by Iraqi forces in September 1980 was not linked to the ongoing U.S. military commitment to this vital region.

It is clear that the fall of the Shah of Iran in February 1979 and the Soviet invasion of Afghanistan in late December of that year were watershed events in the use of U.S. military force in this volatile region. This chapter analyzes major implications of the Gulf War, particularly in terms of U.S. military policy as it evolved in the Gulf over the past decade. An assessment is also made of how the United States organized its forces for the difficult mission of protecting U.S.-flagged Kuwaiti oil tankers, a mission that many claimed was not clearly defined at the outset—at least in terms of goals and strategy—and that was burdened with political constraints and intense media criticism. The conduct of U.S. maritime escort policy is analyzed within the context of examining how active U.S. involvement during late 1987 and early 1988 impacted on Iran's decision to agree to a cease-fire. In this respect, the evolving rules of engagement covering the postreflagging operations are particularly pertinent. Further, the role played by Congress in either hindering or facilitating these operations, especially regarding struggles with the White House over varying interpretations of the War Powers Resolution and its application to deployment of U.S. naval forces in the Gulf conflict, merits close scrutiny. Finally, and of greatest importance to theorists and practitioners of the art of war, some lasting lessons learned from this experience are posited for critical reflection.

HISTORICAL BACKGROUND

The involvement of U.S. forces in the Gulf goes back much farther than the Iraqi invasion of Iran or even the Soviet invasion of Afghanistan. It is useful to review briefly the sequence of events during the 1970s that led to increased American political and military involvement in the region.[2] A series of seemingly disconnected but nevertheless interrelated events in the late 1970s fostered a fundamental revision in how the United States planned for military contingencies in Southwest Asia. In addition to the Shah's demise and genuine fears over Soviet intentions following their invasion of Afghanistan, a major escalation had occurred in the border dispute between North Yemen and South Yemen (the People's Democratic Republic of Yemen). This long-standing dispute, if extended into open war, could have exerted a direct impact on continued access through the vital chokepoint at the Bab al-Mandeb, just as the Soviet invasion of Afghanistan appeared to threaten free passage through the Strait of Hormuz.

The Gulf region had not escaped the notice of U.S. politico-military planners in the post–World War II period. However, with limited resources at its disposal, particularly after the ignominious withdrawal from Southeast Asia in 1975, the Pentagon placed primary emphasis on the defense of Europe through the collective security arrangements of the North Atlantic Treaty Organization. Other regional hot spots were dealt with on what appeared to many to be an ad hoc basis. Some commentators have even asserted that when military force was used as a token of earnest in the execution of American foreign policy, it was very often simply a case of the squeakiest wheel getting the most grease.

This was not the case with U.S. policy in the Gulf in the postwar period. Essential to understanding how the United States organized its military forces for the Gulf conflict, particularly for the conduct of the critical and controversial maritime escort operations from August 1987 to July 1988, is the realization that the United States pursued a coherent and consistent foreign policy, coupled with an appropriate military presence, in this vital region for over four decades.

One immutable fact undergirds U.S. policy in the Gulf. Throughout the past 40 years the U.S. military presence in and near the Gulf has directly reflected American strategic, economic, and political interests in the region. Moreover, the United States has maintained a permanent naval presence in the Gulf—the Middle East Force—throughout this period and has received varying degrees of support and encouragement from regional states. The U.S. military presence has been specifically fashioned to prevent regional domination by powers hostile to the United States or to its Western allies in the Gulf.

THE CARTER DOCTRINE, THE RDJTF, AND CENTCOM

One does not have to be either a George Kennan or a George Patton to divine that U.S. policy had the adversarial relationship with the Soviet Union as its principal consideration. The U.S. military presence was designed early on with the preeminent objective of impeding Soviet advances in the region. During 1971–79, through the "twin pillars" policy conceived and promulgated by President Nixon, the United States assisted the military development of our two closest friends in the Gulf, Iran and Saudi Arabia. However, by the mid–1970s the single pillar of Iran under Shah Reza Pahlavi had become the policeman of the Gulf. While the United States maintained a modest military presence in the region and remained capable of deploying an aircraft carrier battle group during crisis periods, security of the Gulf in the 1970s largely fell under the Shah's purview.

With the Shah's fall and the Soviet invasion of Afghanistan, the United States was forced to reevaluate its strategy and military operational presence in the region. On January 23, 1980, President Jimmy Carter declared: "Let our position be absolutely clear: An attempt by any outside force to gain control of the Persian Gulf region will be regarded as an assault on the vital interests of the United States of America, and such an assault will be repelled by any means necessary, including military force."[3] The so-called "Carter Doctrine" signalled anew continuing resolve by the United States to defend its vital interests in the Gulf with whatever military means were considered necessary. Key to this declaration, however, was the establishment of a specific military organization to execute this policy, the Rapid Deployment Joint Task Force (RDJTF), popularly albeit incorrectly known as the Rapid Deployment Force (RDF). The mission and organization of the RDJTF have been analyzed elsewhere.[4] It is important to note that this initial nucleus of a military planning headquarters—which evolved into a unified command, the United States Central Command (CENTCOM), on April 1,

1983—became the operational catalyst for facilitating substantially increased U.S. military presence in the Gulf during the height of the Iran-Iraq conflict from 1987 through 1988. CENTCOM was established to plan and coordinate U.S. military operations throughout Southwest Asia and to demonstrate America's commitment to stability in the region. CENTCOM's geographical area of responsibility stretches from Pakistan in the east to Egypt in the west and Kenya in the south and encompasses some 19 countries in all. This is an area nearly twice as large as the continental United States and is geographically complicated with nearly impossible lines of communication and some of the most inhospitable terrain in the world. As the immediate past commander of CENTCOM stated in 1988, the "overall mission [of CENTCOM] is to put military capability behind the national commitment."[5]

It was CENTCOM that responded on January 29, 1987, when President Reagan approved Secretary of Defense Weinberger's recommendation that the United States should reflag Kuwaiti oil tankers, and that appropriate military/naval protection should be provided to those vessels. In so doing, President Reagan made a major commitment of U.S. military force to the Iran-Iraq conflict. Whether this constituted a tilt toward Iraq is beyond the scope of this paper; what is relevant here is to examine the organization of CENTCOM's forces and analyze how it executed its difficult and dangerous mission.

The United States had maintained a modest naval presence in the Gulf since 1949 with its Middle East Force. The mission of this force, which did not change appreciably following the establishment of the RDJTF and its evolution into CENTCOM, was to act as the forward military presence in carrying out principal objectives of American policy in the region. The sine qua non of U.S. Gulf policy, regardless of the threat, has been to ensure the unimpeded flow of oil through the Strait of Hormuz. Petroleum from the Gulf remains critical to the American economy, as well as to those of Western Europe and Japan. Beyond oil, U.S. policy and its military presence have been designed to ensure freedom of navigation through the Gulf for U.S. vessels and those of its allies and to protect the security and stability of the moderate states of the region.[6]

THE GULF WAR

While the initial impetus for establishing the RDJTF was apprehension over Soviet expansionism into the region, it became increasingly apparent that the threat to American interests and to these objectives in the region was Iran. Until late 1986 the Iran-Iraq War had been contained; that is, it had been limited locally to a destructive, bloody, and wasteful conflict between the belligerents and, except for limited attacks on oil tankers in the Gulf, had exerted little impact on other states. However, the Iranian decision in the fall of 1986 to increase military pressure on Kuwait marked a decisive turning point in prompting active U.S. involvement in the conflict.[7]

The significant rise in Iran's bellicose rhetoric and in its attacks on Kuwaiti and Kuwait-bound shipping prompted Kuwait on January 13, 1987, to request that the United States reflag 11 Kuwaiti oil tankers, thereby putting them under U.S. protection. In September 1987 the Iranians deployed Chinese Silkworm missiles to launch sites near the Strait of Hormuz, sites from which Iran could place U.S. vessels under fire. It might be argued that Iran was merely responding to increased U.S. naval operations in the Gulf—operations that clearly were designed to protect the reflagged Kuwaiti tankers—for at nearly the same time, U.S. forces discovered a major increase in Iranian mining activities and even caught one Iranian vessel, *Iran Ajr*, laying mines in areas that Middle East Force convoys transited. However, such an argument misses the critical point that Iranian forces were threatening neutral shipping in international waters.

In early 1987 U.S. forces in the Gulf were still organized under the Middle East Force umbrella, although a carrier battle group was stationed in the northern Arabian Sea. The tragic, unanticipated Iraqi attack on the USS *Stark* on May 17, 1987, sharply refocused national attention on American interests in the region and led to a major restructuring of U.S. military forces in the Gulf. Whereas the commander of the Middle East Force's (COMIDEASTFOR) flagship and three to five combatant vessels (destroyers and frigates) had been the traditional presence, by September 1987 U.S. naval forces under COMIDEASTFOR had been quickly beefed up to a total of 18 combatant vessels. The mission of this task force was to perform escort duties for the 11 reflagged Kuwaiti oil tankers and to protect them against increasingly hostile Iranian forces. Though initially no U.S. patrol boats, minesweepers, attack helicopters, marines, special operations forces, or mobile sea bases had been included, by the close of 1987 all these units had been sent to the Gulf.

Yet it quickly became clear that the commander of the existing Middle East Force lacked the staff and communications resources necessary to command and control this expanded force. Accordingly, the commander of CENTCOM, with the approval of the Joint Chiefs of Staff, established the Joint Task Force Middle East (JTFME) by combining the Middle East Force with the existing carrier battle group staff and its sophisticated communications resources in the northern Arabian Sea. JTFME was augmented further with personnel drawn from all four services from the Atlantic and Pacific Fleet Headquarters.

Between September 1987 and early July 1988 the commander of JTFME conducted over 100 convoys and operated between 28 and 33 navy combatant vessels serving as escorts in or near the Gulf.[8] Despite Iranian attempts to disrupt the JTFME by mining in the Gulf along known convoy routes, from a military point of view the escort/convoy operations appeared to be a successful venture. However, at home there was less support for these operations, particularly in the Congress, where questions were raised about application of the provisions of the War Powers Resolution to these operations.

Even then Secretary of the Navy James H. Webb, Jr., apparently misunderstanding that service secretaries by tradition were not supposed to "meddle" in operational matters, told Secretary Weinberger in a strongly worded letter in early August 1987 that he did not feel comfortable with his understanding of the policy goals and decisions that had been evolving regarding the escort operations in the Gulf.[9] According to some sources, he somewhat naively complained to Secretary Weinberger that he had been left out of the most sensitive policy deliberations and was very concerned that operational aspects of U.S. involvement in the Gulf were taking on a momentum of their own. Reportedly, he further called on the secretary of defense to lay out very clear long-term principles concerning the use of U.S. forces in the Gulf.

Secretary Weinberger was not amused by Webb's concerns and reportedly was even more upset when portions of Webb's memo were leaked to the *Washington Post*.[10] Ultimately, this fundamental divergence in personal perspective prompted Secretary Webb's resignation.

CONGRESS AND THE WAR POWERS RESOLUTION

The dispute between the executive branch and Congress over the administration's escort policy and the concomitant U.S. military buildup in the Gulf was equally revealing. During heated hearings in the Senate Armed Services Committee on June 5, 11, and 16, 1987, several prominent senators took serious issue with the escort policy. For example, Senator Ted Kennedy stated that "once again, the Administration has leaped before it looked on a sensitive issue in the Middle East, with reckless disregard of the consequences of our military policy and for our foreign policy in the region."[11] Senator John Glenn opined that "the flagging proposal . . . if it is necessary, was a very poor policy to go off on, without considering all the ramifications of what may happen under that flagging policy."[12] Senator Carl Levin correctly, and with an uncanny sense of prescience, stated his certainty that "whether we escort those Kuwaiti ships and coordinate the figleaf of their reflagging, Iran will almost surely treat our ships as Kuwaiti ships and attack them."[13] Later, Senator John Warner, hardly a dove, admitted that he was "having some difficulty determining our policy . . . if we are making a major departure from the basic reasons we have put our people at risk before.

. . . [A]re we doing that in the cause of freedom as we have done traditionally in this country? . . . Or, is it primarily an economic motivation,
and that motivation primarily being oil?"[14]

In addressing these serious concerns, Under Secretary of State Michael
Armacost testified that "our protection of a number of Kuwaiti reflagged
tankers is a limited expansion of our role of protecting U.S. vessels. Our
intent is to deter, not to provoke."[15] During the same hearing Assistant
Secretary of Defense Richard L. Armitage noted that representatives
from the Departments of Defense and State had consulted regularly with
key congressional leaders and their staffs during March and April about
the expanding U.S. military role, and he argued that there never had
been any intention in the executive branch to avoid consulting with
Congress, as required by the War Powers Resolution.[16] The position of
the Reagan administration was consistent throughout these hearings:
Protection of these 11 Kuwaiti ships under the U.S. flag was not part of
an open-ended unilateral commitment to defend all nonbelligerent shipping in the Gulf; rather, the policy was a limited but effective signal of
American determination to stand up to intimidation, to support our
friends, and to help contain, and eventually end, the Iran-Iraq War.[17]

The War Powers Resolution states that "the President in every possible instance shall consult with Congress before introducing United
States Armed Forces into hostilities or into situations where imminent
involvement in hostilities is clearly indicated by the circumstances, and
after every such introduction shall consult regularly with the Congress
until United States Armed Forces are no longer engaged in hostilities
or have been removed from such situations."[18] To answer congressional complaints and criticism that the administration was ignoring
the War Powers Resolution, the standard policy response contended
that the War Powers Resolution was not applicable to the Gulf situation, simply because imminent involvement of U.S. forces in hostilities
was not clearly indicated. In any case, although the administration
claimed that the War Powers Resolution did not apply to U.S. forces
in the Gulf, it kept congressional committees informed through briefing papers and by several informal briefings, beginning on March 12,
1987, with the House Foreign Affairs Committee and the Senate Foreign Relations Committee. As one who personally participated in for-
mulating those briefing papers and in meetings with congressional
staff members, I can say that it became clear from the outset that the
deployment of American military forces in the Gulf was peripheral to
the critical debate. The gut issue concerned a general power struggle
between the executive and legislative branches over who would exercise ultimate authority for employing American military force in support of U.S. foreign policy.

Perhaps most interesting about this power struggle is that it proved the old adage that success has many fathers, but failure is a foundling. The proximate cause for the debate in Congress was not a philosophical assessment of the pros and cons of the escort policy but rather the egregious Iraqi attack on the USS *Stark*. At that time, rallying against U.S. Gulf strategy was popular among the liberal fringe in Congress. The administration, however, stayed the course. In so doing, it emboldened and stiffened the spines of certain regional Arab leaders, without whose support the U.S. Navy and CENTCOM could not have accomplished the mission. When gradually it became clear that the maritime protection policy was working—particularly when American forces in the Gulf came under fire from Iranian gunboats in the fall of 1987— congressional heat lessened considerably.

What turned the tide of public opinion at home, especially in the Congress, and in the Gulf regarding the actual conduct of maritime escort operations? Unknown to the American public, the administration had sent very specific warnings to Tehran that if its forces persisted in hostile activities in the Gulf, namely, mining and missile attacks on tankers, U.S. forces would have no recourse but to take Iranian forces under fire. In other words, a subtle shift occurred from a strictly defensive protection policy to one that permitted on-scene U.S. commanders in the Gulf much more latitude in responding to the Iranian military threat. This development did not come overnight, nor did it constitute a fundamental change to the rules of engagement that governed the JTFME.

To understand how this happened, one must have some sense of how rules of engagement are formulated. All American forces operate in peacetime under a common or generic set of rules of engagement devised in concert by the unified commanders and approved by the Joint Chiefs of Staff (JCS). These rules cover those situations in peacetime operations when U.S. troops may employ force, for example, in self-defense and immediate defensive retaliation. In a given theater of operations, that is, a specific geographic location where there is a greater danger of a hostile act by the enemy, the rules of engagement are somewhat more specific and are usually classified so that the enemy will not know what to expect if he commits a hostile act. With tighter rules of engagement, the on-scene commanders are free to take immediate action without asking permission of the highest commanders, up to and including the White House. Furthermore, congressmen and their staffers love to second-guess the theater commanders; with loose rules of engagement, there is always friction over who is in command.

By late 1988 any naysayers in Congress were clearly in the minority. Iranian mining activities had become so blatant that American units in the Gulf were virtually forced to respond to these Iranian hostile activities, particularly in view of the stricter rules of engagement. The denouement to this "paper-scissors-rock game" began on April 14, 1988, when the American frigate USS *Roberts* struck an Iranian mine off the coast of Qatar. In a measured response on April 18, JTFME units attacked two Iranian oil platforms in the Gulf that had been serving as command and control bases for Iranian missile-boat attacks. Iranian forces countered with a missile attack against U.S. aircraft flying cover and against the guided missile cruiser USS *Wainwright*. Finally the die had been cast, and President Reagan authorized a major retaliation.

For reasons still unknown, most of the Iranian navy left their ports of Bushehr and Bandar Abbas on the morning of April 18, steamed toward JTFME forces in the vicinity of Dubai, and clearly "displayed" hostile intent when they fired missiles at American vessels. By the end of the day JTFME forces had sunk five Iranian fast patrol boats and one frigate and had severely damaged another frigate. Thus a near-fatal blow had been dealt to Iranian naval capability.[19]

The atmosphere in the Pentagon briefings to the Senate late in the afternoon of April 18 was one of jubilation and congratulation. When the administration informed Congress four days later that it would begin protecting neutral foreign ships requesting U.S. assistance, the final chapter was opened for American policy during the Gulf War. More important, any possible congressional confrontation over the War Powers Resolution quickly evaporated in the victorious euphoria that was pervasive in Washington.

The decisive act in this bushido-like tragedy occurred on July 3, 1988, when the guided-missile cruiser USS *Vincennes* mistakenly shot down an Iranian Airbus commercial jetliner flying between Bandar Abbas and Dubai. When the world community failed to condemn this tragic mistake as aggression, Ayatollah Khomeini reportedly began to see that his military situation was bleak at best. Matters deteriorated when Iraqi forces apparently employed chemical weapons later that week against Iranian forces along the front. The international reaction to Iraq's use of chemical warfare was similarly surprisingly mild to nonexistent. Vituperative Iranian rhetoric finally had backfired on the Khomeini regime. The late ayatollah was forced to drink his "cup of poison" after nearly eight years of fighting. While the diplomatic maneuvering over terms of the ceasefire, withdrawal of forces, and exchange of prisoners and the sick and wounded would remain subject to protracted Iranian intransigence, the war's end was clearly a victory for American foreign policy and for JTFME forces in the Gulf that had executed that policy.

CONCLUSION

Several objectives of projecting American military force in the Gulf were outlined at the beginning of this chapter. It should now be clear that U.S. involvement in the Gulf during the Iran-Iraq War, particularly during the so-called "tanker war" following the reflagging of Kuwaiti tankers, was part of a long-standing continuum of American foreign policy. Projection of American military force, first under the umbrella of the RDJTF and later under CENTCOM's Joint Task Force Middle East, was not precipitated by the Iran-Iraq War per se; the catalysts for establishing a specific unified U.S. command responsible for the Gulf region came in 1979 with the fall of the Shah of Iran and the Soviet Union's invasion of Afghanistan. Nonetheless, if CENTCOM had not been available, and if the United States had not had standing contingency plans to deal with the full spectrum of regional hostilities, it would have been very difficult indeed to have achieved the military success that American foreign policy in the Gulf ultimately attained.

What military lessons were learned in the Gulf that might apply to future similar conflicts of this nature, either in the Gulf or elsewhere? Critics of CENTCOM in the early 1980s contended that with a theater of operations some 8,000 to 10,000 miles distant from its headquarters at MacDill Air Force Base, Florida, and with severe constraints on sealift and airlift assets, CENTCOM would be unable to get to the war on time with sufficient forces to confront the enemy, then presumed to be the Soviet Union. Military planners in the Pentagon and at CENTCOM took on this challenge and employed creative methods of mobility to plan for a major military contingency in the region; by 1984–85 they had begun to consider several smaller conflict scenarios. Critical to all of these contingency plans, however, were sound imperatives: reliable communications for real-time command, control, communications, and intelligence in a combat situation. Virtually from its founding, successive commanders of CENTCOM had adopted this necessity as their number one priority for funding requests. They correctly argued that considerations of mobility, firepower, command relationships, and force structure were practically peripheral issues; if command and control could not be exercised over one's forces, then those forces could not and should not be committed to combat situations.

Regarding rules of engagement, with the tragic loss of the Iranian Airbus, internal debate still exists in the Pentagon over how strict those rules of engagement should be. On the other hand, in a continually hostile environment, and given the equally tragic incident of the USS *Stark*, the argument must be made that decision makers in Washington should not tie the hands of the on-scene commanders. The enemy must know that U.S. forces will no longer err on the side of discretion. This is a minimum prerequisite to ensuring that U.S. forces have at least a fair chance when confronting potential adversaries in a combat situation.

Finally, a thought on the role of Congress. When viewed from the perspective of the national mood and congressional atmospherics following our silver-medalist performance in Southeast Asia and the failure of our presence mission in Lebanon, one can understand the initial reluctance of Congress to become involved in the Gulf conflict; the situation was viewed by many as just another "big muddy" in which America might become mired. What remains clear, however, is that the War Powers Resolution is flawed and should be redrafted, amended, or abolished. The president is the duly elected commander in chief; Congress has the power to raise armies and approve treaties. The latter powers invest Congress with sufficient authority for its participation in shaping American foreign and defense policy. To further hamstring the president's ability to commit U.S. forces abroad in defense of vital national interests runs contrary to the Constitution and to practical military considerations for the United States throughout the world. The unmistakable success of the U.S. military effort in the Gulf War during 1987–88 clearly suggests this conclusion.

NOTES

1. *Washington Post*, July 21, 1988, p. A1.

2. See, for example, Anthony Cordesman, *The Gulf and the Search for Strategic Stability: Saudi Arabia, the Military Balance in the Gulf, and Trends in the Arab-Israeli Military Balance* (Boulder, Colo.: Westview Press, 1984); Bruce R. Kuniholm, *The Persian Gulf and United States Policy: A Guide to Issues and References* (Claremont, Calif.: Regina Books, 1984); Thomas McNaugher, *Arms and Oil: U.S. Military Strategy and the Persian Gulf* (Washington, D.C.: Brookings Institution, 1985); James H. Noyes, *The Clouded Lens: Persian Gulf Security and U.S. Policy*, 2d ed. (Stanford: Hoover Institution Press, 1982); and J. E. Peterson, *Defending Arabia* (London: Croom Helm, 1986).

3. President Jimmy Carter, "State of the Union Address," January 23, 1980.

4. Maxwell Orme Johnson, *The Military as an Instrument of U.S. Policy in Southwest Asia: The Rapid Deployment Joint Task Force, 1979–1982* (Boulder, Colo.: Westview Press, 1983).

5. General George B. Crist, speech to the World Affairs Council in Boston, Massachusetts, February 23, 1988.

6. Under Secretary of State for Policy Michael H. Armacost, in *U.S. Military Forces to Protect "Re-Flagged" Kuwaiti Oil Tankers*, Hearings before the Committee on Armed Services, United States Senate, 100th Cong., 1st Sess, June 5, 11, 16, 1987, p. 27 (Hereafter cited as *Kuwaiti Tanker Hearings*).

7. Assistant Secretary of Defense Richard L. Armitage, news briefing at the Pentagon, February 16, 1988.

8. Combatant vessels include those ships whose primary mission is to sail in harm's way and take the enemy under fire when required. Thus the term refers to aircraft carriers, battleships, cruisers, destroyers, and frigates, as well as amphibious ships and submarines, but does not include support ships. The convoys were conducted by a combination of anywhere from four to seven combatants as a general rule, much in the same manner as convoys in World War II operated.

9. Jim McGee, "Naval Secretary Questioned U.S. Persian Gulf Policies," *Washington Post*, September 6, 1987, p. A30.

10. Ibid.

11. Remarks of Senator Ted Kennedy, in *Kuwaiti Tanker Hearings*, p. 8.

12. Remarks of Senator John Glenn, in *Kuwaiti Tanker Hearings*, p. 13.

13. Remarks of Senator Carl Levin, in *Kuwaiti Tanker Hearings*, p. 7.

14. Remarks of Senator John Warner, in *Kuwaiti Tanker Hearings*, p. 23.

15. Testimony of Secretary Armacost, in *Kuwaiti Tanker Hearings*, p. 31.

16. Testimony of Assistant Secretary of Defense for International Security Affairs Richard L. Armitage, in *Kuwaiti Tanker Hearings*, p. 32.

17. Secretary of Defense Caspar Weinberger, *A Report to Congress on Security Arrangements in the Persian Gulf*, June 15, 1987.

18. War Powers Resolution, Public Law 93–148, 87 Stat. 555 (H. J. Res. 542).

19. *Washington Post*, April 19, 1988, p. A1.

9

Moscow and the Gulf War

Mark N. Katz

The Soviet role in the Gulf has certainly increased as a result of the Iran-Iraq War. Nevertheless, Soviet influence in the Gulf did not appreciate significantly during this period.

When the war broke out in September 1980, the Soviets had very close relations with Iraq, which in turn had very poor relations with the United States. The Soviets had sent substantial quantities of arms and advisers to Iraq and also had a treaty of friendship and cooperation with Baghdad. Yet, though Soviet-Iraqi relations were very close, Moscow did not enjoy predominant influence over Iraq, as evidenced by the Baath Party's crackdown on the Iraqi Communist Party, Iraqi criticism of Soviet military involvement in the Horn of Africa and Afghanistan, and Iraqi initiation of the war with Iran—something the Soviets did not want to see happen at all. However, Iraq remained the one country in which the Soviets retained significant influence. Although revolutionary Iran had recently thrown off American influence—a move the Soviets welcomed—Moscow's relations with Iran were also troubled. The Ayatollah Khomeini regularly denounced both superpowers as "Satans." Finally, the Soviets had virtually no influence with the conservative Arab states of the Gulf Cooperation Council (GCC). These states looked primarily to the United States and the West for their defense. Except for Kuwait, no GCC state even had diplomatic relations with Moscow. Soviet influence in the region at the beginning of the war, then, was relatively limited.

By the time fighting ended in August 1988, the Soviet Union still provided Iraq with most of its external military assistance. Indeed, Baghdad became extremely dependent on the Soviet Union for this aid once Iranian forces had crossed into Iraq. This dependence, however, failed to prevent Iraq from dramatically improving relations with the United States and the West over the course of the war. While Western states may not have gained strong influence in Baghdad—indeed, the relationship remains an uneasy one—improved Iraqi-Western ties have served to reduce the previous exclusivity of Soviet-Iraqi relations. During the war the Soviets strove to improve relations with Iran. While some improvement did occur, Moscow failed to transform Tehran's hostility toward the United States into an alliance or even friendship with the USSR.

Moscow's one consolation was that U.S. efforts to improve relations with Iran were even less successful than Soviet attempts. The Soviet Union did improve its ties to the GCC states during the war. Moscow opened diplomatic relations with Oman, the United Arab Emirates (UAE) and Qatar during this period. Soviet contacts with Saudi Arabia and Bahrain also increased. Finally, Kuwait's request that the USSR protect part of its oil shipping led to a significant increase in Moscow's naval presence in the Gulf. Nevertheless, improved Soviet relations with the Gulf states did not lead the GCC to reduce its reliance on U.S. and Western protection. Indeed, this reliance increased during the course of the conflict.

The Soviets, then, did not markedly enhance their influence in the Gulf during the Iran-Iraq War. On the other hand, their clout in the region suffered no great decline either. The Soviets did not lose an important ally as a result of this conflict, as they had earlier in the Middle East (Egypt) and the Horn of Africa (Somalia). But they had sought to achieve more than just retaining their existing influence in Iraq. They had hoped to expand their importance in the region generally and to bring about the reduction of U.S. influence there. This chapter examines how the Soviets specifically pursued these goals during the Iran-Iraq War and sets out the reasons for the resultant degrees of success and failure that they met. The chapter concludes by exploring prospects for future Soviet influence in the Gulf now that hostilities have ended.

SOVIET POLICY OBJECTIVES

Throughout the Gulf War Soviet foreign policy pursued contradictory goals. Even before the conflict began, Soviet foreign policy sought inconsistent objectives in the Gulf region, such as attempting to improve relations with established conservative governments while concurrently promoting revolution against them or their neighbors. Although Moscow did gain influence with the revolutionary regimes that came to power in Iraq, North Yemen, and South Yemen, leftist revolution failed to spread elsewhere. At the same time, monarchies in the Gulf grew apprehensive of Soviet diplomatic initiatives because of these efforts to promote revolution.

By 1979 a major Soviet foreign policy goal in the area was to preserve Moscow's alliance with Iraq. In doing this, the Soviets did not feel constrained from supporting Iraq's neighbor and antagonist, Syria, which was ruled by a rival wing of the Baath Party. When the Ayatollah Khomeini came to power in 1979, the Soviets seemed hopeful that Islamic revolution could be transformed along increasingly Marxist and pro-Soviet lines. The Soviets especially anticipated that closer cooperation or even an alliance with Iran could be cultivated on the basis of common anti-American foreign policies. This aspiration, however, became seriously compromised when Moscow's ally, Iraq, launched its attack on Iran in September 1980.[1]

At this point the Soviets sought to achieve several policy objectives. Above all, they wanted to prevent the return of U.S. influence to Iran. Similarly, they sought to salvage efforts to improve relations with Iran. Almost immediately after the war began, Moscow cut off its direct supply of arms to Iraq and apparently began facilitating arms transfers to Iran. By providing overland transit facilities, the Soviets thwarted U.S. attempts to impose an economic blockade against Iran.[2] It is important to realize that the Soviets viewed Iran as being strategically far more important than Iraq because Iran borders on the USSR, has a long coastline on the Persian Gulf and Indian Ocean, and possesses a relatively large population.

Yet Moscow also wanted to retain Baghdad as an ally. The Soviet arms cutoff to Iraq and aid to Iran, of course, greatly rankled Baghdad. The Soviets sought to mollify Saddam Hussein by allowing indirect shipments of Soviet arms to reach Baghdad through third parties.[3] As the Kremlin leadership undoubtedly calculated, Iraq was not in a position to expel the Soviets in the same manner that Egypt and Somalia had done. Iraq could not turn to the West for significant military aid. Its relations with the West were poor to begin with, and virtually no Western nation supported Iraq's offensive actions against Iran. Iraq, then, could not afford to dispense with its Soviet connection. The GCC states, in contrast, were extremely nervous about Soviet support to Iran, as well as the scenario of a victorious Iraq turning its attention toward them. During the war's initial two years most of the GCC states continued to dread Soviet actions in the region, despite the fact that Moscow had ceased efforts to promote revolution against them.

SOVIET WARTIME STRATEGIES

Notwithstanding Soviet efforts to aid Iran—efforts that were not popular among most Arab states—Moscow was not able to gain much influence in Tehran. It was during these early years of the war, when Iran was on the defensive and arguably was most in need of Soviet help, that Khomeini brutally suppressed the Tudeh (Iranian Communist) Party, gave military assistance to Afghan mujahedin groups, and generally continued to denounce the USSR as the other great Satan.[4]

During 1982 Khomeini's forces pushed the Iraqis out of Iran back into their own territory. The prospect of an Iranian victory over Iraq suddenly arose. This outcome would have posed serious problems not only for the West and moderate Arab states, but also for the Soviets. Replacement of the Baath regime by a pro-Iranian government in Baghdad would have spelled the loss of a long-standing, albeit difficult, Soviet friend. Nor could the Soviet leadership expect to acquire influence over a victorious Iran, given that they had been unable to do so even when Iran was on the defensive. The Soviets consequently resumed direct military assistance to Iraq in 1982—a move that they thought would also improve their ties to the GCC states. But the Soviets also sought to ensure that resumption of direct arms transfers to Iraq would not prompt Iran to turn back to the United States. As a result, Soviet arms shipments continued to reach Iran indirectly via North Korea, Vietnam, Syria, Libya, and even some East European countries.[5]

From mid–1982 through early 1985 the Soviet Union definitely tilted toward Iraq. This policy shift did little to enhance Soviet influence in Iraq. The GCC states also remained cool to Soviet offers of friendship. Even the Iraqis, who were now more dependent on Moscow than ever before, dramatically improved relations with the United States and the West during this period. Soviet efforts to please all parties in the Gulf to some extent proved less than notably successful.[6] This situation, however, changed after Mikhail Gorbachev came to power. From 1985 through 1987 Gorbachev managed the very difficult balancing act of retaining Soviet influence in Iraq while also improving Soviet relations with both the GCC states and Iran.

Moscow's minimal relations with the GCC states began to expand soon after Gorbachev assumed control. In late 1985 Oman and the UAE agreed to establish diplomatic ties with the USSR. Qatar did likewise in August 1988. The most important Soviet breakthrough, however, occurred with Kuwait. In 1986 Kuwaiti officials asked the United States to protect their oil tankers from increasing Iranian attacks launched in retaliation for Kuwait's support to Iraq. The Reagan administration initially refused, apparently because it did not want to damage its secret venture to establish better ties with Tehran. Kuwait proffered the same request to Moscow, which agreed to it in early 1987. The U.S. government immediately reversed itself and offered to protect all Kuwaiti tankers, clearly a reaction to exclude the Soviet Union from any military role in the Gulf.

In the wake of the Iran-Contra revelations concerning U.S. transfers of arms to Iran, Washington was anxious to restore its credibility as the principal protector of the GCC states against Iran. The Kuwaiti government, however, decided that it would receive a stronger U.S. commitment if the Reagan administration had to compete for Kuwait's affections with the Soviet Union. Thus Kuwait chartered 3 Soviet oil tankers and transferred 11 of its own vessels to American registry.[7]

For the Soviet Union, the Kuwaiti invitation marked an important milestone in Moscow's efforts to improve relations with the conservative GCC states. Although the Kuwaitis had purchased Soviet weapons since the mid-1970s, they had remained wary of moving too close to the USSR. Kuwait had only agreed to permit Soviet military advisers into the country for the first time in early 1985, after Washington had very publicly denied a Kuwaiti request to purchase Stinger shoulder-fired antiaircraft weapons, and even then, only ten Soviet advisers were admitted.[8]

By agreeing to protect Kuwait's oil exports, the Soviet Union secured for the first time ever an active role in defending the GCC states—a role that previously had been played exclusively by the United States and Great Britain. The Soviets may have calculated that if it undertook this protector role for the Kuwaitis, other GCC states, especially Saudi Arabia, might also come to regard the USSR as a potential ally. In addition, Moscow may well have hoped that this increased involvement with Kuwait would promote expanded Soviet arms sales to Kuwait and the initiation of arms transfers to other GCC states.

The Soviets, however, kept their arrangement with Kuwait in perspective. Moscow opted not to compete with Washington as the superpower with the most naval vessels protecting the most tankers in the Gulf. The Kremlin realized that a rapid Soviet naval buildup in the Gulf would not only prompt a much greater U.S. naval presence but would also provoke renewed apprehensions by the GCC about the USSR—developments that would clearly be contrary to Soviet interests. Even more important, Moscow was reluctant to improve relations with the GCC at the expense of its long-standing ambition of bettering ties with Iran. Tehran was clearly angry that the Soviets had agreed to protect Kuwaiti shipping. In May 1987 a speedboat reportedly operated by the Revolutionary Guards attacked a Soviet freighter. The Soviets, however, chose not to retaliate publicly and instead played down the incident.

Soviet media mentioned the attack but insisted that no one had been injured and little damage had occurred.[9] Nor did Moscow raise a public fuss when another Soviet vessel struck a mine a few days later.[10]

Soviet minimization of the risks of conflict with Iran, as well as restraint in not retaliating militarily for these two incidents, stood in stark contrast to U.S. behavior toward Iran. When one of the reflagged Kuwaiti tankers struck a mine in July 1987, the U.S. government moved greater naval force into the region. Provocative Iranian actions were met with increased U.S. force levels, and open suggestions were made by U.S. officials regarding what military means might be used for retaliation against Iran in different situations.

As the war of nerves between Washington and Tehran escalated during the summer of 1987, the Soviet navy continued to maintain a low profile in the Gulf. Then, suddenly, in early August 1987 Moscow and Tehran announced a major economic cooperation accord. The Soviets agreed to build a pipeline to carry Iranian oil to the Black Sea. A second connection between the Soviet and Iranian railway system was also planned.[11]

During the summer of 1987 the United States launched a major campaign to isolate Iran internationally as punishment for continuing the war. The Reagan administration succeeded in getting a U.N. Security Council resolution adopted (with Soviet approval) that called on both sides in the conflict to accept a cease-fire. As anticipated, Iraq accepted the resolution, but Iran did not. The United States then proposed a Security Council resolution calling for an arms embargo against Iran until it accepted a cease-fire. The Soviet Union, however, refused to vote in favor of an arms embargo. Iran's acceptance of the cease-fire in August 1988 made the issue a moot point.[12]

By thwarting U.S. efforts to impose an embargo against Iran, Moscow sought to mollify Tehran's displeasure over Soviet protection of Kuwaiti oil shipping and aid to Iraq. The Soviets also sought to persuade Iran that while the United States was its enemy, the USSR was actually its friend. The Soviets, moreover, tried to convince all states in the region that U.S. actions against Iran only exacerbated prospects for increased conflict, but that the USSR—not the United States—could help bring peace to the Gulf. Moscow contended that peace between Iran and Iraq was necessary so that the Muslim world could again focus its undivided attention on Israel, the common enemy. The Soviets claimed, in sum, that continuation of the Iran-Iraq War served American and Israeli interests by distracting Muslims from the Arab-Israeli conflict.[13]

In 1987 the Soviets appeared to succeed in improving relations with all states in the Gulf simultaneously, even though Iranians and Arabs remained bitterly opposed to each other. Both Iranians and Arabs were unhappy and clearly apprehensive about Soviet assistance to the other party. Nonetheless, a certain logic persisted as to why each would want good relations with the Soviet Union in any event. As mentioned before, Iraq had no choice: It could not afford to abandon Soviet assistance, even though Moscow was also aiding Tehran. This became especially evident when the Iraqis were fighting desperate defensive actions on their own territory in 1987.

Iran by 1987 had become less sanguine about its being internationally isolated and without friends as it had been during the early 1980s. Tehran recognized that it needed diplomatic allies and political support. Its hostile relations with both the United States and Iraq made improved relations with the USSR all the more important. Finally, Khomeini appeared to realize that his efforts to bring about the downfall of Saddam Hussein also necessitated improved Soviet-Iranian relations. Since it was mainly with Soviet weapons that Iraq was thwarting Khomeini's aims, Iran had to provide Moscow with some incentive to at least moderate its arms aid to Baghdad.

Even the GCC states had a strong incentive to improve relations with the USSR in 1987. They were particularly concerned about what an Iranian victory could mean for them. They were much less capable of defending themselves than Iraq was. Although receiving U.S. military assistance, the GCC states hoped that the USSR might somehow restrain Iran. The Gulf monarchies sought this because they were not completely confident about the American commitment to their defense. They also understood that improved Soviet-GCC relations, especially the tanker lease agreement, served to increase U.S. willingness to help the GCC states, as Washington was concerned about losing influence to the Soviets otherwise. Finally, the GCC sought to improve relations with Moscow in order to give the Soviets an incentive to moderate their aid to Iran.

Each party in the Gulf, then, felt the necessity to rely upon the USSR to a greater or lesser extent. Nevertheless, each party continued to distrust the Soviets because Moscow persisted in aiding its enemy. All the Gulf states consequently sought to avoid complete dependence on the USSR. The Soviets hoped that Tehran would be grateful to Moscow for not approving the American-sponsored arms embargo resolution. But the Iranians could not forget that it was with Soviet arms that Iraq attacked them, and that the USSR remained Iraq's primary arms supplier. Similarly, the Soviets hoped that Iraq would be appreciative for its arms supplies. But the Iraqis could not overlook the fact that the Soviets had cut back their arms supplies to Baghdad from 1980 to 1982 and had tried to improve relations with Tehran since at least 1985. Finally, the Soviets reckoned that the GCC would be grateful that Moscow no longer was supporting revolutionaries or issuing hostile propaganda against them, for protecting Kuwaiti shipping, and for being in a better

position than the United States to negotiate an end to the conflict between Iran and Iraq. But the GCC governments still harbored memories
of Moscow's former hostility to them. They appreciated the small Soviet
naval presence in the Gulf but remained wary about Moscow's efforts
to bring about an end to the American naval presence there. The GCC
states (as well as Iraq) were also extremely unhappy over Soviet refusal
to approve the American-sponsored arms embargo against Iran.[14] In the
end, Iran agreed to a cease-fire despite Soviet refusal to approve the
arms embargo, though the prospect of continued Soviet military aid to
Iraq undoubtedly played a role in Khomeini's decision.

SOVIET GULF POLICY: AN EVALUATION

The Soviets attempted to achieve several goals in the Gulf: to preserve
their influence in Iraq, to gain influence with the GCC and Iran, and to
reduce American influence in the region. Clearly, some of these goals
were contradictory. Yet the United States was also pursuing disparate
goals in the region, some of which also were contradictory: to preserve
American influence in the GCC, to increase American influence with
Iran and Iraq, and to minimize Soviet influence in the region. The distinction between U.S. and Soviet policies, however, was that the Americans subordinated some goals to others while the Soviets seemed to
pursue all theirs with equal priority. For Washington, the most important
policy objectives were to preserve U.S. influence with the GCC states
and to minimize Soviet influence. Subordinate to these was the effort
to increase American influence with Iraq. Subordinate to all was increasing American influence with Iran. The Iran-Contra revelations terminated the U.S. effort to increase its sway with Iran's leadership not only
because that policy was unpopular with the American public, but also
because its prosecution threatened the preservation of American influence in the GCC. Indeed, it can be argued that the United States attempted to improve relations with Iran in part to bring the war to a
close, thus reducing the threat to our GCC allies. At no time during the
conflict was the United States willing to support either Iraq or Iran to
such an extent that the GCC might feel endangered.

The Soviets, in contrast, were confident from the outset that Iraq
would not be lost as an ally though it disapproved of Moscow's policies.
This presumption gave the Soviets the maneuvering room to improve
relations with Iran, as well as with the GCC. The primary Soviet priority
was that neither Iran nor Iraq should be defeated. The Soviets actually
declared this policy openly, as they called on both sides repeatedly to
end the war. The Soviets attempted to bolster their influence throughout
the region by portraying themselves as a more credible peacemaker than
the United States. The GCC governments, while willing to listen to this

argument, eventually came to realize that the USSR was reluctant to pressure Iran into accepting a cease-fire. Moscow was more intent on improving relations with Iran than on fostering a negotiated peace or protecting GCC interests. Indeed, the GCC, Iraqi, and Iranian governments may well have concluded that the Soviets really did not wish an end to the war because its continuation served to enhance Soviet influence throughout the region. Thus, while the Soviet Union attained some success in projecting its influence with all the Gulf parties, none of them in 1988 regarded Moscow as a reliable ally.

CONCLUSION

What are the prospects for Soviet foreign policy in the Gulf now that the fighting has stopped? The war bolstered Soviet standing in the region. Will its termination lead to declining Soviet influence? Not necessarily. Although the hostilities have ended, tensions between Iran and Iraq remain high. Iraqis fear that Iran will use the cease-fire as a time to build up their military forces again. As in the past, Baghdad cannot afford to alienate the USSR or end its dependence on Soviet arms supplies.

Similarly, Iran must improve relations with the USSR to give the Kremlin an incentive for moderating its support to Iraq. Tehran also desires to better political ties with Moscow while its relations with the United States remain strained. Neither Iran nor Iraq, however, are likely to rely upon the Soviets to the same extent that they did during the war. During the conflict the highest priority for both belligerents was to obtain means for prosecuting the war—a goal that both came to regard the USSR as being essential for achieving. With hostilities over, the need for securing arms has become less immediate. As a consequence, Iran and Iraq are turning attention to rebuilding their war-ravaged economies. For this effort, both states, but particularly Iran, will require massive economic assistance and restoration of commercial contacts with the outside world. The level of economic aid and trade available from the Soviet Union is relatively limited, especially since Gorbachev has cut back on foreign economic assistance in order to preserve resources for his ambitious domestic programs. Iran and Iraq must both look primarily to the wealthy Gulf states, Western Europe, and Japan for economic assistance and trade. The longer the cease-fire holds, the more likely Iraq and Iran are to put increasing emphasis on economic reconstruction at the expense of defense programs.

Both Iraq and Iran are likely to continue to seek better relations with the Soviet Union. Even so, their need for foreign economic assistance and increased trade will nudge them to expand relations with the West far into the future. Both states would undoubtedly like to obtain Soviet aid and trade if available, but it simply is not—at least not nearly to the extent that it is from the West and the GCC.

The GCC states have even less dependence on the Soviets than Iran or Iraq. With the war over, there is less need for the Soviets to restrain or moderate Iranian behavior. Nor are the GCC states dependent on the Soviets for arms supplies; they can obtain weapons easily from the West, though not always from the United States. Still, the GCC states are not necessarily anxious to expel the Soviets from the Gulf. They are less intimidated by the Soviets than in the past. The Soviet Union's withdrawal from Afghanistan and Eastern Europe makes Moscow appear much less threatening. The GCC states do, however, view relations with Moscow as useful for keeping Washington concerned about losing influence in the region.

The Soviets used the Iran-Iraq War to enhance their influence in the Gulf. Nevertheless, the gains that were made were not particularly significant. The Soviets did not succeed in reducing U.S. influence in the region. Nor did they gain significant political sway with either the GCC or Iran. While Soviet relations with Iraq remain strong, their position has become somewhat eroded owing to Baghdad's continued pursuit of improved relations with the West. In sum, the Gulf War permitted the Soviets an opportunity to expand influence and project power into the region. Now that the Iran-Iraq War has ended, the Soviet Union confronts fewer opportunities as well as greater obstacles for extending political and military influence in the Gulf.

NOTES

1. For a useful account of Soviet relations with Iran, Iraq, and the Arabian Peninsula countries during the 1970s and early 1980s, see Aryeh Y. Yodfat, *The Soviet Union and the Arabian Peninsula* (New York: St. Martin's Press, 1983).

2. Ibid., chap. 4.

3. William B. Quandt, *Saudi Arabia in the 1980s: Foreign Policy, Security, and Oil* (Washington, D.C.: Brookings Institution, 1981), p. 21.

4. Yodfat, *Soviet Union and the Arabian Peninsula*, pp. 123–31.

5. David K. Shipler, "Level of World Arms Sales to Iran Regarded as Largely Unchanged," *New York Times*, April 11, 1987, p. 2.

6. Joseph G. Whelan and Michael J. Dixon, *The Soviet Union in the Third World: Threat to World Peace?* (Washington, D.C.: Pergamon-Brassey's, 1986), pp. 145–67.

7. Don Oberdorfer, "Soviet Deal with Kuwait Spurred U.S. Ship Role," *Washington Post*, May 24, 1987, p. 1.

8. Mark N. Katz, *Russia and Arabia* (Baltimore: Johns Hopkins Press, 1986), p. 165.

9. Bernard E. Trainor, "Soviet Ship Attacked by Iran in Gulf, U.S. Says," *New York Times*, May 9, 1987, p. 1, and *Trud* (Moscow), May 12, 1987, p. 3.

10. See TASS commentary in U.S. Foreign Broadcast Information Service, *Daily Report: Soviet Union* (hereafter cited as *FBIS-SOV*), May 17, 1987, p. H1.

11. Philip Taubman, "Iran and Soviet Draft Big Projects, Including Pipelines and Railroad," *New York Times*, August 5, 1987, p. 1.

12. "Gorbachev's Gulf, Too," *Economist*, October 24, 1987, pp. 13–15.

13. See, for example, TASS commentary in *FBIS-SOV*, June 25, 1987, pp. E1–E2.

14. High-level officials in Saudi Arabia, Kuwait, Bahrain, and Qatar made this point during conversations with the author while he visited these countries in February–March 1988.

PART II

Diplomatic and Legal Dimensions

10

Choice and Duty in Foreign Affairs

The Reflagging of the Kuwaiti Tankers

David D. Caron

The U.S. naval presence in the Persian Gulf that accompanied the U.S. decision to reflag and escort eleven Kuwaiti tankers is credited by many with hastening the end of the Iran-Iraq War. As Robert C. McFarlane wrote shortly after Ayatollah Khomeini's July 1988 endorsement of a cease-fire: "The purpose of that intervention—too often clouded by extraneous declarations of principle—was to prevent either side from winning and, by succeeding in that strategy, to bring them both to a negotiated settlement."[1] Nothing is as praiseworthy as success, and that result is not challenged here. Instead, this chapter examines two questions and challenges two lessons that otherwise might be drawn too hastily from the success of the U.S. strategy.

The first question is, What are the implications of implementing a foreign policy on the basis of a duty rather than a choice? A distinctive characteristic of U.S. Gulf strategy was that it was implemented precisely on the basis of what McFarlane termed "extraneous declarations of principle." The United States justified its presence in the Gulf on the basis of a duty to defend vessels flying the flag of the United States. The rhetoric of U.S. officials often resounded of policy and choice: It was stated to be in the interest of the United States to oppose the expansionist desires of revolutionary Iran, to support the moderate Arab Gulf states, to exclude the Soviets from the Gulf, and thereby to maintain the stability of the Gulf region. Ultimately, however, the naval presence and actions of the United States were justified on the basis of a duty to protect vessels flying its flag. The fact that performance of the duty also promoted other U.S. interests was only a bonus.

Given that U.S. interests in a reflagging operation were to be hotly debated in Congress, the assertion of a duty by the executive made the implementation of U.S. Gulf policy a politically much easier task. An apparent lesson for diplomacy and statecraft, therefore, would be that controversial international policies, such as those involving armed forces, may be more easily implemented by an executive if the policy is characterized as a duty rather than a desirable course of action supporting national interests. I argue that ease of implementation is only the seductive first part of a story whose motif is loss of control.

The second question is more specific to the reflagging operation. It asks how strongly international law respects the cloak of nationality that a flag places over a vessel. More generally, it asks how strongly international law respects any fictions during armed conflict. The United States claimed the rights of a neutral and the expectation that the 11 tankers flying its flag would be regarded by Iran as impartial in the war. The validity of this expectation rested upon the assertion that Kuwait's ownership and control of these tankers was irrelevant. The apparent lesson is that during armed conflict a vessel of a state that at least financially aids one of the belligerents may gain the status of a neutral by taking on the flag of a neutral. The strength of this cloak of neutrality, however, is not so clear. The reflagging operation is troubling because although the link of the United States to these tankers was contrived, Congress was unable to express in legal terms the falseness it perceived. I argue that the international legal issue was not framed correctly during the reflagging debates in the United States. In essence, there was a failure to distinguish between the respect customary international law accords fictions during peace and its lack of tolerance for such formalities during armed conflict. In this way the second question returns us to the first, for international law's piercing of fictions during armed conflict may dispel an asserted duty and thus help expose the underlying choice.

DUTY AND CHOICE

A state confronted with a difficult international situation can choose between a number of possible responses. It is the task of diplomacy and international relations to suggest the methodology by which the best response is chosen. One common approach would call for an assessment of the state's interests and the selection of that course of action that best would support those interests. Duties, whether they be moral or legal,

national or international, reflect the institutionalization of what a community regards as the required choice to be made in certain situations.
Thus an executive can argue that the choice of a certain course of conduct
is suggested by an assessment of present interests or that it is required
by a duty. In this chapter I refer to the former decision as policy based
upon a choice and the latter as policy based upon a duty.[2] The reflagging
operation offers four propositions concerning the implications of basing
a policy upon duty rather than choice.

It Is Easier to Implement a Controversial Policy If It Is Based upon a Duty Rather Than a Choice

The Iran-Iraq War began in September 1980, shortly after the revolutionary Islamic regime of Ayatollah Khomeini assumed power in Iran.[3]
In 1984 Iraq intensified its effort to disrupt Iran's oil-export operations,
and the Persian Gulf "tanker war" began in earnest.[4]

In September 1986 Iran seemed dangerously close to a breakthrough
in the land war. Apparently in an effort to intimidate Kuwait from
continuing its logistical and financial support of Iraq, Iran focused attacks
upon Kuwait's territory and shipping.[5] With the nearby al-Faw peninsula
held by Iran and another major Iranian offensive in the offing for January
1987, Kuwait sought protection of its economic and security interests.

On December 10, 1986, the Kuwait Oil Tanker Company requested
the U.S. Coast Guard to provide it with U.S. reflagging requirements
and informed the United States on December 23, 1986, of its interest in
reflagging. (Apparently, Kuwait approached all the permanent members
of the Security Council at this time expressing a similar interest.) On
January 13, 1987, Kuwait asked the United States whether reflagged
Kuwaiti-owned vessels would receive U.S. naval protection.[6]

In January and February 1987 several interagency policy meetings were
held at the White House to discuss the Kuwaiti requests. Then in late
February the Reagan administration learned that the Soviets had agreed
to reflag and protect 5 Kuwaiti tankers. On March 2 Kuwait asked the
administration to put 6 other Kuwaiti tankers under the U.S. flag. The
administration responded on March 7 with an offer to protect all 11
vessels. Thus, to be fair to the Reagan administration, it was Kuwait
that set up the "duty" trap by requesting that the United States reflag
Kuwait's tankers. The bait for the trap was the preventing of such reflagging by the Soviets.

On April 21 Ambassador Richard W. Murphy, assistant secretary of
state for Near Eastern and South Asian affairs, briefed the House Foreign
Affairs Committee on the reflagging operation. It is fair to say that at
this point the U.S. public and Congress were aware of a choice by the
executive to reflag 11 Kuwaiti tankers. I do not believe that the public

or a majority of the Congress appreciated, however, the implications of that choice. Thus the Congress and the nation did not really focus on the reflagging until May 17, when missiles fired from an Iraqi F-1 fighter jet struck the USS *Stark*, killing 37 U.S. servicemen. This incident prompted extensive executive consultations with Congress.

In part, what followed was an education of many members of the Congress as to the relationship of a flag state to its vessels. A ship is said to have the nationality of the state under whose laws it is registered.[7] Nationality is a prime, if not conclusive, factor in determining what state may exercise executive, legislative, and judicial jurisdiction over the vessel; what state may espouse a diplomatic protection claim concerning the ship; and what state may come to the defense of the vessel.[8] In general, each state under international law decides for itself the basis upon which it will grant its nationality to vessels. In this case the executive had decided to allow 11 Kuwaiti tankers to gain U.S. nationality through reflagging.

The administration's policy was set forth in mid-June by Secretary of Defense Caspar Weinberger[9] and Under Secretary of State for Political Affairs Michael Armacost.[10] Both asserted that U.S. economic, strategic, and political interests were being threatened by the escalation of the Iran-Iraq War. These interests included maintaining the principle of freedom of navigation in international waters and an unimpeded flow of oil through the Gulf; defending the security, stability, and cooperation of the moderate Arab states in the region; and limiting the Soviet Union's influence and presence in the Gulf. To protect these interests, the administration asserted that it was following a two-track policy: (1) diplomatic efforts in the United Nations to galvanize international pressure to persuade Iran and Iraq to negotiate an end to the war, and (2) active measures to protect U.S. interests and help protect the security of moderate, friendly Arab states in the Gulf. The second track of the policy essentially consisted of the reflagging and protecting of the 11 Kuwaiti tankers.

Ultimately, however, it was not the enumerated interests that were put forward to justify the decision that U.S. naval vessels at great cost would escort and defend Kuwait's tankers. Rather, the United States agreed to do so because, as Secretary Weinberger's report to Congress stated, "US-flag ships have received U.S. protection since the beginning of the U.S. Navy and will continue to have this protection as long as they fly the U.S. flag."[11] In this sense, the presence of the U.S. flag upon the tankers was invoked to justify the policy.

SENATOR KERRY: What is it about a Kuwaiti ship that is so precious, as distinct to an American asset, an American owned ship? What is the distinction? . . .

SECRETARY WEINBERGER: . . . It has . . . followed our laws, which permit the placing of the American flag on other foreign owned ships, and when that flag is on those ships, those ships are entitled to and receive the protection of the United States.[12]

Because the ships were to be reflagged shortly as Kuwait requested, there was in the administration's official view no choice for the United States but to defend them. Although the executive did not speak in terms of a legally enforceable right, it did speak repeatedly of the U.S. obligation and the vessels' entitlement.[13] Consequently, the original choice to reflag the vessels, at least in the public's view, became obscured; that choice had been made, and afterwards the United States could only fulfill its duty to protect U.S. vessels. But even if it may have been the United States' duty to protect the *Bridgeton*, it was the administration's choice, not its duty, to reflag the tanker formerly known as *al-Rekkah*.

The extent of the commitments the United States accepted in the Gulf would have been much more apparent if, instead of reflagging the vessels, the United States had had the time to place the decision in the context of a defense assistance agreement whereby it would have escorted and defended the tankers. To justify that agreement, the administration would have had to present a complex argument pointing to the strategic value of the Gulf and of Kuwait in particular, to the necessity of regaining leadership in the Gulf region, to the importance of keeping the Soviets out, and so forth. It is one thing to say to the public that a duty must be fulfilled; it is quite another to convince the Congress and the public of the wisdom of a complex choice and to ask them in essence to personally take on the responsibility of concurring in that choice.

As the first U.S. convoy prepared to sail in July 1987, the United Kingdom discussed a similar request by Kuwait to place other Kuwaiti vessels under the British flag.[14] As with the Reagan administration, the British government acknowledged the obligation of the flag state to protect its vessels as its capabilities allowed. The British government went a step farther in saying that it had no choice, however, as the following extract from the House of Commons debate on July 21, 1987 reveals:

Mr. Jonathan Aiken: Can [the Foreign Secretary] confirm reports that the Government of Kuwait have made a formal request to Britain to have some of their vessels reflagged under our flag? What will be our policy in response to such a request...?

Sir Geoffrey Howe: ... If there were any question of registering..., it would be a purely commercial and procedural arrangement.... There is no need for a formal decision by the Government.

Mr. Tony Banks: ... Surely the Foreign Secretary must understand that when there is any application for reflagging there are also very important political and military considerations to take into account?

Mr. Gerald Kaufman: . . . [Is the Foreign Secretary] saying, that, if there were a purely commercial reflagging arrangement between British and Kuwaiti interests, the Royal Navy and British foreign policy would be dragged along behind such a private commercial arrangement? . . .

Sir Geoffrey Howe: . . . The question of re-registering . . . is, as it has long been, a purely commercial and procedural arrangement in respect of which there is a wide range of legal and other implications that must be complied with.[15]

In essence, the British government stated that it had no choice but to grant its flag if administrative formalities were met and no choice but to defend that flag once granted. This position was not only an effective tactic against domestic questioning but also a proclamation of "we have no choice" to Iran, which had warned Britain not to protect Kuwaiti tankers.[16] In effect, to invoke a duty is to assert that one has no choice.[17]

The Specific Course of Action Suggested by a Duty May Be Quite Different from the Course Suggested by Analysis of Interest

One should not assume that the duty used to ease implementation of a controversial policy will generate a course of action congruent with the interest analysis that may have suggested the controversial policy in the first place. Presumably, if a nation's past calculation of interest correctly led to the formation of a duty, then that nation's analysis of its present interests should not lead to a policy less extensive than that which flows from the duty.[18] Present interest may suggest, however, that more than one's duty should be undertaken. Once this is seen, a new light is cast on the commentary on the U.S. Gulf policy because much of the criticism of the U.S. reflagging operation rested upon the divergence between a policy aimed at defending vessels flying one's flag and policies that would further what the administration stated to be its objectives in the region.

This font of criticism was recognized by Under Secretary of State for Political Affairs Michael H. Armacost, for example, in a statement before the Senate Foreign Relations Committee on June 16, 1987: "We have not always articulated as clearly as we might the distinction between our comprehensive policy to protect all our interests in the gulf, on the one hand, and the specific interests advanced by the decision to reflag a limited number of ships, on the other."[19] Thus it was argued that if the United States was there to protect freedom of navigation, why did it not join in efforts to protect all shipping, and if the United States was there to protect American interests, why did it not protect U.S.-owned vessels sailing under foreign flags?[20] Consequently, this form of criticism in one sense is misplaced because it assumes that the course of action was chosen to further one's interests as much as possible rather than to fulfill a duty that coincidentally more or less also furthered one's interests.

That there may be a divergence between a duty-generated and choice-generated course of action does not mean necessarily that the difference is a bad thing. Whether the divergence is good or bad will depend upon the situation and may change over time, an example of the type of fortuity generally regarded with distrust by policy planners. The divergence was advantageous in the reflagging operation because the duty-generated course of action was clearer and narrower than the course of action suggested by choice. In the Gulf the United States projected an image of successfully defending a preferred group because the duty that generated the policy happened to define a group of manageable size. To appreciate this effect, one must realize that for a variety of reasons, particularly labor and taxation, a U.S. flag is expensive and therefore rarely used outside of U.S. coastal trade, where it is required by U.S. law. Consequently, when the United States declared that it stood ready to defend U.S.-flagged vessels, the United States as a practical matter committed itself to defend the 11 Kuwaiti tankers.

The formality of the flag defined the group. If instead the group had been defined so as to protect U.S. interests, then the refusal to defend U.S.-owned vessels flying foreign flags would have been very difficult to justify.[21] Likewise, if the U.S. interest was to protect the free flow of oil, U.S. policy should have been to protect all such shipping. But as one senior Pentagon official reportedly stated: "If we increased our protection mission, we would have to increase our force structure, and that would take gobs of money."[22]

Instead, because the flag defined a relatively small group, it defined a group that the United States had a good prospect of successfully defending. Unlike the situation in Lebanon in 1983–84 where U.S. goals were uncertain and the commitments broad, the United States in the Persian Gulf was committed to defend only 11 ships. From a military standpoint the United States defined a target it had a more than reasonable chance of defending. From an image perspective the United States gave itself a more than reasonable chance of "success" in projecting force overseas.[23]

Criticism based upon the divergence between duty and choice is valid, however, in assuming that even if a duty were invoked to ease the implementation of a course of action, one may argue later that analysis of interests justifies increasing the scope of the policy. Indeed, the reflagging operation seems to suggest that criticism based upon interest analysis will tend to pull the duty-based policy toward the choice-based policy. For example, the U.S. decision to protect only U.S.-flagged vessels was embodied in its rules of engagement. These rules, by defining a small group, narrowed the Navy's mission. The pressure for enlarging the scope of these rules to include the U.S.-owned foreign-flag vessels, or indeed any vessel under attack, grew throughout the operation. Finally, the United States altered its rules of engagement in April 1988 to permit Navy ships to protect any neutral merchant ships that came under attack.[24] Of course, the consequence of this change was to increase the scope of the Navy's mission, the likelihood that the Navy would come into conflict with Iranian forces, and the likelihood that U.S. forces would cease to project an image of "success." Indeed, the tragic downing of Iran Air Flight 655 was incidental to the U.S. Navy's protection not of a U.S.-flagged vessel, but rather a Danish one.

The Course of Action Suggested by a Duty Is Not Altered by Changes in One's Interests

I have argued that the course of action suggested by a duty may or may not coincide with the course suggested by a calculation of one's interests. Even more, however, it must be recognized that the course of action suggested by a duty will not be responsive to changes in the country's objectives. Thus an initial coincidental match between duty and interests may diminish over time. Indeed, continuation of the course of action dictated by the duty eventually may run counter to a state's interests. This shift is precisely what occurred just prior to the Iranian acceptance of the cease-fire in July 1988.

In reconsidering the reflagging operation in July 1988, Shireen Hunter wrote that if "its purpose has been to contain Iran, shore up Iraq and reassure the Arabs, then this has already been achieved."[25] In this sense, if the United States was acting in accordance with appraisals of its changing interests, it should have reduced its involvement during the summer of 1988. Iran no longer was close to a breakthrough in the land war. Indeed, Iraq had recaptured al-Faw Peninsula in April 1988 and continued recapturing territory throughout May and June.[26] Simultaneously, Iraq continued its use of chemical weapons not only against Iranians, but also against its own Kurds. It is at this point that the reflagging operation became counterproductive. The picture carefully drawn by many countries had been that of an Iran unwilling to accept reasonable terms of peace proffered by Iraq. Indeed, Iraq in 1986 probably would have gone far to accommodate many of Iran's demands for an end to the war. But in the summer of 1988 Iraq regained a sense of strength. Consequently, continued U.S. support of Iraq via the reflagging operation led not only to Iran's acceptance of the U.N. cease-fire, but also to Iraq's intransigence in the peace talks that followed.[27] Since the United States had made it its duty to indirectly help Iraq, it had no levers by which to influence Iraq. As one State Department official reportedly stated: "It's a mistake to suggest we have a tremendous amount of influence on Iraq."[28] U.S. interests were to contain a revolutionary Islamic Iran, not to humiliate it, and certainly not to become a tool of Iraq.

It Can Be Difficult to Terminate a Course of Action Based upon the Existence of a Duty

The real implication of invoking a duty and stating that one has no choice is to assert also that one is not in control of the policy. In the reflagging operation the circumstances underlying the duty were controlled by Kuwait, which chose to aid Iraq and to keep its tankers under the U.S. flag, and by Iran, which hoped to intimidate Kuwait by attacking Kuwaiti tankers. "I believe that we run the risk of once again having our entire policy become hostage to Iran."[29] Indeed, when Senator Pell inquired of Secretary Weinberger under what circumstances he would consider the U.S. mission completed, the secretary replied, "When there is no longer any threat, any obvious, overt threat to the passage of free nonbelligerent, innocent commerce over these international waters."[30]

In the summer of 1988 it became increasingly apparent both that the escorting had accomplished what the United States sought and that the escorting could not be terminated because symbols of the United States imprinted upon these tankers would be left behind.[31] In July 1988 Democratic Senator Adams observed: "We do not know how to tell if we have won; we do not know how to tell if we have lost. All we know is that we are there and will be there for a long time."[32] Republican Senator Lugar observed: "I think we are there until the threats to shipping and commerce cease."[33] The United States was fortunate in that it did not take a long time for the threats to shipping and commerce to cease.[34]

FORM AND SUBSTANCE

The invocation of duty by the United States to defend vessels flying its flag was troubling to many because it seemed contrived—an artifice.[35] After all, the tankers were Kuwaiti-owned and controlled, and Kuwait was an important financial and logistical supporter of Iraq. Moreover, the choice to not protect the free flow of oil generally in the Gulf harmed Iran, given the fact that Iraq initiated and maintained the tanker war in order to limit Iran's ability to generate oil revenues. Consequently, the decision to escort and reflag the Kuwaiti tankers quite correctly was seen as a sharp tilt in U.S. policy toward Iraq.[36]

The perception that the United States' duty to the tankers was an artifice was of great concern to the Reagan administration. The administration repeatedly declared itself neutral in the Iran-Iraq War[37] and asserted that the reflagged tankers partook of this neutral status. As a corollary, the administration asserted that the U.S. naval presence in the Gulf was purely defensive. "Our general strategy from the beginning has been, and remains, based entirely on the theory of deterrence."[38]

Internationally, the United States desired a neutral image so as not to foreclose further the possibility of normalizing relations with Iran in the future or, as importantly, to avoid pushing Iran toward the Soviet Union. "We do not seek confrontation with Iran. We hope, with time, to improve our relations with that strategically important country."[39] Domestically, the administration was faced with the possibility of congressional action under the War Powers Resolution. The defensive posture enabled the administration not only to repeat its established position that the Resolution was unconstitutional but also to add that the Resolution simply did not apply by its own terms because U.S. forces were not in a situation of "imminent hostilities" but rather were merely responding defensively to acts that, although individually hostile, were not part of continuing hostilities.[40]

That the image of neutrality and reluctant defender would be desirable is understandable. The question, however, is why international law did not help to lay bare the contrived nature of this arrangement. Although the contrived nature of the duty to defend the reflagged tankers was palpable, the falseness failed to be expressed in legal terms.

A number of commentators and legislators attempted to argue that the United States could not validly grant its flag to these vessels because there was no "genuine link."[41] As mentioned earlier, each state generally decides for itself the basis upon which it will grant its nationality to vessels.[42] Significantly, a large number of states will grant their nationality to vessels not owned by their nationals. As a consequence, there is an international market of sorts in flags. International law does place a few limitations on the attribution of nationality by the flag state, however. The limitation argued by many to be relevant to this inquiry is that of a "genuine link" between the flag state and the vessel.

The push for a genuine-link limitation arose in response to states who liberally granted their nationality to ships.[43] It was argued that without a genuine link, there would be "flags of convenience" facilitating the use of unsafe and undermanned vessels. This limitation, as set forth in Article 5(1) of the 1958 Convention on the High Seas, provides that there "must exist a genuine link . . . in particular, the state must effectively exercise its jurisdiction and control in administrative, technical and social matters over ships flying its flag."[44] The precise content of the genuine-link requirement was to be addressed by the 1986 Convention on Conditions for Registration of Ships, although it is accepted generally that the compromises that yielded the 1986 convention lead it only to provide general guidance rather than specific norms.[45]

Whether the reflagged Kuwaiti vessels possessed a genuine link to the United States was addressed in the secretary of defense's report to Congress. The report reviewed the vessel registration laws of the United States[46] and the required Coast Guard compliance inspections then ongoing and concluded that "under international and U.S. domestic law, these prerequisites to and incidents of U.S. registration establish effective jurisdiction by the United States over commercial vessels of its flag. In practice, they provide the 'genuine link' with the United States that under international law impresses authentic U.S. nationality on the Kuwaiti tankers."[47] Contesting this conclusion, Professor Jordan Paust, for example, asserted that the plan to reflag "violates international law" because "transfer of title 'temporarily' to a United States holding company patently demonstrates that there is no real or 'genuine' link between the Kuwaiti vessels and the United States, but an attempted subterfuge of international law."[48] Abraham D. Sofaer, the State Department Legal Adviser, replied to Paust, writing that the tankers had been inspected and generally met U.S. standards. Where standards were not met, "national defense" waivers were granted—but only where the U.S. specifications *exceed* internationally accepted standards, and only for a limited time."[49]

Although minor points could be debated, it seems clear to me that the reflagged Kuwaiti tankers met the minimum international legal requirement of a genuine link with the United States.[50] Among other things, it should be noted that no state officially questioned that the United States effectively exercised jurisdiction over the tankers. However, the focus on the "genuine-link" question was misplaced for a more important reason. In particular, the debate overlooked that a state under international law may not refuse to recognize the nationality of a vessel because of a dubious genuine link between the ship and the flag state.[51] In discussing the genuine-link limitation in the 1950s, the International Law Commission rejected a proposal that would have allowed a state not to recognize a ship's nationality if it believed that a genuine link did not exist. A state that suspects the lack of a genuine link must instead "report the facts to the flag State," which must then investigate the allegation.[52] In other words, even if the United States' link to the tankers was questionable, it was not Iran's right under the genuine-link doctrine to challenge the validity of the U.S. flag. Thus the international community regards the genuine-link requirement as soft both in that the content is vague and its enforceability is weak. The much clearer rule is that the importance of nationality to public order on the high seas requires that states not challenge apparent nationality because of unilateral suspicions.

There is a yet more fundamental reason, however, why a focus on the "genuine-link" doctrine is misplaced. In particular, a focus on the "genuine-link" doctrine overlooks the fact that this doctrine arose only after World War II. Perhaps it is the ahistorical way in which international law is taught that accounts for the oversight, but it must be remembered that before there was concern over "flags of convenience" in peacetime there was far greater concern over "flags of refuge" during war.[53] It is this last observation that leads to the right focus: If Kuwait is a belligerent on the side of Iraq, does the reflagging alter the legal character of either the vessels or their cargoes?

The question must be approached with care because the laws of neutrality and belligerency present at the beginning of the century find new limits in contemporary international law for two reasons. First, before World War II international law allowed for both peace and war, the latter being the subject of extensive rules to regulate, among other things, relations between belligerents and neutrals. The U.N. Charter, however, outlawed the use of force except in self-defense or as collectively authorized under the Charter. In theory, at least, there no longer would be neutrals; all collectively would oppose the "aggressor."[54] The view, however, that neutrality was incompatible with the charter soon was questioned. The dominant view that emerged was that if the U.N. Security Council cannot or will not act in regard to an armed conflict, then the traditional laws of war and neutrality continue to apply.[55] Second, the content of the laws of war is intimately related to the technology of war and the means by which states may be said to be assisting one another. In this regard, the laws of war originating primarily around the turn of the century surely are dated and deserve more critical attention than is possible in this chapter.

With these doctrinal concerns in mind, one starts with the proposition that a state, under the laws of war, is either a belligerent or neutral. "A 'neutral State' is one which in a war between other States sides with neither party."[56] A neutral state "must not furnish either belligerent with troops, ships, munitions of war, money, or indeed with anything which may aid him in the war."[57] As to the status of Kuwait, suffice it to say here that it can be argued that Kuwait was a belligerent on the side of Iraq, and that a large number of significant persons referred to Kuwait as such.[58] Indeed, Under Secretary of State Armacost testified that Iran had stated publicly that it had singled out Kuwaiti vessels so as "to force Kuwait to quit supporting Iraq with financial subventions and permitting goods bound for Iraq to be offloaded at a Kuwaiti port."[59] On the other hand, Under Secretary of State Armacost also stressed that the United States does "not consider Kuwait a belligerent—nor does Iran, formally."[60] He went on to state that the United States does "recognize, however, that Kuwait provides financial support for Iraq."[61] Secretary Weinberger asserted: "The United States will be in full compliance with international law[, which] clearly recognizes the right of a neutral state to escort and protect its flag vessels in transit to neutral ports. The tankers will carry Kuwaiti oil to neutral ports and will return in ballast; they will not carry contraband for either of the belligerents."[62] The secretary's statement is somewhat unclear, however, as to the source of the neutral character of the tankers. In particular, are they neutral because the flag state, the United States, is neutral or because Kuwait is neutral?

The respect to be given a neutral flag in time of war was debated widely in the last century. The generally accepted rule, as stated by Sir Samuel Evans in 1918 in *The Hamborn*, was: "It is a settled rule of prize law . . . that [it] will penetrate through and beyond forms and technicalities to the facts and realities. . . . This rule . . . means that the Court is not bound to determine the neutral or enemy character of a vessel according to the flag she is flying."[63] Lord Summer of the Privy Council on appeal wrote: "The criteria for deciding enemy character in the case of artificial person . . . can . . . only be the conduct of those who act for or in the name of the artificial person. . . . [T]he right and power of control may form a true criterion."[64] Another formulation that reaches the same conclusion is contained in Article 57 of the 1909 London Declaration.[65] That article provides that "the neutral or enemy character of a vessel is determined by the flag which she is entitled to fly." This provision, however, was subject to broad exceptions in the case of transfer of flag. In the case of reflagging during war, Article 56 of the same Declaration provided that "the transfer of an enemy vessel to a neutral flag effected after the outbreak of hostilities is void unless it is proved that such transfer was not made in order to evade the consequence to which an enemy vessel, as such, is exposed." In the words of the U.S. Navy in 1917, such a transfer would only be valid if it is "accompanied by a payment sufficient in amount to leave no doubt of good faith; that it is absolute and unconditional, with a complete divestiture of title by the vendor, with no continued interest, direct or indirect, of the vendor, and with no right of repurchase by him; and that the ship does not remain in her old employment."[66]

In the case of the U.S. reflagging operation, the 11 tankers continued to be owned and controlled by Kuwait. Under either formulation of the laws of war, if Kuwait is characterized as a belligerent, the character of the tanker was not altered by the U.S. reflagging, and Iran would not have been required by international law to respect the neutral character of the U.S. flag.[67]

Consequently, the fact that the reflagging operation worked (albeit with great delays in transit times and at considerable expense) does not appear to be so much a result of Iranian respect for the neutral character of reflagged Kuwaiti tankers as it is a reflection of Iranian respect for the U.S. power present and the very limited naval and air capabilities of Iran.[68] It is not at all clear that a more powerful Iran would have been as reticent or unsuccessful in the attacks it made.

Form and reality were confused greatly in the case of the U.S. reflagging decision. Consequently, the most apparent lessons to be drawn can be quite wrong. In particular, it would be a mistake to conclude that a belligerent's vessels can or should gain a measure of protection under international law by their transfer to the flag of a neutral state. Laws of war, if they are to be respected at all by the warring states, necessarily reflect closely the interests of the belligerents, and belligerents logically find it necessary to look beyond formalities to realities.

CONCLUSION

Invocation of a duty eases implementation of policy by cutting short debate on the wisdom of the policy. In many cases this is of little consequence because the duty was originally reviewed by the polity. Treaty obligations, for example, receive the advice and consent of the Senate. Invocation of the kind of duty that can be assumed in a discretionary fashion by the executive, however, runs counter to the notion of participatory politics. The question therefore arises as to whether the administration might have moved toward its objectives in the Gulf in a more forthright way. It is not at all clear that the Congress and the public would have been convinced of the wisdom of protecting Kuwaiti tankers, although perhaps they ultimately might have agreed to the protection of American interests in the region. Far more acceptable would have been American participation in a multilateral or U.N. effort to end the war and preserve freedom of navigation generally in the Gulf. Such a policy, however, would not necessarily have supported the administration's goals of keeping the Soviets out of the Gulf, demonstrating to the moderate Gulf states that the United States (despite the Iran-Contra affair) was a reliable partner, and ensuring that Iran did not win the war. Of course, exploration of alternatives was not particularly feasible in this instance, given the way in which Kuwait constructed the "duty" trap.

Regardless of whether a more forthright alternative existed in this case, however, it does seem clear that executives and their foreign policy advisors deeply question whether forthright participatory politics will yield what they believe to be the desirable course of action. Whether this view is correct or can be justified is not the subject of this chapter. Rather, this chapter cautions that the seductive call of a duty as a means to sidestep participatory politics carries with it great risk. Duties take on an existence of their own. A realist might say that a duty only raises limits in theory, and that just as the duty was invoked when needed, it also could be sidestepped when needed. In fact, however, the reflagging operation tells us that denying the existence of a duty or limiting its scope will not be easy or, most likely, even considered. The duty comes to form the way we and others talk and think about the policy. In this way duties become an independent source of one's policy.

The reflagging operation was not a brilliant strategy. The operation in fact was quite risky and can be said to have failed to the extent that it encouraged Iraq's later intransigence in the peace talks. The success of the operation (to the degree it was a success) was a result of the carefully restrained execution by the United States of this risky strategy and of the fact that Iran lacked the means to truly challenge the cloak of neutrality that the United States at Kuwait's request placed over the 11 tankers.

NOTES

1. R. McFarlane, "A Crusade Stalled, A Risk Averted: By Its Role in Gulf, U.S. Has Helped Ayatollah to Break Faith," *Los Angeles Times*, July 27, 1988, sec. 2, p. 7. For a similar earlier description by a former ambassador to the United Arab Emirates, see M. Sterner, "Doing Something Right in the Gulf," *New York Times*, January 27, 1988, p. 25.

2. Duty-based policy and choice-based policy are of course not watertight categories. For example, the institutionalization of what a community regards as the required choice to be made in certain situations presumably reflects, at least in some measure, the community's past or present calculation of what is in its best interest.

3. On the Iran-Iraq War generally, see Anthony Cordesman, *The Iran-Iraq War and Western Security, 1984–1987* (Royal United Services Institute for Defence Studies, Jane's Press, 1987); and U.S. Senate Committee on Foreign Relations Staff Report, *War in the Persian Gulf: The U.S. Takes Sides* (1987).

4. On the tanker war, see C. Danzinger, "The Persian Gulf Tanker War," *U.S. Naval Institute Proceedings*, 1985, p. 160.

5. C. Weinberger, *A Report to the Congress on Security Arrangements in the Persian Gulf*, June 15, 1987, p. 7 (hereafter *Weinberger Report*), reprinted in U.S. Senate Committee on Foreign Relations, *U.S. Policy in the Persian Gulf*, 100th Cong., 1st sess., 1988, pp. 294, 307.

6. Statement of Ambassador Richard W. Murphy, "International Shipping and the Iran-Iraq War," U.S. Department of State Current Policy no. 958, May 1987, p. 3.

7. See generally D. Caron, "Ships: Nationality and Status," in R. Bernhardt, ed., *Encyclopedia of Public International Law*, vol. 11 (New York: North-Holland, 1989), p. 289.

8. See A. D. Watts, "The Protection of Merchant Ships," *British Yearbook of International Law* 33 (1957): 52.

9. See *Weinberger Report*.

10. Statement of Michael H. Armacost, "U.S. Policy in the Persian Gulf and

Kuwaiti Reflagging," June 16, 1987, reprinted in *Department of State Bulletin*, August 1987, p. 78.

11. *Weinberger Report*, p. 299.

12. Testimony of Secretary Caspar Weinberger, October 23, 1987, *U.S. Policy in the Persian Gulf*, pp. 163–64; Testimony of Ambassador Richard W. Murphy before the Senate Foreign Relations Committee, May 29, 1987, *U.S. Policy in the Persian Gulf*, p. 42. Kuwait totally agreed with the administration's position and reportedly stated, "They are your vessels now, it is your responsibility to protect them." *War in the Persian Gulf: The U.S. Takes Sides*, p. 38.

13. Testimony of Ambassador Murphy, ibid. See also *Weinberger Report*, p. 299 (U.S. flag ships "will continue to be protected. . . . This is our responsibility and obligation as the leader of the Free World.").

14. Ultimately, three Kuwaiti tankers were placed under the British flag. See H. Pick, "Britain denies policy shift on reflagging," *Guardian*, July 13, 1987, p. 8; H. Pick, "Britain quick to renew Embargo Backing," *Guardian*, July 22, 1987, p. 6; P. Brown, "Kuwaitis apply to fly British flag on their Gulf oil tankers," *Guardian*, July 23, 1987, p. 6; H. Pick, "Gulf help near after UK lobby," *Guardian*, August 27, 1987, p. 1; D. Fairhall, "Second Kuwaiti Tanker reflagged," *Guardian*, October 20, 1987, p. 8; and "2 Kuwait Tankers get British Flag," *New York Times*, October 27, 1987, p. 2.

15. 120 *H. C. Weekly Hansard* (July 21, 1987), cols. 205–16. See also C. Gray, "The British Position in Regard to the Gulf Conflict," *International and Comparative Law Quarterly* 37 (1988): 420–28.

The United States was more cautious in characterizing the initial decision to reflag:

SENATOR SARBANES: . . . The real question is how can you broaden our military obligations in this way, through [the reflagging] provision of the law which I would assume was put there for purposes totally unrelated to military protection?

AMBASSADOR MURPHY: I think the only reply that I could make, Senator, is that there is . . . not a surge of requests for our flagging. . . . the answer will have to be on a case-by-case basis. . . .

SENATOR SARBANES: . . . You, in effect, are going to make an administrative decision to place the American flag on these vessels . . . and thereby impose on the military an obligation of protecting them.

AMBASSADOR MURPHY: . . . [I]t is the right of another country to come to us and ask for reflagging.

U.S. Policy in the Persian Gulf, pp. 42–44.

16. D. Hirst, "Tehran Warns Britain against Protecting Kuwaiti Tankers in Gulf," *Guardian*, July 16, 1987, p. 7.

17. To say that one has no choice but to defend the vessels is, of course, also to assert a very credible threat. See generally T. Schelling, *The Strategy of Conflict* (Cambridge, Mass.: Harvard University Press, 1960), pp. 187–88.

18. The difficulty arises, of course, when the calculation of present interest, including the consequences of the breach of the duty, points in a different direction than fulfillment of the simple duty.

19. M. Armacost, *Department of State Bulletin*, August 1987, p. 78. Senator Sam Nunn's detailed critique of the administration's policy offered a similar view:

Senator Sam Nunn, "Response to the Weinberger Report," reprinted at *International Legal Materials* 26 (1987): 1464, 1472.

20. L. Daniels, "U.S. Companies Seek Shield for Their Foreign-Flag Ships," *New York Times*, October 16, 1987, p. 6.

21. For example, on October 15 a U.S.-owned tanker flying the Liberian flag was struck by an Iranian missile while in Kuwaiti waters. While the administration described the attack as a "very hostile action toward Kuwait," retaliation was ruled out because the ship was not in international waters nor flying the American flag. E. Sciolino, "Iran Missile Hits a Gulf Tanker Owned in U.S.," *New York Times*, October 16, 1987, p. 1.

22. E. Sciolino, "A Failed Bid for Safe Passage in the Gulf," *New York Times*, January 10, 1988, sec. 4, p. 8.

23. It could be argued that analysis of interests, such as manageability of the group to be defended, would yield the same limited policy. It could be difficult to justify one's choice, however, as to which manageable group would be defended. The duty provides a legitimate basis for singling out a group.

24. R. Pear, "U.S. Will Increase Its Gulf Defense of Merchant Ships," *New York Times*, April 23, 1988, p. 1.

25. S. Hunter, "U.S. Must Make Up Its Mind on Gulf Goals," *Los Angeles Times*, July 6, 1988, sec. 2, p. 7.

26. B. Trainor, "Iraqi Offensive: Victory Goes Beyond Battlefield," *New York Times*, April 20, 1988, p. A8; B. Trainor, "Iraq Retakes Land near Border Port," *New York Times*, May 26, 1988, p. A3; Y. Ibrahim, "Iraqi Units Continue a String of Victories by Taking Oil Field," *New York Times*, June 26, 1988, sec. 1, p. 1.

27. P. Lewis, "Iraq Balks, Deadlocking Gulf Peace Plan," *New York Times*, July 29, 1988, p. A4; P. Lewis, "Cease-Fire Plan of U.N. Leader Rejected by Iraq," *New York Times*, August 3, 1988, p. A1; P. Lewis, "Gulf Peace Negotiations Hit a Potentially Serious Snag," *New York Times*, August 27, 1988, p. 3.

28. R. Pear, "U.S. Presses Iraq for a Cease-Fire," *New York Times*, August 5, 1988, p. A4.

29. Testimony of Robert S. Hunter, June 16, 1987, *U.S. Policy in the Persian Gulf*, p. 106.

30. Testimony of Secretary Weinberger, *U.S. Policy in the Persian Gulf*, p. 130.

31. "Lending our flag and honor to Kuwaiti boats makes them extraterritorial outposts of the United States." Allan Gerson, "U.S. Should Quit Kidding Itself about Reflagging," *Beaumont Enterprise*, September 19, 1987, p. 7B.

32. R. Pear, "U.S. Called Entangled without Orderly Policy," *New York Times*, July 5, 1988, p. A7.

33. S. Rasky, "Legislators Say Airbus Case Underlines Inability to Act," *New York Times*, July 7, 1988, p. A6.

34. R. Pear, "U.S. Welcomes Move by Teheran and Hints Gulf Fleet Could Be Cut," *New York Times*, July 19, 1988, p. A1; J. Cushman, "Navy to End Convoys in Gulf But It Will Still Protect Ships," *New York Times*, September 17, 1988, p. A2.

35. See, for example, Statement of Senator Kerry, *U.S. Policy in the Persian Gulf*, p. 142 ("a kind of 'shammish' transaction").

36. See, for example, R. K. Ramazani, "The Iran-Iraq War and the Persian Gulf Crisis," *Current History* 87 (1988): 61, 63 ("Reflagging the tankers, Wash-

ington believed, would help save Iraq from defeat and the other Arab gulf states from falling, one after another, like dominoes").

37. M. Armacost, *Department of State Bulletin*, August 1987, p. 80 ("The United States remains formally neutral in the war. With one aberration, we have sold weaponry to neither side").

38. Testimony of Secretary Weinberger, *U.S. Policy in the Persian Gulf*, p. 124.

39. M. Armacost, *Department of State Bulletin*, August 1987, p. 79.

40. See *U.S. Policy in the Persian Gulf*, pp. 144, 145, 153–54. As for the second trigger of the War Powers Resolution, introduction of U.S. armed forces "into the territory, airspace or waters of a foreign nation while equipped for combat," Secretary Weinberger replied that U.S. forces were not in such areas but rather "turn over our convoys after we finish escorting them 20 nautical miles from the shores of Kuwait." Ibid., p. 146.

41. See, for example, T. Phillips, "Exchanging Excuses for Uses of Force: The Tug of War in the Persian Gulf," *Houston Journal of International Law* 10 (1988): 275, 280.

42. See *Muscat Dhows* case (Fr. v. G.B.) (Perm. Ct. Arb., 1905), reprinted in James Brown Scott, ed., *The Hague Court Reports* (New York: Oxford University Press, 1916), pp. 93, 96 ("Generally speaking it belongs to every sovereign to decide to whom he will accord the right to fly his flag and to prescribe the rules governing such grants"); *Lauritzen v. Larsen*, 345 U.S. 571, 584 (1953) ("Each state under international law may determine for itself the conditions on which it will grant its nationality to a merchant ship").

43. This push was in part inspired, and certainly strengthened, by the International Court of Justice's recognition of such a limitation on the granting of nationality to individuals in the *Nottebohm* case. *International Court of Justice Reports*, 1955, p. 4.

44. This provision is repeated in Article 91(1) of the 1982 Law of the Sea Convention.

45. Convention on Conditions for Registration of Ships, done at Geneva on February 7, 1986, reprinted in *International Legal Materials* 26 (1987): 1229. As to the convention, see M. McConnell, " 'Business as Usual': An Evaluation of the United Nations Convention on Conditions for Registration of Ships," *Journal of Maritime Law and Commerce* 18 (1987): 435 ("Although the present text includes requirements relating to state of registry participation in management and manning and/or ownership, a close study of these requirements shows them to be without effect," p. 449).

46. As to U.S. vessel registration, see generally A. E. Henn, P. J. Pluta, and T. H. Gilmour, "Reflagging Foreign-Flag Vessels to U.S. Flag: Past, Present, Future," *Marine Technology* 24 (April 1987): 164; and M. Hathorn, "The Vessel Documentation Act of 1980," *Maritime Lawyer* 7 (1982): 303.

47. *Weinberger Report*, p. 313.

48. J. Paust, "Under International Law, Reflagging Doesn't Fly" (Letter to the Editor), *New York Times*, July 26, 1987, p. 26E.

49. A. Sofaer, "Complied with U.S. Law" (Letter to the Editor), *New York Times*, August 16, 1987, p. 24E. As to Sofaer's legal analysis, see A. Rubin, "Up the Gulf without a Paddle of International Law," *New York Times*, August 30, 1987, p. 26.

50. Accord M. Nordquist and M. Wachenfeld, "Legal Aspects of Reflagging Kuwaiti Tankers and Laying of Mines in the Persian Gulf," *German Yearbook of International Law* 31 (1988), p. 138.

51. See, for example, *The Virginius* (1893), John Basset Moore, *Digest of International Law*, vol. 2 (Washington, D.C.: Government Printing Office, 1906), pp. 895–900. See also *Lauritzen v. Larsen*, 345 U.S. 571, 584 (1953).

52. See Article 94(6), 1982 Law of the Sea Convention.

53. See, for example, B. Boczek, *Flags of Convenience: An International Legal Study* (Cambridge, Mass.: Harvard University Press, 1962), p. 8.

54. E. Korovin, "The Second World War and International Law," *American Journal of International Law* 40 (1946): 742, 754 ("With aggression an international crime, neutrality becomes a form of connivance at this crime").

55. See, for example, Phillip Jessup, *A Modern Law of Nations* (New York: Macmillan, 1949), pp. 203–4.

56. P. H. Cobbett, in H. H. L. Bellot, ed., *Leading Caes on International Law*, vol. 2, 4th ed. (London: Sweet and Maxwell, 1924), p. 400.

57. Ibid., p. 402. See also Lassa Oppenheim, in H. Lauterpacht, ed., *International Law: A Treatise*, vol. 2, 7th ed. (London: Longmans 1952), p. 656 ("Neutral States are bound by certain duties of abstention, *e.g.*, in respect of loans"); C. Colombos, *International Law of the Sea*, 5th ed. (London: Longman's, 1962), pp. 589–90 ("Neutrality is violated by any assistance . . . to one of the belligerents").

58. See, for example, R. Hunter, "United States Policy in the Middle East," *Current History* 87 (1988): 49, 59 ("At best, [Kuwait's] relationship with Iraq was ambiguous, at worst, it was a co-belligerent").

59. See M. Armacost, *Department of State Bulletin*, August 1987, p. 79. See also letter from the Permanent Representative of the Islamic Republic of Iran to the United Nations addressed to the Secretary General (August 11, 1987), reprinted in *International Legal Materials* 26 (1987): 1481, 1483 ("Resolution of the crises [requires] strict observance of neutrality on the part of all littoral states, particularly Kuwait").

60. M. Armacost, *Department of State Bulletin*, August 1987, p. 80.

61. Ibid. See also *Weinberger Report*, p. 307.

62. *Weinberger Report*, p. 321.

63. *The Hamborn Law Reports (Probate Division)*, 1918, pp. 19, 22.

64. *The Hamborn A.C.*, 1919, p. 993. See also R. W. Tucker, *The Law of War and Neutrality at Sea*, Naval War College International Law Studies (Washington, D.C.: Government Printing Office, 1955), p. 76.

65. Declaration Concerning the Laws of Naval Warfare, done at London, February 26, 1909.

66. G. Hackworth, *Digest of International Law*, vol. 6 (Washington D.C.: Government Printing Office, 1943), p. 529 (quoting from Instructions for the Navy of the United States Governing Maritime Warfare [1917]). See also J. Garner, "The Transfer of Merchant Vessels from Belligerent to Neutral Flags," *American Law Review* 49 (1918): 321; Tucker, *Law of War and Neutrality at Sea*, pp. 79–81.

67. This is not to say that there may not be other limits upon Iran. See, for example, W. J. Fenrick, "The Exclusion Zone Device in the Law of Naval Warfare," *Canadian Yearbook of International Law* 24 (1986): 91; and M. Jenkins, "Air

Attacks on Neutral Shipping in the Persian Gulf: The Legality of the Iraqi Exclusion Zone and Iranian Reprisals," *Boston College International and Comparative Law Review* 8 (1985): 517.

68. R. Hunter, "United States Policy in the Middle East," p. 51; Ramazani, "Iran-Iraq War," p. 87.

11

The Law of Maritime Warfare and Neutrality in the Gulf War

Boleslaw Adam Boczek

The international legal dimension of the Iran-Iraq War has not been adequately explored in terms of the law of maritime warfare and the belligerents' attacks on neutral shipping.[1] This chapter examines the applicability of maritime warfare law to the Iran-Iraq conflict, particularly the lawfulness of the belligerents' treatment of neutral shipping transiting Gulf waters and the Strait of Hormuz during the conflict.

MILITARY OPERATIONS AT SEA

Upon the outbreak of war, Iraq tried to avoid confrontation with the stronger Iranian navy that had bombarded the port of Basra and destroyed two oil terminals near al-Faw. On the war's first day Iran proclaimed a naval blockade of Iraq. This effectively isolated the two Iraqi naval bases of Basra and Umm Qasr and cut off the Shatt al-Arab waterway from the Gulf, thus interrupting Iraq's contact with the world via its narrow sea outlet.[2] Until the tanker war began in February 1984, both belligerents showed restraint in their actions against commercial shipping, limiting attacks to vessels in the northern zone of the Gulf.

The Iranian navy began seizing neutral vessels suspected of carrying contraband destined for Iraq. Iraq, for its turn, mined the channel between Bandar-e Khomeini and Bandar Ma'shur and on January 14, 1982, warned neutral shipping to keep clear from the northern part of the Gulf west of those ports.[3] This act marked the first step toward Iraq's proclamation of a war (exclusion) zone on August 12, 1982, that extended up to 65 kilometers from Kharg Island, Iran's main oil terminal, in which ships were liable to attack. On November 25, 1983, Iraq again warned that all merchant vessels should avoid the "war zone" in the northern Gulf, or they would be subject to attack. On January 29, 1984, Iraq proclaimed one broad "exclusion zone" encompassing (ostensibly in addition to the northern end of the Gulf in the area of Bandar-e Khomeini) a 50-mile-radius section of the Gulf around Kharg Island.[4]

Iranian reaction came in May 1984, after Iraq had started air and missile attacks on Iran-bound neutral vessels. Iran retaliated by striking neutral shipping sailing to Kuwait and Saudi Arabia, setting ablaze a Saudi-flagged vessel in Saudi Arabia's territorial sea.[5] Iran also proclaimed an exclusion (war) zone in which merchant ships would be subject to visit and search and, if ultimately Iraq-bound, would be seized or attacked.

Attacks on neutral ships by both belligerents continued, not only in their respective zones but also beyond them. The war escalated in mid-1984 when Saudi aircraft shot down one or possibly two Iranian planes in Saudi airspace.[6] During that dangerous period at least 71 tankers and other merchant ships were attacked by sea and air, mostly by Iraq.[7] This tense situation prompted the United Nations Security Council to adopt two resolutions upholding freedom of navigation in the Gulf.[8]

In 1985 fewer than 50 attacks occurred on commercial shipping in the Gulf; a marked deterioration followed in 1986 and 1987 when 111 and 174 ships, respectively, were hit. In 1987 a serious escalation occurred in the Gulf war at sea. The Iranian navy received orders to fire missiles at any neutral ship bound for Kuwait. (Occasionally, Iranian warships did so even after having stopped a ship for visit in search of contraband according to the traditional rules.) Iran also laid mines in international shipping lanes in the Gulf, ostensibly to "defend its coastlines."[9] Although some ships were damaged by mines, the increasing hit-and-run raids by patrol boats manned by the Revolutionary Guards using rocket-propelled grenades were more dangerous.[10]

In response to Iranian attacks on neutral shipping, during 1987 France, Italy, Belgium, the United Kingdom, the United States, and the Soviet Union sent warships to the region to escort their respective shipping to neutral ports in the Gulf.[11] The U.S. Navy especially increased its profile following an apparently accidental attack in May 1987 by Iraqi missiles upon the destroyer *Stark*.[12] In July 1987 Kuwait transferred 11 oil tankers to the U.S. flag, thus obtaining the U.S. Navy's protection against attacks.[13] Nevertheless, one reflagged tanker, the *Bridgeton*, struck a mine near the Iranian island of Farsi on the first U.S. convoy to Kuwait.[14]

The U.S. Navy soon clashed with Iranian naval forces. In these hostilities Iranian boats and minelayers were sunk or captured, and unidentified vessels suspected of hostile intent were fired upon. A retaliatory strike was even undertaken in reprisal for an Iranian attack in Kuwaiti territorial waters on a reflagged tanker, the *Sea Isle City*, in October 1987, in which U.S. warships, after a warning, destroyed an Iranian military platform in the Gulf, but beyond Iran's territorial sea.[15]

During the resumed "War of the Cities" in early 1988, neutral shipping enjoyed a three-week lull from attacks. However, the tanker war soon resumed, and 96 ships were attacked prior to the cease-fire's entry into force on August 20, 1988. A final significant clash occurred in which the U.S. naval forces destroyed Iranian oil platforms and sank or severely damaged six Iranian warships.[16]

THE LAW OF MARITIME WARFARE

The laws of war at sea have confronted serious challenges during this century and have sometimes proved unrealistic and outdated given technological advancements and modern warfare. Yet a binding body of international law for maritime warfare still exists, dating back to the Declaration of Paris of 1856. The law of naval warfare[17] is principally constituted by six of the Hague Conventions of 1907: VI, VII, VIII, IX, X, and XI,[18] as well as Convention XIII Concerning the Rights and Duties of Neutral Powers in Naval Warfare. Convention X was revised and substantially enlarged by Geneva Convention II of 1949 for the Amelioration of the Condition of Wounded, Sick, and Shipwrecked Members of Armed Forces at Sea and subsequently complemented by some provisions of Protocol I of 1977. Finally, operations of submarines, surface warships, and also aircraft with respect to merchant vessels are, under the so-called London Protocol of 1936, still governed by Part IV (Article 22) of the 1930 Treaty of London for the limitation and reduction of naval armaments. Thus there exists no single instrument that comprehensively deals with the law of maritime warfare.

Neither Iran nor Iraq are parties to any of the Hague Conventions. They are, however, parties to the London Protocol of 1936, which reaffirms the validity of Part IV of the 1930 London Treaty dealing with operations against merchant vessels. They are also parties to the four Geneva "Red Cross" Conventions of 1949, including the convention governing protection of victims of war at sea.

The Hague Conventions are declaratory of customary law; as such, they bind belligerents in an armed conflict at sea, regardless of whether determination of aggression has been made by the U.N. Security Council. Of major importance are two general principles that govern maritime warfare: (1) considerations of humanity and respect for life as far as possible without unacceptable risk, and (2) respect for the rights of neutrals, with reasonable accommodation between conflicting rights and interests of the belligerents and neutrals.[19]

THE REGION AND THEATER OF WAR IN THE GULF

A distinction is sometimes made between "region" and "theater" of war.[20] The region of war is the area where belligerents might prepare and execute hostilities against each other. The theater of war is that part of the region of war where hostilities are actually taking place. The Gulf was the region of war in the Iraqi-Iranian naval hostilities and encompassed the internal waters and the territorial seas of the belligerents and the high seas, including the superjacent airspace of these zones. But according to the law of war and neutrality, excluded were waters and superjacent airspace of neutral states along the Gulf's littoral.[21]

Hostilities tended to concentrate around Kharg Island and along shipping lanes, but they also occurred elsewhere in the Gulf and in the Strait of Hormuz. Consequently, the distinction between a region and a theater of war virtually disappeared during the Gulf War, and the two zones became practically coextensive.

THE WAR (EXCLUSION) ZONES

Despite various terms used by belligerents to proclaim war zones, such zones retain a common purpose, namely, to control an area of sea and its superjacent airspace so as to limit neutrals' freedom of navigation by means less than those required for maintaining an effective blockade under traditional international law.[22] Both Iraq and Iran proclaimed war (exclusion) zones in the Gulf War. The strategic rationale for these zones soon evolved into economic warfare at sea. In their geographical location and specific purposes, however, the zones differed. As depicted on the War Zone map, Iraq's zone was actually established off Iran's northeast coast in the Gulf and clearly failed to qualify as a defense zone, which would have encompassed only waters off a proclaiming state's territory. Similarly, while the Iranian zone extended contiguous to Iran's coast, its rationale exceeded pure defense.

The primary objective of Iraq's exclusion zone was to halt Iran's exports, thus depriving Iran of revenues needed to purchase war material. Cutting Iran's maritime supply route might have been an additional objective. Iraq's zone was directed not only against Iranian tankers shuttling oil from Kharg Island, but also against neutral shipping. To enforce zone restrictions, Iraq relied primarily on its air force, though some mining was done in the narrow channel leading to Bandar Ma'shur and Bandar-e Khomeini and near Kharg Island.

War (Exclusion) Zones in the Gulf War

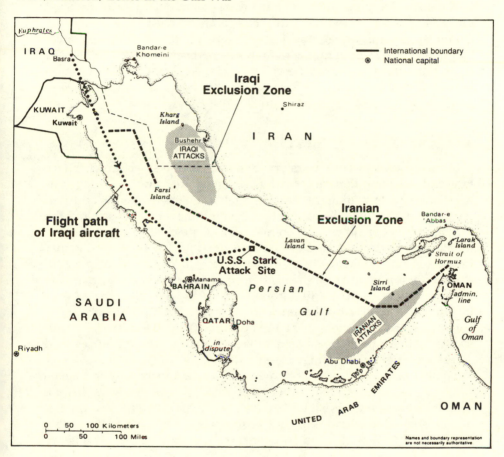

Source: U.S. Department of State, *U.S. Policy in the Persian Gulf*, Special Report No. 166, July 1987, p. 4.

The Iraqi zone could have been considered legitimate if Iraq had observed the requirement of "reasonableness," especially with regard to its treatment of neutral shipping. However, Iraq made no provisions for safe passage routes and showed no concern for safety of crews. To the extent that Iraq failed to observe the requirements of reasonableness, its zone was unlawful under international law.

The Iranian zone did not seriously impede free navigation through the Strait of Hormuz since neutral vessels were still able to transit it using Omani waters, where a traffic separation scheme was available. Under the circumstances, Iran's zone might be considered reasonable. Although vessels entering it without Iran's permission were threatened, few Iranian attacks occurred there; Iran's actions against neutral shipping remained concentrated mainly in Gulf waters outside Iran's exclusion zone.

ATTACKS ON ENEMY MERCHANT SHIPS

In naval warfare both warships and merchant vessels are primary targets. Under traditional international humanitarian law applied to maritime warfare, only military targets—that is, enemy warships and military aircraft on the high seas, or those within the territorial sea and the internal waters of either belligerent—may be attacked on sight. Enemy merchant vessels may be attacked and destroyed if they persistently refuse to stop or submit to visit and search following request by an enemy warship. A merchant ship attempting to evade or resist an enemy warship acts at its peril.[23] In addition, an enemy merchant vessel may be attacked and destroyed even without prior warning if it sails under convoy escorted by enemy warships or aircraft, or if it is armed offensively.[24] Attacks on enemy merchant vessels in other circumstances (and *a fortiori* on neutral shipping) are prohibited.

Traditional maritime warfare envisages special procedures and measures for dealing with enemy merchant ships. Belligerent warships are authorized the right of visit and search at sea, but not in neutral waters. A ship suspected of carrying contraband is to be taken into the belligerent's port for adjudication by a prize court. Only in case of military necessity may a seized ship be sunk, provided, however, that the crew, passengers, and ship's papers have first been safely removed. But prize proceedings must still follow to determine the lawfulness of a seizure and sinking.[25] Unfortunately, the prevalent practice during the two world wars demonstrated that seizure with all its formalities became the exception, and attacking and sinking enemy merchant vessels without warning and regard for the safety of passengers and crew was widespread. Both sides usually rationalized their actions on grounds of reprisals against illegal acts by the enemy.[26]

Assuming that the World War II practice resulted in customary international law, Iraq's on-sight attacks against Iranian-flagged vessels could be justified in Iraq's exclusion zone and beyond, in cases where the target ship was armed, sailed under convoy of Iranian warships or was escorted by Iranian military aircraft, or was otherwise integrated into Iran's war-sustaining effort (for example, by transporting oil that financed Iran's military operations). However, Iraq violated international humanitarian law when its air force failed to assist the rescue of survivors, for example, by communicating locations of attacks to those who could render direct assistance. With regard to Iran, nearly all its targets were neutral ships sailing to and from neutral ports in the Gulf.

THE LEGALITY OF WEAPONS AND METHODS OF WARFARE

Fundamental to international humanitarian law are restrictions on the right of belligerents to choose methods and weapons of warfare. Methods and weapons that cause superfluous injury or unnecessary suffering are prohibited. Another basic principle distinguishes between combatants and noncombatants and between military and nonmilitary objectives. Articles 49 and 57(4) of Protocol I of 1977 to the 1949 Conventions specifically apply this rule to sea warfare. Though neither Iran nor Iraq is party to the Protocol, they were bound to observe these general principles because they reflect customary international law.

Mines

One weapon potentially causing indiscriminate damage to neutral merchant shipping is mines.[27] The desire to protect neutral shipping against destruction by mines led to the adoption in 1907 of Hague Convention VIII concerning the laying of automatic submarine contact mines. The Convention, however, was largely disregarded in both world wars; moreover, modern mine technology (for example, acoustic and magnetic devices that explode without contact) has rendered obsolete the types of mines regulated by Convention VIII, to which neither Iran nor Iraq is a party. Yet the underlying general principles of Hague Convention VIII are still considered binding customary law. Every possible precaution must be taken for the security of peaceful shipping; mines must be made harmless within a limited time; and when a minefield is not under surveillance, notification of the danger zones must be made to shipowners and governments as soon as military exigencies permit. These principles were disregarded by Iran when, purportedly to defend its coastline, it laid mines in several international shipping channels.

International law permits a neutral country whose ships are put at risk by belligerent mines to take reasonable measures in self-defense. In 1987, after a U.S. helicopter had observed an Iranian craft, the *Iran Ajr*, engaging in nighttime mine laying in the Gulf near U.S. naval units, the United States had reason to believe that its ships were intended targets. Although strafed by U.S. helicopters, the Iranian boat resumed mining; in the engagement that followed, it was disabled and boarded by U.S. forces, who found nine mines on deck.[28] U.S. action against the Iranian craft engaged in mine laying may reasonably be regarded as legitimate self-defense and was justified accordingly by the United States. This legal position, however, did not go unchallenged.[29]

Early in the Gulf War Iraq also resorted to mine warfare. In 1982 it mined the channel near Bandar-e Khomeini, but it had announced the operation. Consequently, this action did not expose shipping to as great a risk as did Iran's secret mining operations in the more heavily trafficked southern Gulf and Strait of Hormuz. Still, five neutral ships were damaged by Iraqi mines.

Missiles

A major weapon used in the Gulf War, especially by Iraq, was the long-range guided missile. However, because they are relatively new as weapons technology, missiles are not yet regulated by specific rules of international law. They are, in principle, a legitimate weapon, but care must be exercised to use them in a way and in circumstances minimizing accidental risk to neutrals, especially in international shipping lanes. The ostensibly accidental missile attack on the U.S. frigate *Stark* by an Iraqi aircraft underscores the need to draft international-law rules to govern missile warfare at sea.

Neutrality and "Nonbelligerency"

Failure by the U.N. Security Council to designate the aggressor in the Gulf War made it possible for other states to assume the status of neutrality. The traditional law of neutrality, based on impartiality toward the belligerents, was codified at the Second Hague Conference in 1907 in two conventions: (1) Convention V Respecting the Rights and Duties of Neutral Powers and Persons in Case of War on Land; and (2) Convention XIII Concerning the Rights and Duties of Neutral Powers in Naval War.

Yet in actual practice traditional strict neutrality has given way to varied gradations of conduct by countries outside the conflict, ranging from meticulous impartiality to partiality to and support for a belligerent short of active participation in the hostilities. During World War II the term "nonbelligerency" emerged for this ill-defined halfway house between neutrality and war. In this status a nonbelligerent state would, without direct participation in the hostilities, give a belligerent financial and material support but still expect to enjoy traditional advantages of neutrality.

What nonbelligerency means in strict legal terms is unclear. While it lacks defined legal status, it is not without legal consequences. For example, a belligerent may claim that a "neutral" has forfeited its status of neutrality by giving assistance to the other belligerent; hence it cannot be entitled to benefits of neutral status. As far as the United Nations is concerned, the Security Council in considering the "situation" and later the "armed conflict" between Iran and Iraq was careful to use a generic phrase, "states that are not parties to the hostilities." But even this collective security organ deplored attacks on "neutral" ships in Resolution 598 of July 1987. It remains uncertain whether the term "neutral" was employed as a legal term referring to the traditional status of neutrality or was only a short generic expression.

Third-Country Policies

States not parties to the hostilities were eager to stress their neutrality in the Gulf War, but apparently no formal declarations of neutrality were made. The conduct of many "neutrals" in the war, however, more closely resembled nonbelligerency than neutrality.

The United States announced observance of "a strict and scrupulous attitude of neutrality" when the Gulf War broke out in September 1980.[30] Nonetheless, U.S. policy favored Iraq. For example, U.S. satellite information was made available to Iraq during 1985 and 1986.[31] Furthermore, the presence of U.S. military forces in the Gulf and the reflagging of Kuwaiti tankers brought the United States dangerously close to open armed conflict against Iraq's enemy.[32] The Soviet Union assiduously tried to appear neutral, but it was the principal supplier of war material to Iraq,[33] with which it has a friendship and cooperation agreement. China claimed to be "strictly neutral,"[34] but it was the largest supplier of weapons to Iran; in 1987 alone China provided Iran with as much as $1 billion worth of weapons, including Silkworm missiles shipped from North Korea.[35] France backed Iraq from the war's outset, furnishing it with credits and large quantities of munitions. The lease of Super Etendard aircraft and sale of Exocet missiles is well known.[36]

Although officially neutral, most Arab states, especially Jordan and Kuwait, strongly supported Iraq. Kuwait's role as the major transshipment point for cargo bound for Iraq seriously undercut its claim of neutrality. One must add, however, that Kuwait was obliged to assist Iraq in this way under a bilateral transit agreement entered into in 1972.

The traditional law of neutrality does not forbid private citizens and firms of neutral states from supplying war material or granting loans to a belligerent; only states are prohibited from assisting belligerents in this way. Under Article 7 of Hague Convention V, a neutral power is not required to prevent export or transit of arms or munitions to belligerents, implying that it is prohibited from delivering such materials itself. Article 6 of Hague Convention XIII expressly prohibits a neutral state from supplying belligerents with war material.

The distinction between state and private activity is obsolete in today's era of governmental control; consequently, a state asserting neutrality has the duty to take reasonable measures to prevent private persons from supplying war material and other assistance to belligerents.[37] It remains questionable whether a nonbelligerent (and not strictly neutral) state may assert traditional rights of neutrality vis-à-vis a belligerent against which it practices discrimination.

BELLIGERENTS AND RIGHTS OF NEUTRALS IN THE GULF WAR

The Neutral's Freedom of Navigation: The War (Exclusion) Zones

The law of war at sea holds that neutral ships may not be denied the right of navigation on the high seas and through international straits. This right, however, is not absolute and must be accommodated to legitimate defense exigencies of the belligerents and risks entailed by navigation in the locale of war. For example, neutral vessels and aircraft must accept certain restrictions for their own safety near the vicinity of naval operations established by a belligerent. Similarly, state practice accords belligerents the right to control movement of neutral shipping within defense zones, provided that such zones are publicized and neutral ships are not unduly put at risk. On the other hand, war (exclusion) zones are justifiable only if they are directed mainly against the enemy and do not unreasonably interfere with the neutrals' freedom of navigation in peaceful pursuit of commerce.

In practice, however, war (exclusion) zones have mainly infringed upon the rights of neutrals. During the two world wars (and also in the Gulf War), such zones allowed a belligerent to circumvent the strict traditional rules of lawful blockade and contraband control. In the Gulf War previous observations about the Iraqi and Iranian exclusion zones apply by analogy to the status of neutral shipping in these zones. Nonetheless, both Iran and Iraq attacked neutral shipping outside their designated exclusion zones and, in exceptional cases, even in the territorial waters of neutral states in the Gulf.

Treatment of Neutral Shipping

International humanitarian law protects all merchant ships, both enemy and neutral. The latter, however, enjoy special protection. Any hostilities against neutrals, including attacks on neutral ships, are considered acts of war, not merely breaches of neutrality.[38] An even more serious violation is armed attack on a neutral vessel or installation in the territorial waters of a neutral country. Under the Hague codification belligerents are obliged to respect neutral waters,[39] and in general, "the territory under the sovereignty of neutral Parties is inviolable" and must not become a theater of operations. Therefore, Iranian attacks on Kuwait's Sea Island terminal and on Saudi- and U.S.-flagged vessels in Saudi and Kuwaiti waters respectively violated international law. In such cases the neutral country—assuming that it really is neutral—has the right of self-defense, as Saudi Arabia did in 1984 when its air force responded to Iranian aerial intrusions in Saudi airspace.

A major difference exists between the legal status of enemy and neutral vessels. Whereas the former may be seized and captured as prize irrespective of their cargo or destination, neutral merchant vessels are not normally subject to capture as prize unless they refuse to stop or submit to visit and search, violate a blockade, carry contraband, or perform "unneutral service."[40] These rules governing treatment of neutral vessels were largely disregarded in the Gulf conflict, despite the Security Council's demand in 1984 that "there be no interference with shipping to and from countries not parties to the conflict."[41]

In the Gulf War vessels were simply attacked rather than subjected to traditional search, visit, and seizure procedures governing contraband control. Some commentators have held that the right of visit and search may be exercised even during the time of cease-fire or armistice until the conclusion of a peace treaty.[42] This was also Iran's position, as its navy stopped and searched a neutral vessel as late as December 1988.

No reliable data are available on the number of ships searched and cargo seized by Iran as contraband, that is, goods prohibited by a belligerent from reaching its enemy on grounds that they contribute to the conduct of war.[43] Since the traditional distinction between "absolute" contraband (that is, articles clearly of military character, such as weapons) and "conditional" or "relative" contraband (that is, articles such as food or fuel that can be used both for peaceful purposes and in the war effort) had collapsed by the end of World War I, nearly every item may be considered for wartime use. In practice, the Iranian navy could determine which particular articles should be treated as contraband;[44] in reality, most cargo removed by the Iranians from ships stopped and searched during the Gulf War probably could qualify as contraband. Many vessels were permitted to proceed after search. Furthermore, under the doctrine of continuous transportation, Iran retained the right to seize neutral goods as contraband going from one neutral port to another port if it determined that the goods had an ultimate enemy (that is, Iraqi) destination, either by sea transshipment or, in the case of the Kuwait-Iraq connection, by overland route.[45] It was in this context that the Iranian foreign minister asserted before the U.N. General Assembly in 1984 that "Iran will no longer tolerate the passage of vessels loaded with war munitions for the Iraqi regime through the Strait of Hormuz toward certain ports in the southern part of the Persian Gulf."[46] In fact, most vessels stopped and searched by the Iranian navy were in transit to Kuwait. However, political expedience sometimes overrode impartial treatment of neutral cargoes. It is known, for example, that Iranian warships allowed boatloads of Soviet arms, ultimately destined for Iraq, to continue on their way to Kuwait.[47]

It remains unclear whether either belligerent set up prize courts. Under traditional international law these courts have final authority to adjudicate the lawfulness of prizes, that is, captured neutral vessels suspected of carrying contraband or running a blockade. Failure to establish such courts is considered a breach of customary law for maritime warfare and neutrality. Nevertheless, attacks on merchant shipping— instead of the normal legal procedure of bringing the capture for adjudication—virtually eliminated the role of prize courts in the Gulf War. Whether and how neutrals will pursue claims for damage and loss of life in the conflict remains to be seen, but past experience points to the futility of such efforts, particularly since shipowners can recover claims from marine insurance under war-risks provisions.

A distinction is warranted between Iraqi and Iranian tanker attacks in the Gulf War. Most commentators agree that Iraqi attacks against neutral vessels—mostly tankers sailing to and from Iranian ports, both within and outside the proclaimed Iraqi exclusion zone—cannot be legitimized on grounds of being integrated into Iran's war-sustaining effort. Thus these attacks would not be acceptable under international law. The opposite view rationalizes the legality of such attacks by stretching the "unneutral service" concept to suggest that carrying Iran's oil exports incorporates a neutral ship into Iran's war effort. While allowance should be made for state practice in twentieth-century wars, it remains uncertain whether customary law has indeed eroded the neutrals' rights to such a degree. In one commentator's view Iraqi practice "touches the outer limits of legal acceptability and may well overstep the boundary."[48]

A compromise solution for this vexing legal problem appears more acceptable than more extreme views.[49] In this compromise approach Iraqi attacks on chartered shuttle tankers under neutral flags transporting Iranian oil from Kharg Island to points south are justifiable on the grounds that these vessels were performing unneutral service through integration into Iran's war-sustaining effort. The same applies to neutral vessels (wherever they were located) under Iranian military convoy or escort. Yet the concept of integration into the enemy's war effort must not be construed so extensively as to include other neutral tankers, specifically those that carried oil from points outside the Iraqi exclusion zone and over which Iran's control was limited purely to aspects of navigation.

Regarding Iranian attacks on neutral shipping, consensus exists that these attacks—most of which took place outside any proclaimed exclusion zone—could not be justified even under the most liberal interpretation of international law. The proper choice for Iran to follow was the traditional procedure of visit and search, which the Iranian navy did institute but often exceeded by resorting to strikes against neutral shipping on sight, even after conducting visit and search.

Might the Iranian attacks be defended as legitimate reprisals? As a belligerent, Iran retained the right to take belligerent reprisals—that is, to retaliate against the enemy for acts of warfare committed in violation of the law of war, in order to enforce future compliance with recognized rules of this law.[50] If Iranian attacks on neutral shipping were treated as belligerent reprisals, then they were certainly unlawful. These attacks were directed against neutrals and not Iraq, the perpetrator originally violating the laws of war. While Iran may have had legal grounds to retaliate against Iraq for its illegal attacks in waters off Iran, it did not have any lawful right to apply belligerent reprisals against neutrals.

Rationalizing attacks on neutral shipping or territory as legitimate reprisals short of war is also untenable on legal grounds; armed reprisals are illegal in contemporary international law since they violate the U.N. Charter's prohibition on the use of force. But even assuming lawfulness of such retaliation, reprisals must meet three conditions: There must have been an illegal act by the offending state; an unsatisfied demand for redress must have been made; and the reprisals must be reasonably proportionate to the injury suffered.

The legal relationship between Iran and neutral countries was complicated by the need to differentiate between impartial, traditionally neutral states and partial, "nonbelligerent" neutrals. While a vast majority of countries whose ships became targets of Iranian attacks could be regarded as bona fide neutrals, some, particularly Kuwait, were not strictly neutral. They were clearly partial to Iraq and subsidized its war effort with billions of dollars worth of munitions. The question therefore arises: Did Iran have the right to disregard Kuwait's claim to neutrality, or to interpret Kuwait's partiality as an implied waiver of claim to protective neutral status under the traditional law of neutrality? Could Iran then regard Kuwait (or any other state in similar circumstances) as a participant in the conflict with all the attendant legal consequences?[51]

When the "tanker war" began, Iran alluded to this situation in a letter to the U.N. Security-General in which it referred to "some States in the area and beyond" that "pour extensive financial and material resources into Iraq, . . . and yet they wish to remain secure from the consequences of their obvious backing of the aggressor Iraq."[52] The danger here is that an aggrieved belligerent might find its patience exhausted and resort to armed self-help that is rationalized as self-defense against aggression.

Neutral Convoys

Several states, including the United States and the Soviet Union, sent warships to the Gulf to provide armed escort for their respective flag vessels. This situation raises the issue concerning the legal status of neutral convoys in maritime warfare.[53] The right of a neutral state to convoy its merchant ships and defend them against illegal attacks has historically been recognized, but whether the right of visit and search may be exercised on neutral vessels under convoy of neutral warships of the same nationality "remains an unsettled matter in State practice."[54] Most naval powers, although not Great Britain, have recognized the so-called "right of convoy" whereby neutral merchant vessels under national convoy are exempt from search if the convoy commander declares that no contraband is on board the convoyed vessels. During both world wars, however, Great Britain insisted upon the right to carry out visit and search of neutral merchant vessels under the convoy of their warships. In the Gulf War France and the United States opposed Iranian visits and searches. The United Kingdom recognized Iran's right to such procedures, but only on the basis of self-defense and not on grounds of belligerent rights.[55] The United States asserted that the vessels under its convoy carried no contraband.[56]

Neutral vessels under convoy of a belligerent's warships are subject to different rules. Under the law of maritime warfare, acceptance by a neutral ship of a belligerent's protection in this manner results in the neutral ship acquiring enemy character and consequent liability to capture.[57]

CONCLUSION

The Iran-Iraq War pointed out how significantly new circumstances had modified traditional rules of maritime warfare and neutrality. The Gulf conflict also underscored the danger of belligerents taking advantage of uncertainties and gaps between law and state practice.

Almost from the beginning of the Iran-Iraq War military operations in the Gulf concentrated on economic warfare at sea, and neutral shipping became the primary target. As international attention focused on the tanker war in the Gulf, the war confirmed that far from being obsolete, the concept of neutrality was very much alive. The rights of neutral nations to free navigation and peaceful commerce were constantly invoked and emphasized even by the U.N. Security Council. They were regrettably disregarded in large part by the belligerents. It was ironic to hear the Iraqi delegate at the U.N. General Assembly debate accuse Iran of understanding the rules of international law and free navigation "only in so far as they serve its military objectives."[58] Precisely the same charge could be applied to Iraq.

Apart from neutral rights in maritime warfare, the Gulf War also raised questions about the substantive content of neutrality policy, specifically, the duties of neutrals. It is common knowledge that many neutrals in the Iran-Iraq War ignored the requirement of impartiality and, in favoring one belligerent with military and other supplies, pursued a policy of "nonbelligerency" rather than strict neutrality. This situation generated serious repercussions, especially for the relations between Iran and Kuwait.

These questions highlighted by the Gulf War suggest the need to review, revise, and possibly recodify the law of war at sea and the related law of maritime neutrality. The need exists to adapt this law to contemporary conditions. Issues such as war (exclusion) zones, employment of air power against shipping, the use of new weapons (for example, guided missiles), and the boundaries of permissible belligerent measures against neutral vessels "integrated" into the enemy's war-sustaining effort stand out as key subjects for such an undertaking. However, compliance with the laws of war at sea will ultimately depend on the wartime objectives, national interests, and good will of the belligerents.

NOTES

1. See Maxwell Jenkins, "Air Attacks on Neutral Shipping in the Persian Gulf: The Legality of the Iraqi Exclusion Zone and Iranian Reprisals," *Boston College International and Comparative Law Review* 8 (1985): 517–49; Thomas S. Schiller, "The Gulf War and Shipping: Recent Developments," in Brian A. H. Parritt, ed., *Violence at Sea* (Paris: ICC, 1986), pp. 109–27; Rainer Lagoni, "Gewaltverbot, Seekriegsrecht, und Schiffahrtsfreiheit im Golfkrieg," in Walther Fürst, Roman Herzog, and Dieter Umbach, eds., *Festschrift für Wolfgang Zeidler* (Berlin: W. de Gruyter, 1987), pp. 1833–67.

2. Efraim Karsh, *The Iran-Iraq War: A Military Analysis*, Adelphi Papers 220 (London: International Institute for Strategic Studies, Spring 1987), pp. 40–41.

3. Henry Degenhardt, *Maritime Affairs—A World Handbook* (Harlow, Essex: Longman, 1985), p. 235.

4. Karsh, *Iran-Iraq War*, p. 29.

5. Degenhardt, *Maritime Affairs*, p. 236.

6. *Britannica Book of the Year, 1985*, p. 494.

7. For ships attacked through July 13, 1986, see appendix 2, "Chronology of Attacks—Gulf War and Terrorist," in *Violence at Sea*, pp. 242–56. The U.N. secretary-general asked governments to provide information on incidents. At least 13 countries responded, and 6 of them (Greece, Kuwait, Japan, Switzerland, Turkey, and the United Kingdom) provided specific details on incidents involving rockets, missiles, mines, and bomb attacks, as well as death and injury to crews and passengers and damage to vessels under their respective flags. See U.N. Document S/16877 and Addendum 1, reported in *UN Chronicles* 22, no. 1 (1985): 14. Attacks were also made on ships registered in Australia, the Bahamas, Belgium, China, Cyprus, Denmark, Federal Republic of Germany, India, Italy, Liberia, Malta, Maldive Islands, Norway, Pakistan, Panama, Philippines, Poland, Romania, Saudi Arabia, Singapore, South Korea, Spain, Sri Lanka, Syria, the United States, and the Soviet Union.

8. See U.N. Security Council Resolutions 540 (October 31, 1983) and 552 (June 1, 1984). The former affirmed the right of free navigation and commerce in the region of the Gulf. The latter was prompted by a letter to the Security Council from the Gulf Cooperation Council (GCC) that complained of attacks on neutral shipping plying the Gulf to and from Kuwait and Saudi Arabia. Resolution 552 condemned such attacks, demanded that there be no interference with shipping to and from countries not parties to the conflict, and called upon all states to respect the right of free navigation and the territorial integrity of nonbelligerents.

9. *Christian Science Monitor*, October 20, 1987, p. 32.

10. Such lightly armed speedboats attacked with rocket-propelled grenades a Singapore-registered tanker, the *Norman Atlantic*, which became the first ship sunk in an Iranian raid. All 33 crew members were rescued, however. *Christian Science Monitor*, December 10, 1987, p. 12.

11. In early 1988 the United States had approximately 30 warships in the area, about the same number as West European and Soviet naval units. *New York Times*, January 8, 1988, p. 3. The Soviet Union provided naval escort for its merchant ships after an Iranian warship had stopped and searched a Soviet arms carrier in September 1986. R. K. Ramazani, "The Iran-Iraq War and the Persian Gulf Crisis," *Current History* 87 (February 1988): 61, 86.

12. "U.S.S. Stark Hit by Iraqi Missiles," *Department of State Bulletin* 87 (July 1987): 58.

13. See Michael Armacost, "U.S. Policy in the Persian Gulf and Kuwaiti Reflagging," *Department of State Bulletin* 87 (August 1987): 78. The United States did not protect American-owned vessels under foreign flags. *New York Times*, January 10, 1988, p. 3.

14. Ramazani, "Iran-Iraq War," p. 86.

15. "U.S. Response to Iranian Attacks," *Department of State Bulletin* 87 (December 1987): 74. The United States justified this action as self-defense under Article 51 of the U.N. Charter.

16. See *New York Times*, April 15, 1988, p. 3, and "How to Waste a Navy," *Economist*, April 23, 1988, pp. 41–42.

17. See L. Oppenheim, in H. Lauterpacht, ed., *International Law: A Treatise*, vol. 2, 7th ed. (London: Longmans, Green, 1952), pp. 457–515; C. John Colombos, *The International Law of the Sea* (London: Longmans, Green, 1967),

pp. 477–853; R. Tucker, *The Law of War and Neutrality at Sea*, U.S. Naval War College, International Law Studies (1957); Marjorie Whiteman, ed., *Digest of International Law*, vol. 10 (Washington, D.C.: Government Printing Office, 1968), pp. 599–790; D. P. O'Connell, in I. A. Shearer, ed., *The International Law of the Sea*, vol. 2 (1984), pp. 1094–1140; and R. L. Bledsoe and B. A. Boczek, *The International Law Dictionary* (Santa Barbara, Calif.: ABC-Clio, 1987), pp. 347–405.

18. Convention VI Relating to the Status of Enemy Merchant Ships at the Outbreak of Hostilities; Convention VII Relative to the Conversion of Merchant Ships into Warships; Convention VIII Relative to the Laying of Automatic Submarine Contact Mines; Convention IX Respecting Bombardment by Naval Forces in Time of War; Convention X (replacing a convention of 1899) for the Adaptation to Maritime Warfare of the Principles of the Geneva (1906) Convention; and Convention XI Relative to Certain Restrictions with Regard to the Exercise of the Right of Capture in Naval War. See Bledsoe and Boczek, *International Law Dictionary*, pp. 376–77.

19. Whiteman, *Digest*, Vol. 10, pp. 791–95.

20. See Oppenheim, *International Law*, vol. 2, p. 237.

21. Kuwait, Oman, and Saudi Arabia claim 12 miles. The United Arab Emirates and Bahrain claim only 3 miles. U.N. Office for Ocean Affairs and the Law of the Sea, *Law of the Sea Bulletin*, March 1985, pp. ii–iv.

22. See W. J. Fenrick, "The Exclusion Zone Device in the Law of Naval Warfare," *Canadian Yearbook of International Law* 24 (1986): 91–126; Ross Leckow, "The Iran-Iraq Conflict in the Gulf: The Law of War Zones," *International and Comparative Law Quarterly* 37 (1988): 629–44.

23. Oppenheim, *International Law*, vol. 2, pp. 465–66.

24. International Military Tribunal, *Trial of the Major War Criminals*, vol. 1 (Nuremberg, Germany, 1947), 310, 313, cited in Whiteman, *Digest*, vol. 10, pp. 647–49.

25. Oppenheim, *International Law*, vol. 2, pp. 481–97.

26. Whiteman, *Digest*, vol. 10, p. 65.

27. On the legal status of mines, see J. J. Reed, "'Damn the Torpedoes': International Standards Regarding the Use of Automatic Submarine Mines," *Fordham Law Journal* 8 (1985): 286–322; A. G. Y. Thorpe, "Mine Warfare at Sea—Some Legal Aspects of the Future," *Ocean Development and International Law* 18 (1987): 255–78.

28. "Letter of President Reagan to Congress," September 24, 1987, *Department of State Bulletin* 87 (November 1987): 44.

29. See Alfred Rubin, "The U.S. Is Not the Mine-Sheriff of the Gulf," *Christian Science Monitor*, October 5, 1987.

30. Statement of U.S. delegate at the Meeting of the Security Council, *UN Chronicle* 17, no. 9 (November 1980): 7.

31. Ralph King, *The Iran-Iraq War: The Political Implications*, Adelphi Papers 219 (London: International Institute for Strategic Studies, 1987), p. 54.

32. Former President Carter believed that by its naval presence in the Gulf, the United States was acting "in fact as a belligerent." Ramazani, "Iran-Iraq War," p. 86.

33. King, *Iran-Iraq War*, pp. 49–50.

34. Statement of the Chinese delegate in the Security Council debate on Resolution 598, *UN Chronicle* 24, no. 4 (November 1987): 21.

35. *New York Times*, March 13, 1988, p. 7.

36. King, *Iran-Iraq War*, pp. 55–56.

37. Wolfgang Friedmann, *The Changing Structure of International Law* (New York: Columbia University Press, 1964), pp. 346–48.

38. Oppenheim, *International Law*, vol. 2, p. 685.

39. Hague Convention XIII, Articles 2 and 3.

40. "Unneutral service" is any act or conduct by a neutral vessel that furthers the interest of the enemy, such as operating under charter to the enemy or transporting enemy armed forces. In serious cases of "unneutral service," the neutral vessel may be captured and condemned according to prize law, but under general principles of international humanitarian law, it cannot be sunk. Oppenheim, *International Law*, vol. 2, pp. 831–46.

41. U.N. Security Council Resolution 552 (October 4, 1982).

42. Oppenheim, *International Law*, vol. 2, pp. 848–49.

43. A list of neutral ships stopped and searched by the Iranian navy, based on Lloyd's List and Lloyd's Casualty Report, is compiled in Schiller, "Gulf War and Shipping," pp. 114–18.

44. See Oppenheim, *International Law*, vol. 2, pp. 799–813.

45. Ibid., vol. 2, pp. 818–19; Colombos, *International Law of the Sea*, pp. 680–86.

46. *UN Chronicle*, Special Supplement, March 1984, p. 1.

47. Ramazani, "Iran-Iraq War," p. 86.

48. Fenrick, "Exclusion Zone Device," p. 121.

49. Lagoni, "Gewaltverbot," pp. 1856–57.

50. Oppenheim, *International Law*, vol. 2, pp. 561–65.

51. In September 1985 Iran stated that it considered Kuwait to be a belligerent. Schiller, "Gulf War and Shipping," p. 115.

52. Letter of May 25, 1984, United Nations Document S/16585. See *UN Chronicle* 21, no. 5 (1984): 5.

53. See Oppenheim, *International Law*, vol. 2, pp. 849–51, 858–59.

54. U.S. Department of the Navy, *Law of Naval Warfare*, cited in Whiteman, *Digest*, vol. 11, pp. 37–38.

55. Leckow, "Iran-Iraq Conflict," p. 638.

56. "U.S. Policy in the Persian Gulf," *Department of State Bulletin* 87 (October 1987): 39.

57. Colombos, *International Law of the Sea*, pp. 710–11.

58. *UN Chronicle* 22, no. 10/11 (November/December 1985): 52.

12

The Role of the United Nations in the Iran-Iraq War

Anthony Clark Arend

During the eight years that it lasted, the Iran-Iraq War inflicted incredible destruction on both sides.[1] Estimates indicate that somewhere between 420,000 and 1 million lives were lost in the conflict, and thousands more were injured.[2] Indeed, during the conflict some of the worst horrors of war occurred—civilian populations were targeted, chemical weapons were used in violation of the 1925 Geneva Gas Protocol, and neutral shipping in the Persian Gulf was attacked.

Throughout this bloody conflict the United Nations attempted repeatedly to bring an end to the fighting. No less than nine Security Council resolutions were passed between 1980 and 1988 calling upon the parties to stop the Gulf War. Two secretaries-general, Kurt Waldheim and Javier Perez de Cuellar, offered their good offices to the belligerents. But all efforts were futile until July 1988, when Iran accepted Security Council Resolution 598 and agreed to a cease-fire. On August 20 the cease-fire was finally put into effect, and the United Nations was universally praised for its accomplishment.

The purpose of this chapter is to explore the role played by the United Nations in the Iran-Iraq War. To do this, the study first examines actions by the United Nations during the war. It then evaluates the United Nations' role in the Gulf conflict, with a view toward assessing the implications for the organization and distilling lessons about the effectiveness of the United Nations in resolving regional disputes.

U.N. ACTIONS DURING THE WAR

To appreciate the role played by the United Nations in the Gulf War, it is useful to divide the conflict into three phases. Phase one encompasses the period from the beginning of the war in 1980 through early July 1988. Phase two begins in July 1988, when Iran agreed to a cease-fire, and ends on August 20, 1988, when the cease-fire began. Phase three then runs from August 20, 1988, through the present.

Phase One (September 22, 1980–July 16, 1988)

During the first phase of the war the United Nations was involved in two major activities. First and foremost, it engaged in efforts to persuade the parties to cease hostilities and to settle their dispute peacefully. Second, the United Nations was involved in investigating and policing violations of the laws of war that were reported to it.

When the fighting began on September 22, 1980, the organization responded quickly. Secretary-General Kurt Waldheim immediately offered his good offices to both parties. In a letter to the presidents of each state, he called upon each government to "heed the appeals addressed to you with a view to ending the bloodshed and destruction immediately, and to avail yourself of the various good offices which have been offered with a view to assisting the two Governments to settle their differences by peaceful means."[3] On September 28 the Security Council adopted Resolution 479.[4] In this resolution the Council called upon "Iran and Iraq to refrain immediately from the further use of force and to settle their dispute by peaceful means and in conformity with principles of justice and international law." It further urged the parties "to accept an appropriate offer of mediation or conciliation or to resort to regional agencies or arrangements or other peaceful means of their own choice that would facilitate the fulfillment of their Charter obligations." Finally, the Council expressed support for the efforts of the Secretary-General directed toward bringing about a settlement of the dispute.

These initial U.N. actions are quite revealing. They demonstrate a clear reluctance on the part of the organization to serve as a collective security body. Under the theory of limited collective security that undergirds Chapter VII of the U.N. Charter, when there is a threat to the peace, breach of the peace, or act of aggression, the Security Council is to investigate the matter, determine the guilty party, and order appropriate enforcement measures. Here, as in numerous instances in the past,[5] the Council declined to take that course of action. It did not characterize the situation as a threat to the peace, breach of the peace, or act of aggression, nor did it claim to be acting under authority granted by Chapter VII. Instead, the Security Council called upon both sides to end the fighting and to avail themselves of the various means available for the peaceful settlement of the dispute.[6]

As the fighting wore on, the United Nations continued to prefer the role of mediator to that of judge or enforcer. In November 1980 Waldheim appointed former Swedish Prime Minister Olof Palme as his personal representative in the mediation effort. In that capacity Palme made numerous trips to the area to meet with Iranian and Iraqi officials. During these talks he outlined various U.N. plans for a cease-fire and troop withdrawals. Unfortunately, Palme's efforts were largely unsuccessful. They may have facilitated some exchanges of prisoners of war and aided in the release of certain foreign ships that had been trapped in the Shatt al-Arab at the beginning of the war,[7] but they did not induce the parties to accept a cease-fire. During the early months of the war Iraq clearly held the advantage. It had seized considerable Iranian territory and was reluctant to stop a war it seemed to be winning.[8] In a slightly different vein, Iran had converted the war into a religious mission against Saddam Hussein and was also unwilling to stop.[9]

In December 1981 the United Nations underwent a change of leadership when Javier Perez de Cuellar was elected Secretary-General. The organization's predominant role in the Iran-Iraq War, however, remained largely the same. Several more Security Council resolutions were adopted to deal with the conflict.[10] All these resolutions, while addressing new issues, followed the same basic approach to ending the war as had Resolution 479. They reminded the parties of their obligations to settle their disputes peacefully and to refrain from the use of force and then called upon both Iran and Iraq to institute a cease-fire. They went beyond Resolution 479 by calling for a withdrawal to "internationally recognized borders." They thus expressed a desire for a return to the pre–September 1980 boundaries. None of the resolutions, however, characterized the situation as falling under Chapter VII of the Charter, nor did any attempt to assess responsibility for starting the war.

In 1987 U.N. efforts to settle the conflict underwent a slight change. In January Perez de Cuellar held a press conference and called for a new approach to ending the Iran-Iraq War. Specifically, he called upon the Security Council, and the permanent members in particular, to make a special concerted effort to resolve the conflict.[11] In February 1987 the permanent members began working jointly to formulate a framework for settling the conflict. The fruit of this effort was Security Council Resolution 598, which was adopted unanimously on July 20, 1987.[12]

Resolution 598, while building upon previous resolutions, went further. Finally, the U.N. Security Council assumed the role of a collective security body, albeit in very circumscribed fashion. In pertinent part, this resolution provided:

The Security Council,

. . .

Determining that there exists a breach of the peace as regards the conflict between Iran and Iraq.

Acting under Articles 39 and 40 of the Charter.

1. *Demands* that, as a first step towards a negotiated settlement, the Islamic Republic of Iran and Iraq observe an immediate cease-fire, discontinue all military actions on land, at sea and in the air, and withdraw all forces to the internationally recognized boundaries without delay;

2. *Requests* the Secretary-General to dispatch a team of United Nations observers to verify, confirm and supervise the cease-fire and withdrawal and further requests the Secretary-General to make the necessary arrangements in consultation with the Parties and to submit a report thereon to the Security Council;

. . .

4. *Calls upon* Iran and Iraq to co-operate with the Secretary-General in implementing this resolution and in mediation efforts to achieve a comprehensive, just and honourable settlement, acceptable to both sides, of all outstanding issues, in accordance with the principles contained in the Charter of the United Nations;

. . .

6. *Requests* the Secretary-General to explore, in consultation with Iran and Iraq, the question of entrusting an impartial body with inquiring into responsibility for the conflict and to report to the Council as soon as possible;

. . .

8. *Further requests* the Secretary-General to examine, in consultation with Iran and Iraq and with other States of the region, measures to enhance the security and stability of the region.

This resolution was quite significant for several reasons. First, it represented the first time that the Security Council declared that there had been a "breach of the peace" and that it was acting under Articles 39 and 40 of the Charter, the provisions of Chapter VII dealing with the collective security function of the organization. Second, it marked the first time that the Council had expressed a concern to determine "responsibility" for the initiation of the war. In this case the resolution suggested the use of an "impartial" body to make that determination. Presumably, this provision was included in the resolution to appeal to

Iran. Since the beginning of the conflict Iran had argued that the war had been started by Iraq and that, consequently, any cease-fire would have to be preceded by a determination that Iraq was the aggressor.[13] Third, Resolution 598 used language that was much stronger than that contained in previous resolutions. It "demanded" a cease-fire and a withdrawal to internationally recognized borders "without delay." Fourth, the resolution specifically called for the establishment of a U.N. observer group to monitor the cease-fire. Fifth, it stressed the need to work closely with both parties to resolve all issues and reach a settlement that would be acceptable by both states. In other words, while the resolution was more concerned about assessing blame for the conflict than were previous resolutions, it still emphasized the need for the agreement of both parties to resolve the conflict ultimately. In short, Resolution 598 contained elements of collective security, but they remained muted, presumably to guard against either side believing that the United Nations was biased in either direction.

Resolution 598 is also significant because it was the product of great-power cooperation. It represented an effort by the permanent members to come to grips with the conflict. Hence the resolution indicated a unity on the issue that previously did not exist. Backed by this support, the resolution held more sway than previous decisions by the Council.

Following the adoption of Resolution 598, the Secretary-General began his effort to secure its acceptance by the parties. On August 14, 1987, Iraq notified Perez de Cuellar that it was prepared to accept the resolution, but no such response came from Iran. In early September 1987 the Secretary-General visited Tehran and Baghdad, where he presented an outline of his "implementation plan" to the two sides.[14] He subsequently obtained the support of the permanent members of the Council for this plan and met on October 9, 1987, with them to discuss strategy for implementing Resolution 598. Following this, on October 15 Perez de Cuellar presented a finalized implementation plan to the foreign ministers of Iran and Iraq.[15]

Throughout the rest of 1987 and into the first half of 1988, the Secretary-General continued to press Iran and Iraq to accept the U.N. proposal. Iraq was generally receptive to a cease-fire, but Iran remained unresponsive. Iran's reluctance to agree to a cease-fire was probably due to its perception that it was in a better military position than Iraq. Since 1982 Iran had been on the offensive. Despite heavy personnel and economic losses, until mid–1988 Iran seemed to be winning the land war by attrition.[16] This belief, together with its revolutionary fervor, may have convinced Iran's leaders that it could defeat the Iraqis on its own terms. To accept a U.N.-sponsored cease-fire at that point would have prevented Iran from reaching this goal.

While the United Nations was attempting to end the conflict, it also found itself playing another role—that of an investigator. During the war the organization was called upon several times to investigate alleged violations of the laws of armed conflict, the *jus in bello*. Specifically, the United Nations was asked to investigate four types of violations: attacks on civilian populations, use of poisonous gas, abuses of prisoners of war, and interference with neutral shipping.

The first request to investigate attacks on civilians came in October 1982, when Iran asked the Secretary-General to send a fact-finding mission to examine civilian areas in Iran that had allegedly been attacked. The following year such a mission was in fact undertaken, and on June 20, 1983, Perez de Cuellar concluded that there had been major damage to civilian areas in Iran and some damage to certain areas in Iraq.[17] On October 31, 1983, the Security Council condemned "all violations of international humanitarian law, in particular, the provisions of the Geneva Conventions of 1949 in all their aspects" and called "for the immediate cessation of all military operations against civilian targets, including city and residential areas."[18] The organization continued to investigate complaints about the use of force against civilians. Finally, on June 11, 1984, in response to a mission by the Secretary-General to the area, Iran and Iraq agreed to stop targeting civilian populations.[19] U.N. inspectors were subsequently dispatched to verify the agreement. Unfortunately, the agreement did not hold, and what came to be known as the "war of the cities" flared up several more times before July 1988.[20]

A second violation of international humanitarian law that the United Nations was asked to investigate concerned the use of poisonous gas. In March 1984 a U.N. mission was sent to investigate the alleged use by Iraq of gas. Following the report of the mission, the President of the Security Council stated that the Council "strongly condemn[s] the use of chemical weapons reported by the mission of specialists." According to subsequent visits by experts to the area, one as late as July 1988, the use of gas continued. On two other occasions the Security Council formally condemned the use of chemical weapons.[21] Iraq, however, continued to use gas into 1988.

A third potential violation of the laws of war that the United Nations investigated was alleged abuses to prisoners of war. As early as June 1983 Iraq asked the organization to investigate the treatment of prisoners of war. Consultations were held with the International Committee of the Red Cross, and eventually, in January 1985, U.N. missions were sent to Iran and Iraq. On February 22 the missions reported that there were no major abuses of prisoners of war in either country.[22]

A final problem the organization was asked to examine pertained to alleged attacks on neutral shipping in the Persian Gulf. In the spring of 1984 the Gulf Cooperation Council brought the issue to the Security Council. On June 1, 1984, the Council adopted Resolution 552, which called upon states to respect the rights of neutral ships in the Gulf. Unfortunately, attacks on neutral shipping continued. As late as July 1987 the Council noted again that it deplored "attacks on neutral shipping or civilian aircraft."[23] On August 10, 1988, the *New York Times* reported that approximately 600 ships had been attacked; of those, about 90 had been completely destroyed.[24]

In sum, during the initial phase of the conflict the United Nations was occupied with two major tasks: (1) attempting to end the conflict and (2) investigating violations of the *jus in bello*. In the first task the performance of the organization was less than effective. The Security Council's actions and the noble efforts of the Secretary-General did not bring an end to the war or induce the parties to settle their differences peacefully. The parties, or at least one party, remained content to pursue political goals through use of military force, and the organization was unable to convince them otherwise. Importantly, however, the United Nations did establish a framework for dealing with the conflict that came to be quite useful in the second phase of the war. Among other things, the Secretary-General's concerted work with the permanent members of the Council would be crucial in the phase that followed.

As an investigator the United Nations fared only slightly better. By exposing the attacks on civilian population centers, the organization may have limited further attacks for at least a season. It was not, however, very successful in preventing attacks on neutral shipping or use of chemical weapons. The United Nations did focus world attention on these issues and seems to have generated a nearly universal desire to take new steps to control chemical weapons.[25]

Phase Two (July 17, 1988–August 20, 1988)

The United Nations' role in the Iran-Iraq War underwent a dramatic change on July 17, 1988, when Iranian President Seyed Ali Khamene'i sent a letter to Secretary-General Perez de Cuellar indicating Iran's willingness to accept Security Council Resolution 598 as a framework for ending the war. In his letter Khamene'i explained that "the fire of the war which was started by the Iraqi regime on 22 September 1980 through an aggression against the territorial integrity of the Islamic Republic of Iran has now gained unprecedented dimensions, bringing other countries into the war and even engulfing innocent civilians."[26] He then went on to praise the efforts of the Secretary-General to obtain the implementation of Resolution 598 and concluded that "we have decided to officially declare that the Islamic Republic of Iran—because of the importance it attaches to saving lives of human beings and the establishment of justice and regional and international peace and security— accepts Security Council Resolution 598." Ayatollah Khomeini later confirmed Iran's acceptance of Resolution 598, saying it was like swallowing "poison."[27] Now the United Nations assumed two roles. On the one hand, it became an instrument for instituting a cease-fire; on the other, it became a mechanism for establishing a peacekeeping force.

As Perez de Cuellar began U.N. efforts to secure a cease-fire, he was immediately confronted with a serious problem: Iraq remained reluctant to accept the Iranian position. In a radio commentary reported in the *New York Times*, an Iraqi official explained that "we are duty bound to be vigilant and cautious until a clear-cut agreement is reached between Iraq and Iran on peace in its full details."[28] A few days later Iraq added a new precondition for a cease-fire: direct negotiations with Iran. Iraqi Foreign Minister Tariq Aziz explained on July 27 that "we believe the first step for constructive work is face-to-face negotiations between the two parties under the auspices of the U.N. secretary general [sic]."[29] He went on to say that "if the Iranians do not accept the formula, that means they are not sincere about peace."[30] As separate talks between the Secretary-General and the foreign ministers continued, Iraq remained firm. One of Iraq's concerns presumed that the cease-fire would allow Iran a hiatus during which it could prepare for further fighting. Iraq wanted direct talks so that it could probe Iran's motivation for accepting Resolution 598.[31] Another concern may have been that Iraq believed that direct talks "would signal Iran's recognition of the legitimacy of the Iraqi Government,"[32] something that Khomeini had consistently refused to do.

Confronted with Iraqi intransigence, Perez de Cuellar took the rather bold step of stating that he would set a firm date for a cease-fire irrespective of Iraq's unwillingness. On August 1, 1988, after the return of a preliminary military mission sent to the area, he decided to set a date for the cease-fire.[33] Moreover, he made it clear that the establishment of that date was not contingent upon agreement by the parties. Since Security Council Resolution 598 is binding on all members of the United Nations, the Secretary-General could assert it as legal authority for ordering the parties to institute a cease-fire.[34] But after the Secretary-General's statement, Iraq's position seemed unchanged. Demanding "face-to-face talks," Iraqi spokesman Riyadh al-Qaysi asserted that Iraq would "not accept a fait accompli, no matter from which quarter it comes."[35]

Despite this apparent rebuff to the United Nations, Perez de Cuellar remained undaunted in his efforts to stop the war. The Secretary-General requested that the Security Council exert its influence to resolve Iraq's demand for "face-to-face talks with Iran."[36] In particular, he appealed to the five permanent members of the Council. He also attempted to negotiate an agreement whereby the Security Council would offer guarantees to Iraq to ensure its security. Following Perez de Cuellar's lead, the permanent members gave assurances to both sides that they would take action if necessary to see that a cease-fire, once established, was maintained.[37] They also suggested that direct talks could begin pending establishment of such a cease-fire.

All this action coordinated by the Secretary-General bore fruit. On August 6, 1988, Saddam Hussein sent a letter to Perez de Cuellar in which he agreed to a cease-fire prior to direct talks. His only condition was that Iran "declare, clearly, unequivocally and officially, its agreement to enter into direct negotiations with us, in appreciation of this initiative, immediately after the cease-fire."[38] On the following day Iranian Foreign Minister Ali Akbar Velayati assured the Secretary-General that Iran would accept this agreement—cease-fire, then direct talks. With this acceptance by both parties, Perez de Cuellar decided that the cease-fire would begin on August 20, 1988, and set August 25 as the date for the first round of talks under U.N. auspices.

The next task for the United Nations was the establishment of a peace-keeping force to monitor the cease-fire. Preliminary efforts had already begun with the technical team under the leadership of Lieutenant General Martin Vadset of Norway, Chief of Staff of the United Nations Truce Supervisory Organization (UNTSO), that had visited the area in July 1988. Based on information gained from this team, the Secretary-General presented a report to the Security Council outlining his own proposal.[39] Citing his authority under Resolution 598 to "dispatch a team of United Nations Observers to verify, confirm and supervise the cease-fire and withdrawal," Perez de Cuellar called for the creation of the United Nations Iran-Iraq Military Observer Group (UNIIMOG). UNIIMOG, the Secretary-General explained, would have several purposes. First, it would help establish cease-fire lines. Second, it would "monitor compliance with the cease-fire." Third, it would investigate allegations of cease-fire violations and "restore the situation if a violation has taken place." Fourth, it would "prevent, through negotiation, any other change in the *status quo*, pending withdrawal of all forces to the internationally recognized boundaries." Fifth, it would "supervise, verify and confirm the withdrawal of all forces to the internationally recognized boundaries." Sixth, it would then monitor the cease-fire along these internationally recognized boundaries. Finally, UNIIMOG would enter into any special agreements with the parties that might facilitate the reduction of tension. In his report the Secretary-General explained that the force would "act with complete impartiality."[40] He further explained that for UNIIMOG to function effectively, "it must have at all times the full confidence and backing of the Security Council" and "the full cooperation of the parties."[41]

On August 9, 1988, the Security Council adopted Resolution 619, in which it approved the Secretary-General's report and created UNIIMOG for an initial period of six months.[42] Two days later Perez de Cuellar named Major General Slavko Jovic of Yugoslavia to head UNIIMOG as its Chief Military Observer. On August 17 the U.N. General Assembly agreed to fund $35.7 million for the initial three months of UNIIMOG. By August 20 troops from 26 countries—Argentina, Australia, Austria, Bangladesh, Canada, Denmark, Finland, Ghana, Hungary, India, Indonesia, Ireland, Italy, Kenya, Malaysia, New Zealand, Nigeria, Norway, Peru, Poland, Senegal, Sweden, Turkey, Uruguay, Yugoslavia, and Zambia—were in place to carry out the peacekeeping mission.

Given this overview of phase two, it is clear that the United Nations was quite successful. It accomplished facilitating a cease-fire and establishing peacekeeping forces. But why? Why was the United Nations so successful during this stage of the conflict, when it had not been so previously?

The main reason for the United Nations' success at this point apparently was the war weariness of the parties. As noted earlier, when the war began, Iraq enjoyed much success, occupying large portions of Iranian territory. But as the conflict continued, Iraq's military fortune began to change. In 1982 Iranian advances put Iraq on the defensive. Even though Iraq possessed superior equipment and had effectively "won" the air war, it found itself slowly losing the land war.[43] In consequence, Iraq was willing to sue for peace as early as March 1982. Iran, on the other hand, remained content to wage a war of attrition against Iraq. A major turning point, however, seems to have been the failed Iranian offensive against the Iraqi city of Basra in 1987. As Gary Sick observed, "the Iranians expected a decisive victory and, when it didn't occur, they realized they could not win the war."[44] Then, in April 1988 Iraq recaptured al-Faw Peninsula and seized the offensive. Iran was unable to recover. When on July 3, 1988, the USS *Vincennes* accidentally shot down an Iranian Airbus, Iran was near the stopping point. The heavy economic and personnel losses, the growing antiwar sentiment in Iran, and the difficulty in obtaining arms, as well as the increasingly unfavorable military position, all apparently were factors that led Iran to accept the U.N. terms for settlement.[45] Iran was simply tired of battle.

Given these conditions, it is difficult to argue that the United Nations was the major reason Iran agreed to a cease-fire. However, the U.N. framework embodied in Resolution 598 surely did facilitate Iran's acceptance of a cease-fire. For Iran, the cease-fire arrangement outlined in Resolution 598 was something it could live with. Of particular importance seems to have been the provision in the resolution calling for the establishment of an "impartial body" to determine responsibility for initiating the war.[46] Now there was indeed the potential that Iraq could be labeled the aggressor. Additionally, Iran may have been more receptive to a U.N. formulation due to the nature of the world organization.

Since the United Nations maintains an aura of neutrality and internationality, Iran could more readily accept its proposal than that of a single state or even a group of states. Iran could save face and avoid the appearance of capitulation.

Also noteworthy was the crucial role of the United Nations in convincing Iraq to eliminate its precondition for the cease-fire. Under the leadership of the Secretary-General, the United Nations provided a neutral setting in which the permanent members of the Security Council could exert pressure on Iraq. Without the machinery of the United Nations, it remains questionable whether a cease-fire could have been secured as quickly as it was.

Phase Three (August 20, 1988–Present)

Once the cease-fire was in place, the United Nations still faced two formidable tasks. First, it had to coordinate the negotiations between Iran and Iraq with a view toward implementing Resolution 598 and resolving the underlying conflict. Second, it had to serve as a peacekeeper while these negotiations were taking place.

The first of these tasks has thus far proved to be the more difficult. When negotiations began on August 25, 1988, the major goal of the Secretary-General was to see that agreement be reached on carrying out the remaining provisions of Resolution 598. These included securing a troop withdrawal beyond cease-fire lines to internationally recognized boundaries, instituting an exchange of prisoners of war, and mediating "a comprehensive, just and honorable settlement . . . of all outstanding issues."[47] But as the talks began, Iraq took the hard line. On August 26 it claimed that several questions concerning the Shatt al-Arab waterway and freedom of navigation would need to be resolved before the other provisions of Resolution 598 could be considered. First, Iran would have to begin efforts to reopen the Shatt, which had been closed since 1980 due to silt deposits and sunken ships. Second, Iraq wanted Iran to stop searching Iraqi ships passing through the Strait of Hormuz. (Iran had claimed that it had the right under international law to take such action since it was technically still at war with Iraq.) Third, and most extreme, Iran would have to acknowledge Iraqi sovereignty over the entire Shatt al-Arab.[48]

Although there may have been some willingness by Iran to work to reopen the Shatt and even to adopt a new posture regarding the inspection of ships,[49] Iraq's demand for sovereignty over the Shatt was a totally unacceptable precondition for negotiations. Iran cited as its authority the Treaty of Algiers of 1975, under which the waterway was to be divided in the middle. Explained Ali Akbar Velayati, "All border treaties are permanent, unchangeable and decisive."[50] Interestingly enough, Iraq had renounced this treaty when the war began in 1980, claiming that it had been coercively secured by Iran.[51]

Given this new problem, the Secretary-General began looking for areas of compromise. His immediate goal was to obtain a troop withdrawal to internationally recognized boundaries. To obtain Iraq's agreement on this point, Perez de Cuellar suggested that Iran agree to stop searching Iraqi ships and that both sides agree to undertake a study of the question of opening the Shatt al-Arab.[52] The question of sovereignty over the Shatt would presumably be discussed later in the talks. Unfortunately, Iraq was unreceptive to this suggestion.

Throughout the summer and fall of 1988 the talks continued at various levels. In some instances they were coordinated directly by the Secretary-General; in others they were led by his new Personal Representative for the conflict, Jan Eliasson of Sweden. Little progress, however, was made. On October 1 the Secretary-General once again appealed to the parties to move forward to implement Resolution 598. Specifically, he emphasized the need to move forward on such matters as troop withdrawals to internationally recognized boundaries, exchange of prisoners of war, and the clearing of the Shatt al-Arab. On February 2, 1989, Perez de Cuellar reported to the Security Council that Iran and Iraq appeared to "concur in principle on some of these suggestions or aspects thereof."[53] Specifically, he mentioned four points on which there was some agreement: (1) "freedom of navigation on the high seas and in the Strait of Hormuz for ships of both sides"; (2) "expeditious withdrawal of forces to the internationally recognized boundaries"; (3) the value of the "Third Geneva Convention as it pertains to the issue of prisoners of war"; and (4) the "usefulness to both sides of restoring the Shatt al-Arab to navigation."[54] But the Secretary-General concluded, "It should be emphasized that the common ground between the parties on the issues listed above should not be construed as having gone substantially beyond a convergence of views in principle."[55] As the Secretary-General posited,

At present, the parties continue to hold divergent views on what constitutes a cease-fire. They have different views also on when the withdrawal of forces to the internationally recognized boundaries should begin. On the question of restoration of the Shatt al-Arab to navigation, the parties have different positions as to the context and manner in which the matter should be addressed. These divergences emerge in the context of a disagreement on the wider issue of the framework for the conduct of direct talks. The divergent views of the parties illustrate the necessity of creating trust and confidence between them.[56]

In short, the parties were still a long way from even addressing the fundamental issues.

Several plausible reasons suggest why the talks remain stalled. One reason may be Iraq's unwillingness to give up its "winning position" in the war. As indicated earlier, Iraq was doing well militarily when the cease-fire was instituted. Iraq may have seen its demands as a reasonable way of acknowledging this fact.[57] Another reason turns on Iraq's abiding distrust of Iran.[58] Just as Iraq was reluctant to accept a cease-fire because of doubts over Iran's motivation, so too it appears unwilling to move forward with talks until signs of "good faith" are given by Iran. Yet a third reason may lie in the controversy surrounding allegations that Iraq used chemical weapons against Kurdish minorities.[59]

In light of these factors, the United Nations simply has been unable to exert enough pressure on Iraq to back down. Moreover, with the fighting over, the permanent members of the Security Council have appeared less concerned with the future of the negotiations. The issue no longer seems to be one of priority.

While the talks on implementing Resolution 598 have proceeded, the United Nations has been actively engaged in another task: peacekeeping. By February 1989 a total of 409 U.N. military observers had been stationed in the area. This included 350 ground observers, 18 members of an air unit, 37 military police, and 4 medics. There were also 117 international civilian staff members and 41 "local" staff members. The main functions of these forces have been to monitor the cease-fire and facilitate a troop withdrawal. According to the Secretary-General's report of February 2, 1989, "As of 20 January 1989, UNIIMOG had received 1,960 complaints of alleged cease-fire violations."[60] Fortunately, "Most of these were very minor in nature and only approximately 25 percent of them have been confirmed by UNIIMOG as violations."[61] Moreover, the Secretary-General explained that it was "noteworthy that the number of alleged and confirmed violations per month has been steadily declining as UNIIMOG has gained trust and respect."[62] He explained that "cease-fire violations have generally consisted of the movement of troops or the establishment of observation posts or other positions forward of the FDLs [Forward Defense Lines, that is, the cease-fire lines] and engineering works to strengthen defensive positions."[63] According to Perez de Cuellar, "In all such cases UNIIMOG endeavors to persuade the side concerned to stop work and restore the *status quo*. Sometimes UNIIMOG succeeds in this endeavor, sometimes not, but again it is noteworthy that its success rate is steadily increasing."[64]

UNIIMOG thus far has worked reasonably well. Even though several confirmed violations of the cease-fire have occurred, including some "exchange of artillery, small arms and rocket fire" in December 1988, no general resumption of the fighting has taken place. This is no doubt due to a realization by both parties that regardless of their negotiating goals, renewed fighting would be in neither state's interest. Moreover, both sides are less likely to resort to force with neutral U.N. observers on the border.

In sum, the success of the organization during phase three of the Gulf War has been mixed. It has made little headway toward resolving the underlying issues that divide the parties. But it has helped prevent the war from breaking out again. That, certainly, is no small accomplishment.

AN EVALUATION

The United Nations played an extremely active role throughout the course of the Iran-Iraq War. Based on this role, several conclusions can be drawn about the organization's performance.

First, the United Nations continued to be largely ineffective as a collective security organization. The framers of the U.N. Charter intended for the organization to respond quickly to aggression. When one state used force against another, the United Nations was to take necessary action to determine the aggressor state and then stop it. The United Nations was quite reluctant to assume that role in the Iran-Iraq War. Not until 1987 did any resolution of the Security Council even mention the issue of responsibility for the war or declare the matter to be under Chapter VII of the Charter. Even when the Council adopted Resolution 598, it only became a collective security body in muted fashion. It did not immediately determine the aggressor, nor did it take forceful action to end aggression.

The reasons for this unwillingness to be a collective security body are well known. Since the adoption of the Charter in 1945, states have generally been reluctant to brand another state as an aggressor, let alone take action against it. This judgment reflects a political choice that most states do not wish to make. In the Iran-Iraq War there was a clear desire to avoid such a determination, at least initially. This reluctance may have been partly due to a perception that if the United Nations were to "choose sides," it could not play the role of mediator; it would lose its standing as a neutral party. It may also have been due to a desire not to exacerbate the conflict. If the United Nations were to have sided with one party or the other, the war would have involved more states and conceivably produced more casualties. Finally, the organization's inaction must be linked to a general unwillingness by states to become involved in using force. Unless there exists a direct threat to national security or the force in question is at a fairly low level, states tend to refrain from becoming involved in international conflicts.

Second, the United Nations can provide a useful framework for ending armed conflict. Through Resolution 598 and the efforts of the Secretary-

General, the United Nations was able to establish a credible arrangement for establishing a cease-fire. Two major factors made this framework effective: the willingness of the parties to stop fighting, and the pressure imposed by the permanent members of the Security Council. The lesson to be drawn is that the organization can be useful in ending an armed conflict if the permanent members can become unified and if the belligerents are ready. These are clearly two overriding considerations; but without the neutral framework provided by the United Nations, a cease-fire might not have been reached as quickly, even if these conditions had been met.

Third, the United Nations remains good at peacekeeping. Traditionally, peacekeeping has been praised as one of the most successful roles of the organization. Its performance with UNIIMOG seems to confirm this. U.N. peacekeepers have been generally able to keep the parties apart and prevent major fighting. While the organization has not yet facilitated a troop withdrawal, this is largely due to the positions of the parties at the negotiating table.

Fourth, the United Nations still seems capable of exposing major violations of international law and mobilizing the international community about them. The case here concerns the use of chemical weapons during the war. Through U.N. teams the fact that chemical weapons were used was exposed, and efforts were made to strengthen the international regime restricting use of these weapons. Even though the United Nations may not have been able to prevent resort to chemical weapons during the war, exposing their use was certainly an important function.

Fifth, U.N. activities during the war reveal that the world body continues to have difficulty resolving the underlying political issues of a conflict. Even though the organization facilitated a cease-fire, it has not yet been able to produce progress on the substantive issues that divide the parties. On this point lack of enforcement powers appears to be a major difficulty. The United Nations must rely on persuasion to influence the parties. In this case the United Nations has been unable to convince the parties to compromise. Barring an unforeseen development, they will likely remain divided on many issues for some time, including the question of sovereignty over the Shatt al-Arab.

The United Nations became a very important actor during the Iran-Iraq War. While it alone did not end the war, nor has it yet resolved the underlying disputes, the organization has played a crucial role in facilitating and monitoring a cease-fire. It is still too early to determine what the long-term implications of U.N. involvement in the war will be. In the short term, however, the U.N. successes in the Iran-Iraq War, coupled with similar achievements in the western Sahara, Namibia, Angola, and Afghanistan, have greatly enhanced the reputation of the organization. As a consequence, more states seem willing to take disputes to the various organs of the United Nations for settlement than in previous years. The organization is clearly experiencing a political high. This resurgence augurs well for the organization and for the peaceful settlement of international disputes. It is important, however, not to exaggerate claims about the potential of the United Nations in the political realm. Its successes are still largely predicated upon the cooperation of the great powers. The organization will continue to be successful only if this cooperation can be maintained.

NOTES

1. For general discussion of the Iran-Iraq War, see Shahram Chubin and Charles Tripp, *Iran and Iraq at War* (London: I. B. Tauris, 1988); Anthony Cordesman, *The Iran-Iraq War and Western Security, 1984–1987* (London: Jane's, 1987); and Stephen R. Grummon, *The Iran-Iraq War: Islam Embattled* (New York: Praeger, 1982). Much of the factual information in this chapter is taken from press accounts and United Nations information. See especially United Nations Backgrounder, *Chronology of United Nations Negotiations to End the Iran-Iraq War* (New York: United Nations, 1988); *Chronology of United Nations Negotiations to End the Iran-Iraq War Since the Cease-Fire* (New York: United Nations, 1989).

2. See "Iran-Iraq: What the 2 Nations Lost," *New York Times*, August 10, 1988, p. A8.

3. Letter dated September 23 from the U.N. Secretary-General addressed to the presidents of Iran and Iraq, U.N. Document S/14193/Annex (September 25, 1980).

4. U.N. Security Council Resolution 479 (September 28, 1980).

5. Examples would include the Suez crisis, the Goa incident, the Bay of Pigs invasion, the invasion of Czechoslovakia, and the action by the United States in Grenada.

6. I would like to thank Dr. M. Parsadoust for emphasizing the nature of Resolution 479. See Anthony Clark Arend, "The Obligation to Pursue Peaceful Settlement of International Disputes during Hostilities," *Virginia Journal of International Law* 24 (1983): 97.

7. See *Chronology of United Nations Negotiations* (1988).

8. See David Segal, "The Iran-Iraq War: A Military Analysis," *Foreign Affairs* 66 (Summer 1988): 947.

9. Robert Pear, "Radio Broadcast Shows Iran Leader Endorsed Decision for Truce," *New York Times*, July 21, 1988, p. A1.

10. U.N. Security Council Resolution 514 (July 12, 1982); U.N. Security Council Resolution 522 (October 4, 1982); U.N. Security Council Resolution 540 (October 31, 1983); U.N. Security Council Resolution 582 (February 24, 1986); U.N. Security Council Resolution 588 (October 8, 1986).

11. See *Chronology of United Nations Negotiations* (1988), p. 7.

12. U.N. Security Council Resolution 598 (July 20, 1987).

13. See Edward Cody, "Iran Accepts U.N. Plan for Cease-Fire in War with Iraq," *Washington Post*, July 18, 1988, pp. A1, A14.

14. See *Chronology of United Nations Negotiations* (1988), p. 7.

15. Ibid.

16. Segal, "Iran-Iraq War," p. 947.

17. *Chronology of United Nations Negotiations* (1988), p. 3.

18. U.N. Security Council Resolution 540 (October 31, 1983).

19. See "A Chronology of the Gulf War," *Washington Post*, July 19, 1988, p. A14.

20. Statement by the President of the Security Council, March 30, 1984, U.N. Document S/16454.

21. U.N. Security Council Resolution 582 (February 24, 1986); U.N. Security Council Resolution 612 (May 9, 1988).

22. *Chronology of United Nations Negotiations* (1988), p. 5.

23. U.N. Security Council Resolution 598 (July 20, 1987).

24. "Iran-Iraq: What the 2 Nations Lost," p. A8.

25. A new international conference was convened in Paris in January 1989 to address the problems of chemical weapons.

26. Text of Iranian Letter to the United Nations, reprinted in *New York Times*, July 19, 1988, p. A9.

27. Pear, "Radio Broadcast Shows Iran Leader Endorsed Decision for Truce," p. A1.

28. Youssef M. Ibrahim, "Iraq Voices Strong Doubts on Iran's Good Intentions," *New York Times*, July 18, 1988, p. A8.

29. Michael J. Berlin, "Iraq Insists on Direct Peace Talks," *Washington Post*, July 28, 1988, pp. A1, A28.

30. Ibid.

31. Robert Pear, "U.S. Presses Iraqis to Accept Cease-Fire," *New York Times*, August 5, 1988, p. A8.

32. Ibid., quoting Christine M. Helms.

33. Paul Lewis, "U.N. Chief Says He Will Declare a Cease-Fire in the Iran-Iraq War," *New York Times*, August 2, 1988, p. A1.

34. Ibid., p. A9.

35. Paul Lewis, "Cease-Fire Plan of U.N. Leader Rejected by Iraq," *New York Times*, August 3, 1988, p. A1.

36. Paul Lewis, "Iraq Is Said to Use Poison Gas Again," *New York Times*, August 4, 1988, p. A7.

37. Paul Lewis, "U.N. Plans 250 Peacekeepers for Gulf," *New York Times*, August 6, 1988, p. A3.

38. Letter dated August 6, 1988, from the permanent representative of Iraq to the United Nations addressed to the secretary-general, U.N. Document S/20092 (August 6, 1988).

39. *Report of the Secretary-General on the Implementation of Operative Paragraph 2 of the Security Council Resolution 598 (1987)*, U.N. Document S/20093 (August 7, 1988).

40. Ibid., p. 4.

41. Ibid.

42. U.N. Security Council Resolution 619 (August 9, 1988).

43. Segal, "Iran-Iraq War," pp. 957–58.

44. Quoted in Bernard E. Trainor, "Turning Point: Failed Attack on Basra," *New York Times*, July 19, 1988, p. A9.

45. Robert Pear, "Iran Action Linked to Anti-War Mood," *New York Times*, July 22, 1988, p. A6.

46. See Cody, "Iran Accepts U.N. Plan," p. 3.

47. U.N. Security Council Resolution 598, paragraphs 1, 2, 3, 4, 6, and 7 (July 20, 1987).

48. See Paul Lewis, "Gulf Peace Negotiations Hit a Potentially Serious Snag," *New York Times*, August 27, 1988, p. A3.

49. Ibid.

50. Paul Lewis, "Iraq Appears to Toughen Stance on Control of Disputed Waterway," *New York Times*, August 29, 1988, p. 9.

51. Ibid.

52. Paul Lewis, "U.N. Chief Tries New Tack in Gulf Talks Impasse," *New York Times*, September 1, 1988, p. A14.

53. *Report of the Secretary-General on the United Nations Iran-Iraq Military Observer Group*, U.N. Document S/20442 (February 2, 1989), p. 9.

54. Ibid.

55. Ibid.

56. Ibid., pp. 9–10.

57. See Lewis, "U.N. Chief Tries New Tack in Gulf Talks Impasse," p. A14.

58. Paul Lewis, "U.N. Offers Gloomy View of Gulf Talks," *New York Times*, September 2, 1988, p. A3.

59. Clyde Haberman, "Poison Gas Issue: Gulf Talks Snag?" *New York Times*, September 19, 1988, p. A8.

60. *Report of the Secretary-General on the United Nations Iran-Iraq Military Observer Group*, p. 5.

61. Ibid.

62. Ibid.

63. Ibid.

64. Ibid.

13

Iran, Iraq, and the Cease-Fire Negotiations

Contemporary Legal Issues

Charles G. MacDonald

The role of international law in the conflict between Iraq and Iran entered a new phase on August 20, 1988, when a cease-fire between the two states became a reality. The cease-fire was based upon United Nations Security Council Resolution 598 of July 20, 1987. Although Iraq had supported Resolution 598, it was not until midsummer 1988 that Iran decided to accept it following a series of Iraqi battlefield victories. Negotiations between Iran and Iraq, based on Resolution 598, began on August 25, 1988, five days after the cease-fire became effective. The cease-fire set the stage for Iran and Iraq to pursue their differences through peaceful diplomatic means within the accepted legal framework of Resolution 598. It also enabled each state to turn its energies toward reconstruction and away from the long and tragic war that had dragged on for nearly eight years.

This chapter examines the contending international legal claims made by Iran and Iraq in their cease-fire negotiations, as well as the political interests underlying their respective legal positions. It is hoped that some light can be shed on how contemporary international law can facilitate the regulation of relations between the two Third World states. It is also hoped that the nature of the legal dispute between Iran and Iraq will be clarified and that some insights can be gained into the respective approaches that Iran and Iraq take to international law.

The chapter focuses upon selected legal issues in the framework accepted for peace between the two parties—Security Council Resolution 598,[1] passed unanimously on July 20, 1987. First considered are the policies of both Iran and Iraq preceding their eventual acceptance of the cease-fire resolution. The provisions of Resolution 598 are then briefly enumerated, after which the rounds of negotiations sponsored by the United Nations through April 1989 are examined. The legal claims of Iran and Iraq are then appraised in terms of three principal legal issues in contention: (1) discontinuation of all military actions or cease-fire and withdrawal of military forces to "internationally recognized boundaries";[2] (2) release and repatriation of prisoners of war;[3] and (3) a "comprehensive, just and honorable settlement" of "all outstanding issues"[4] (in particular, the question of the Shatt al-Arab or Arvand River boundary). Other issues that are identified by Resolution 598—such as "measures to enhance the security and stability in the region,"[5] "responsibility for the conflict,"[6] and the magnitude of damage and question of reconstruction[7]—have been generally ignored in the negotiations and are unlikely to be given serious attention in the current political atmosphere that exists between Iran and Iraq. The relative legal claims by Iran and Iraq are then analyzed in the context of their broader underlying political interests. Finally, the manner in which international law was used by Iran and Iraq is considered, with a view to explaining both states' legal rationales for their respective policy positions.

PRELUDE TO CEASE-FIRE

The Gulf War, the longest war in modern history since the Battle of Waterloo,[8] raged from September 22, 1980, when Iraqi forces invaded Iranian territory, until August 20, 1988, when a formal cease-fire between Iran and Iraq took effect. The wartime fortunes of each side had ebbed and flowed, with initial Iraqi successes giving way to successful Iranian counterattacks in September 1981, effectively ending Iraq's seige of Abadan. Iran's advance forced Iraq to withdraw from Iran in June 1982. Iraq then called for a cease-fire, but Iran was steadfast in demanding nothing short of the end of Saddam Hussein's regime and significant reparations.

Initially indicating that it was only fighting for self-defense, Iran soon came to envision its religious duty to liberate Iraq's Shi'ite religious shrines from the "evil" Saddam Hussein and crossed the border into Iraq in mid-July 1982. Iran then pursued a policy aimed at seeking an unconditional surrender—no deals with the Saddam Hussein regime.[9]

Even though Iran could have negotiated from a position of strength for quite some time, especially after it seized al-Faw in February 1986 (until it lost it again in April 1988), the Khomeini regime religiously sought to punish the "aggressor."

Iraq, on the other hand, after being forced to take the defensive, sought to expand the war and force the superpowers to impose a cease-fire. Iraq began air attacks on tankers serving Iran in early 1984. Iran responded by hitting tankers serving the Arab side of the Gulf. As the superpowers became drawn into the Gulf to protect neutral shipping, international pressure intensified to find a diplomatic solution. On July 20, 1987, the Security Council adopted Resolution 598, just prior to the U.S. move to escort reflagged Kuwaiti tankers. Iraq quickly announced acceptance of the cease-fire resolution if Iran would do likewise. Iran, however, stated that it would not accept the resolution until a commission had been established to identify the aggressor. The Gulf War became more complicated with increased international involvement in the reflagging and mining activities. The expanded international presence in the Gulf after mid-1987 eventually resulted in armed clashes between Iranian forces and the U.S. Navy.

In February 1988 the "war of the cities" saw 190 Iraqi missiles sent against Tehran, with Iran unable to respond in kind. The missiles raining on Tehran, together with the specter of gas warfare vividly produced in Iranian television accounts of Iraq's horrific gas attacks on Halabja in March 1988, contributed to a demoralization of the Iranian people. The April 17, 1988, Iraqi advance on al-Faw and Iraq's integration of chemical weapons into its offensive military machine signalled that Iran was a defeated nation.

Following a flurry of diplomatic activity, Iran accepted Resolution 598 on July 18. This led to the acceptance by both parties of a cease-fire on August 8, which entered into force on August 20, 1988. Iraq had emerged as the clear battlefield winner when direct negotiations began on August 25. Moreover, Iraq continued to advance against Iran after the cease-fire date had been set. Iraq attempted to take as many Iranian prisoners of war (POWs) as possible to improve its negotiating position in proposed POW exchanges. Iraq also seized additional Iranian territory despite the clearly anticipated requirement in Resolution 598 for troop withdrawals back to recognized boundaries. Relatedly, the day before direct negotiations were to begin, Iraq launched a major drive—a "war of extermination"—against Kurdish rebels in the north, effectively using chemical weapons in the military operation. Iraq moved into the so-called "liberated zones" along the border and reportedly demolished some 1,000 villages. Over 100,000 Kurdish refugees were reported to have fled into Turkey and Iran.[10]

SECURITY COUNCIL RESOLUTION 598: A FRAMEWORK FOR PEACE

When the negotiations began on August 25, 1988, both parties realized that the talks would be long, and agreement would not come easily following such a long and costly war. Iraq was the unmistakable battlefield victor, but Iran remained a bitter and formidable enemy and potentially could be more powerful in the long run. Neither side was willing to trust the other, but both were willing for the fighting to cease.

Resolution 598 provided the legal framework for the U.N.-sponsored negotiations. The preamble to the resolution deplores "the initiation and continuation of the conflict" and "the bombing of purely civilian population centers, attacks on neutral shipping or civilian aircraft, the violation of international humanitarian law and other laws of armed conflict, and in particular, the use of chemical weapons contrary to the obligations under the 1925 Geneva Protocol."[11] Article 1 demands that both "Iran and Iraq observe an immediate cease-fire, discontinue all military actions on land, at sea and in the air, and withdraw all forces to the internationally recognized boundaries without delay." Article 2 provides for the establishment of a peacekeeping force, the United Nations Iran-Iraq Military Observer Group, to oversee the cease-fire and withdrawal. Approximately 350 U.N. personnel assumed positions along the border by the start of the cease-fire. Article 3 urges the release and repatriation of prisoners of war. Article 4 calls for a "comprehensive, just and honourable settlement" of all "outstanding issues," in accordance with the principles contained in the U.N. Charter (including noninterference in the internal affairs of the other state). Article 5 urges other states to refrain from any activities that might widen the conflict. Article 6 requests the Secretary-General to consider, with Iran and Iraq, the establishment of an impartial body to identify the state responsible for the conflict. Article 7 seeks to establish a team of experts to examine the costs of the war and the question of reconstruction. Article 8 requests the Secretary-General to consider regional measures to enhance security and stability. Article 9 asks the Secretary-General to keep the Security Council informed on implementation of the resolution. Article 10 provides for further meetings to ensure compliance with the resolution.[12]

The key issues facing Iran and Iraq involve withdrawal to internationally recognized boundaries and the cessation of all military actions on land, at sea, and in the air; the release of prisoners of war; and the control of the Shatt al-Arab waterway (the Arvand River). The talks initially appeared to get off to a good start. The first day of direct negotiations was called a "serious beginning" by Secretary-General Javier Perez de Cuellar after a six-hour negotiating session between Tariq Aziz, the Iraqi foreign minister, and Ali Akbar Velayati, the Iranian foreign minister. The opening session focused on troop withdrawals, return of prisoners of war, and the schedule for future meetings. The next day, however, the talks stalled on the question of withdrawal. Iraq asserted that the 1975 Algiers accord no longer was valid and demanded that Iran recognize full Iraqi control of the Shatt al-Arab waterway,[13] which would consequently make the cease-fire line the eastern shore of the Shatt al-Arab. Iran responded that questions concerning sovereignty over the river should be considered only after the initial stages of Resolution 598 were implemented, namely withdrawal, repatriation of POWs, and the establishment of a tribunal to determine responsibility for the war.

In addition to withdrawal, the issue of Iran's intercepting Iraqi shipping in the Strait of Hormuz and in the Gulf emerged. With the inception of the cease-fire, Iraq sent two ships into the Gulf. Iran stopped the first, a freighter, and searched it for contraband before allowing it to proceed. The second ship, a tanker, was not stopped. This set the stage for a dispute testing Iraq's demand for freedom of navigation against Iran's claim to enforce security interests in its territorial sea.

The first-round talks became stalemated over withdrawal of troops and freedom of navigation, with the major obstacle being Iraq's insistence that the Algiers accord was void and that Iraqi control of the Shatt al-Arab should be recognized. The talks recessed on September 13, 1988.

A second round of discussions, beginning on September 30, 1988, at the United Nations in New York, made little progress. This session began with Secretary-General Perez de Cuellar presenting a compromise plan to break the deadlock. He asked Iran to guarantee the right of passage for Iraqi shipping in the Gulf and to allow the Shatt al-Arab waterway to be reopened and called on both sides to follow through on mutual withdrawal of occupation forces. He also proposed the return of all prisoners of war. The Secretary-General suggested that the question of sovereignty over the Shatt al-Arab be postponed until a formal treaty had been concluded.[14] Ali Akbar Velayati was quoted as stating that the two countries had agreed in principle to the compromise solution, but that his Iraqi counterpart, Tariq Aziz, "did not have sufficient authority to make a decision."[15]

The impasse in the September discussions gave way to a third round of talks held in Geneva. The third session, commencing on November 1, 1988, brought some apparent progress; an agreement was reached on the exchange of sick and wounded prisoners. The session was adjourned, however, on November 11 because of persistent intransigence over the issue of troop withdrawals and Iraq's claim to full sovereignty over the Shatt al-Arab.

A fourth round of talks convened in Geneva during April 20–23, 1989, but it too broke up with scant progress. The Secretary-General pressed his October 1, 1988, four-point proposal for (1) withdrawal to international boundaries based on the 1975 accord; (2) Iran's self-restraint in searching ships; (3) mutual exchange of POWs; and (4) opening of the Shatt al-Arab. He also suggested a new timetable that called for troop withdrawals within 15 days and an exchange of prisoners of war within 60 days.[16] The Iraqi foreign minister reportedly indicated that withdrawal was not possible until the dredging of the Shatt al-Arab was completed. He blamed Iran for not fully respecting Resolution 598 and for failing "to honor the letter and spirit of the document."[17] Iran maintained that the impasse was due to Iraq's continued obstinate, unacceptable claim to sovereignty over the entire Arvand Rud (the Shatt al-Arab). Iran also complained that Iraq's reluctance to implement Resolution 598 stemmed from the lack of resolve by Security Council members to pressure Iraq, suggesting that Council members were more concerned with their own political interests than with the implementation of justice.[18]

The deadlock in the talks carried over into the summer of 1989 with no breakthrough in sight. Both sides persisted in calling for the implementation of Resolution 598, but with fundamental disagreement on the applicability of the 1975 Algiers accord concerning the boundary of the Shatt al-Arab (the Arvand River). The death of Ayatollah Khomeini on June 3 did not produce any immediate change in the negotiating positions of either side. Reported Soviet support for the Iranian position on the applicability of the 1975 Algiers accord represented a potentially significant development in June 1989, but other Security Council members revealed no interest in pressuring either party.

LEGAL CLAIMS

Cease-Fire and Withdrawal

Iran's approach to negotiations with Iraq is based on the necessity of Iraqi withdrawal to internationally recognized boundaries as determined by the 1975 Algiers accord.[19] Iran contends that no progress can occur in the peace talks until Iraq withdraws. In a letter dated March 10, 1989, to the Secretary-General, the Iranian foreign minister carefully identified "2,663 square kilometres of Iranian territory" that remained under Iraqi occupation.[20] Velayati supported this contention with 42 attached maps. Furthermore, he charged that Iraq had occupied an additional 125 square kilometers of Iranian territory after the cease-fire date had been set.[21] Iran had previously charged that Iraq was occupying more than 2,000 square kilometers of Iranian territory in four provinces.[22]

From its initial assertion that occupation of Iraqi territory was sanctioned by Islamic necessity to liberate the Shi'ite Islamic holy places, Iran now repeatedly claims that it has no desire to acquire any of Iraq's territory and that it has withdrawn all its forces from Iraqi lands.[23] Iranian occupation of Iraqi territory is not an issue at present; even so, the Hussein government is quick to point out that Iran had seized Iraqi territory prior to Iraq's pushing Iran back before the cease-fire.

An issue related to the withdrawal stalemate concerns Iraq's opposition to Iran's stopping of ships in the Strait of Hormuz and in the Gulf. Iraq asserts that such action violates freedom of navigation and represents a military action at sea that must cease under the provisions of Article 1 of Resolution 598. Foreign Minister Velayati responded to the Iraqi position by explaining that "Iraq did not feel content with freedom of navigation in accordance with international law."[24] Velayati charged that Iraq was attempting to acquire "unimpeded passage through the territorial sea of the Islamic Republic of Iran and to deprive Iran of exercising its most basic and universally recognized rights under international law."[25] Moreover, the Iranian foreign minister emphasized that any state transiting the Strait of Hormuz must exercise "innocent passage" through the waterway, presuming then that such shipping would not harm Iran.[26]

In a message on February 8, 1989, to the U.N. Secretary-General, Tariq Aziz detailed Iraq's position on the question of "withdrawal."[27] He stressed Iraq's respect for the territorial integrity of Iran and its desire to reach settlement in accord with Resolution 598. Tariq Aziz carefully identified the extensive areas of Iraq that Iran had occupied and held prior to Iraq's military successes of April 1988. These areas (in square kilometers) included al-Faw (225); al-Shalamjah (175); Majnun with water area (1,447); Makhfar Zayd (56); Safy Sa'd (43); al-Zubaydat (127); Mehran (182); Mahran, Panjwin, and Mawat (1,899); and Haj 'Umran (170).[28] Aziz indicated that Iraq had regained some 4,434 square kilometers on the battlefield between April and July 1988. He explained that in order to remove Iranian forces, Iraqi troops had to penetrate Iranian territory and control certain areas for a "period of time due to military necessity."[29] Aziz said that Iraqi forces had been subsequently withdrawn from these territories, which had amounted to some 9,619 square kilometers.[30] Aziz emphasized that Iraq had no expansionist ambitions and was eager to reach a settlement in accordance with the rules of international law and the provisions of Resolution 598.[31]

Aziz went on to criticize Iran for wanting to annex what it had termed "liberated" Iraqi territory. In that regard, it should be noted that Ayatollah Khomeini in his June 21, 1982, speech to clerics had assertd that if Iran defeated Iraq, "Iraq will be annexed to Iran." He also predicted that the Iraqi people would overthrow Hussein's regime and link themselves with the Iranian nation.[32]

Despite Aziz's claim that Iraqi forces had withdrawn from Iranian territory after necessary military actions, in March 1989 Iraqi President

Saddam Hussein acknowledged the continued presence of Iraqi forces within Iranian territory for defensive purposes. Hussein explained that it was necessary to place army personnel in "observation posts on vantage points some meters away from borders to enable forces to observe enemy movements. As long as the war has not ended with a peace agreement, the presence of such observation posts and the enhancement of the fortifications of defensive positions are not considered acts of occupation in the traditional sense of the word."[33] Hussein went on to suggest that if the Iranians were to move toward a peaceful solution, then all Iraqi troops would be removed.

Release and Repatriation of Prisoners of War (POWs)

The United Nations issued a report on POWs on September 1, 1988. According to the United Nations, Iran held approximately 70,000 Iraqis, and Iraq held about 35,000 Iranians. The United Nations also indicated that Iranian "indoctrination" or "spiritual guidance," essentially "indistinguishable from mental pressure," had transformed some 14,000 Iraqi prisoners into supporters of Ayatollah Khomeini. The United Nations, however, found "no systematic indoctrination" of the Iraqi-held POWs but did identify some "psychological evidence" of indoctrination. In addition to those POWs identified by the United Nations, Iraq claims that Iran holds "more than 30,000" Iraqi POWs who have not been registered with the International Committee of the Red Cross (ICRC).[34] Also notable is the Iranian claim that Iraq had seized 700 Iranians after the cease-fire agreement had been reached.[35]

Iraq and Iran have criticized each other for violations of international law involving mistreatment of POWs. The Iraqi foreign minister repeatedly has charged that Iran has not respected the Geneva Convention on POWs, "either during or after the war," and "has used every brutal method against the Iraqi POWs, including murder, torture, and psychological intimidation."[36] Iran has similarly condemned Iraqi treatment of Iranians, as illustrated in the Islamic government's monograph entitled *Report sur le mauvais traitement des captifs Iraniens en Iraq*,[37] which documents Iranian claims against Iraq.[38] In addition, both sides have taken extreme measures against their own nationals who cooperated with or assisted the enemy. In this regard, Iraq's actions against its Kurds that worked with the Iranians[39] might be juxtaposed to the Iranian actions against the so-called National Liberation Army of the Mujahedin-e Khalq that moved into Iran after the cease-fire. Many of these Mujahedin members were simply executed after their capture.

The POW issue has been a contentious point between Iran and Iraq since the cease-fire agreement was reached. Article 3 of Resolution 598 "*Urges* that prisoners-of-war be released and repatriated without delay after the cessation of active hostilities in accordance with the Third Geneva Convention of 12 August 1949." Since the hostilities supposedly ended with the cease-fire taking effect on August 20, 1988, the ICRC on August 23, 1988, sent a letter to each party stressing the obligation to return POWs. Iraq reportedly responded positively in a letter on September 17, but Iran did not. Prior to the third round of talks between Iraq and Iran, the ICRC sent a memorandum on October 4, 1988, to each country that called for the release of POWs under Article 118 of the 1949 Geneva Convention concerning POWs, in accord with Resolution 598. Iraq reportedly consented to the ICRC proposals, but Iran refused, maintaining that cessation of hostilities would remain in question until Iraq withdrew from all Iranian territory.[40] On March 5, 1989, Iraqi President Saddam Hussein announced in a statement to the International Progress Organization[41] Iraq's continued readiness, "for humanitarian and legitimate reasons, to effect a comprehensive exchange of POWs regardless of the outcome of the peace negotiations and irrespective of the progress in reaching a comprehensive and durable peace."[42] Iran has likewise called for POWs to be exchanged as soon as possible, but within the framework of Resolution 598; Tehran has resisted a comprehensive prisoner exchange until Iraq withdraws from all Iranian territory.

While agreement on the exchange of POWs has been elusive, during the third round of talks an agreement was reached on an ICRC proposal to exchange sick and wounded prisoners on a proportional basis. The November 1988 agreement called for 1,158 Iraqi prisoners to be released by Iran in return for 411 Iranians. The exchange was supposed to take ten days, with 115 Iraqis and 41 Iranians released each day. The exchange of POWs began on November 24 but was suspended by Iran on November 27;[43] Iran asserted that Iraq was not returning the requisite number of POWs and therefore stopped the exchange.[44] During those first three days Iran had sent three groups of 52, 51, and 52, while the Iraqis had sent groups of 19, 18, and 19. The result was the release of 155 Iraqis and 56 Iranians. Iraq, backed by the ICRC, accused Iran of changing the number agreed upon for release in the exchange. In defense of its action Iran indicated that "20 prisoners have refused to return; 61 prisoners have recovered; a decision on the fate of 30 prisoners is pending; 60 prisoners had been released by Iranian authorities without knowledge of the Red Cross (but not turned over to the Iraqi government); the identity of 2 prisoners has not been determined; 8 prisoners have not returned from camp; 2 prisoners have died; and a decision is pending on the fate of 1 Egyptian prisoner."[45]

The Iranian explanation illustrates the problems associated with the disposition of prisoners of war, especially if a significant degree of distrust is involved. Moreover, questions have been raised about the safety of many prisoners of war who have been returned. Iran reported that some Iraqis released by Iran had been taken to a special camp at Habbaniyyah where they were interrogated, drugged, and tortured.[46]

While the agreement on the return of sick and disabled prisoners of war was honored only in part, both Iraq and Iran have subsequently released a considerable number of such prisoners unilaterally. Although figures vary, the Islamic Revolution News Agency reported on April 10, 1989, that following the release of 70 more sick or wounded Iraqis, "Iran in 19 stages has released 1,346 disabled Iraqi POWs, but Iraq has only freed 949 Iranian POWs, including 459 civilians."[47] Some 100,000 POWs remain in captivity despite the cease-fire. Their status is unlikely to change until Iraq withdraws from Iranian territory, which is not anticipated until the controversy over the Shatt al-Arab boundary is resolved.

Sovereignty over the Shatt al-Arab

The key to understanding the impasse in the cease-fire negotiations turns on the validity of the 1975 Algiers accord and the subsequent Treaty Relating to the Boundary and Good-Neighborliness between Iran and Iraq and three protocols signed in Baghdad June 13, 1975.[48] The Iraqi position is clear: Iraq contends that the 1975 Treaty is null and void. The Hussein government asserts that the war was precipitated by Iran's violation of the 1975 agreement. The Iraqi position as described in an *al-Thawra* commentary explains that "Iraq regarded the agreement as annulled after being violated by Iran absolutely when it interfered in its [Iraq's] internal affairs, launched war against it, called in traitors in the north of Iraq and armed and financed them to move rebellion there as well as closed up the Iraqi Shatt al-Arab waterway in September 1980, all of which motivated eruption of the war."[49]

The Iranian position is also clear and was well illustrated in April 1989 by Foreign Minister Velayati's terse explanation: "With regard to the 1975 agreement, I must say that the issue is the river and the thalweg line that divides it. This is a border between Iran and Iraq. . . . This is a valid agreement and all international laws and regulations agree with this."[50] Velayati also asserted that the United Nations had informed Iran that it regards the 1975 accord as valid.[51]

The primary dispute over validity of the 1975 agreement concerns the question of the sovereignty of the river. The 1975 treaty recognizes the *thalweg* or main navigational channel as the boundary between Iran and Iraq. Iraq maintains that since the 1975 treaty is void, the 1937 treaty that recognized Iraqi sovereignty over the entire river is valid. Iran maintains that the 1975 agreement remains valid, and that Iraq's jurisdiction extends only to the *thalweg*.

UNDERLYING POLITICAL INTERESTS

When the legal claims of Iran and Iraq are placed in their broader political context, they become intricately linked to the underlying national interests of each state. First, if attention is given to Iraq's criticism of Iran's occupation of Iraqi territory, one finds that Iraq avoids mention of its own move into Iran at the beginning of the war. Advancing into an area predominately populated by ethnic Arabs, Iraq attempted to seize what Arab nationalists referred to as "Arabistan" in the Khuzistan region of Iran. Iraq wished to take advantage of a weakened Iranian military and move militarily while the balance of power tilted in Iraq's favor. Similarly, Iraq sought to abrogate the Iran-Iraq Treaty of 1975 and reestablish its legal claim to the entire Shatt al-Arab. After all, Iran had unilaterally abrogated the 1937 Iran-Iraq Treaty in April 1969.[52]

When Iraq emerged as the unquestioned battlefield winner in the Gulf War, it sought in August 1988 to take advantage of the situation and turned its attention to the Kurdish problem in the north. Iraq's acceptance of the *thalweg* principle for demarcation of the entire Shatt al-Arab boundary, as provided for in the 1975 Algiers accord, was based upon the Shah's promise to end Iranian (and American and Israeli) assistance to the Kurdish insurrection in the north; nonetheless, Iraq moved to destroy its Kurdish internal resistance once and for all.

Iraq's "war of extermination" against the Kurds began on August 24, 1988, the day before direct negotiations with Iran were set to begin. Press reports indicate that Iraq deployed over 60,000 troops with tanks, artillery, helicopter gunships, fighter-bombers, and chemical weapons. Between August 24 and September 8, 1988, Iraq reportedly used chemical weapons on a widespread basis against the Kurds. The United States confirmed Iraq's "abhorrent and unjustifiable" use of chemical weapons by technical means. Iraq reportedly destroyed more than 1,000 villages and caused some 100,000 Kurdish refugees to flee during this period, as it reclaimed so-called "liberated" zones along the border. Tariq Aziz announced in October 1988 that the Kurdish rebellion was finished forever. The "disappearance" and brutal treatment of Kurdish children, as documented in the March 1989 *Amnesty International Newsletter*, further underscores the Iraqi regime's deep-seated hostility toward its Kurdish opposition. Iraq's actions against the Kurds have not only removed Hussein's most formidable opposition but have also undercut a substantial source of Iranian leverage against Iraq. Now that Iraq does not have to contend with Iranian support to the Kurds, it has resumed its claim to sovereignty over the entire Shatt al-Arab waterway.

Iraq, recognizing that Iran will remain a dangerous enemy over the long term, aims to bolster its strategic position in the south and take advantage of its current military supremacy to reestablish itself in the

Gulf. Iraq's outlet to the Gulf—the Shatt al-Arab—must therefore be opened as soon as possible. Reopening the river will not be easy, even with Iran's assistance. Experts believe that three years may be a modest estimate of the time required for returning the river to full operation. Mines, sunken vessels, chemicals, unexploded ordnance, and other refuse of war promise to make reopening the river a dangerous undertaking. Iran opposes any effort to clear the river as long as Iraqi troops remain in Iranian territory. Iraq's suggestion to divert the river and dry up the Iranian ports of Khorramshahr and Abadan represents a vehicle to increase pressure on Iran.[53]

CONCLUSION

The foregoing analysis suggests that both Iran and Iraq sought to legitimize their policies through international legal claims. Iraq's deliberate approach to international law was carefully based upon the traditional sources of law. Iran, however, exhibited somewhat of a dualistic approach to international law; that is, at times Iran appealed to traditional international legal principles and at times it sought higher Islamic principles to sanction Iranian actions. For example, Iran initially asserted that it fully recognized the territorial integrity of Iraq but was only trying to repel Iraqi soldiers from its territory. Once Iran had successfully forced Iraqi soldiers to withdraw across the border, it claimed the Islamic necessity of liberating the Islamic shrines to justify its occupation of Iraqi territory. Similarly, the late Ayatollah Khomeini's concept of an Islamic world order opposed the very idea of state sovereignty upon which the international legal system is based. Khomeini viewed the subdivision of the Islamic Middle East as an imperialist plot.[54]

Though the Iran-Iraq negotiations remain deadlocked over the issues of withdrawal and validity of the 1975 treaty, it is apparent that neither state wishes to resume the war. The international legal framework supplied by Resolution 598 enables each state to avoid war while remaining in fundamental disagreement over legal issues. Moreover, the current stalemate in the negotiations is unlikely to change unless considerable outside political pressure is brought to bear on one of the parties. Diplomatic gridlock seems likely to continue between Iran and Iraq until a mutual political interest can arise to foster accommodation and compromise between the Gulf antagonists.

NOTES

1. For the text of Resolution 598, see *Middle East Economic Digest*, July 29, 1988, p. 14.
2. See Article 1 of Resolution 598.

3. See Article 3 of Resolution 598.

4. See Article 4 of Resolution 598.

5. See Article 8 of Resolution 598.

6. See Article 6 of Resolution 598.

7. See Article 7 of Resolution 598.

8. For an overview of the war and discussion of the setting of the Gulf conflict as Iran and Iraq began direct negotiations, see *Middle East*, September 1988, pp. 8–12.

9. See interview with Ali Akbar Mohtashemi, Iranian interior minister, in *al-Mustaqbal* (Paris), February 25, 1989, in Foreign Broadcast Information Service, *Daily Report* Near East & South Asia (hereinafter FBIS-NES), FBIS-NES-89–39, March 1, 1989, p. 60. Mohtashemi indicated that Iran adopted the logic that the "aggressor should be punished," as executed during World War II, but the world did not accept the logic as far as Iran was concerned.

10. See *The Winds of Death* (Paris), a special 182–page issue of *Information and Liaison Bulletin of Institut Kurde de Paris*, no. 42 (September 1988).

11. The legal issues raised in the preamble identify numerous legal concerns emanating from the conflict but are beyond the scope of this study.

12. For an Iranian editorial in *Jomhuri Eslami* criticizing the failure of Iran and Iraq to implement fully Resolution 598, see Tehran Iranian News Agency (IRNA) of January 25, 1989, in FBIS-NES-89–016, January 26, 1989, pp. 60–61.

13. It should be noted that the Iranian name for the Shatt al-Arab is the Arvand Rud, a pre-Islamic name for the river. The common Western usage is Shatt al-Arab. Both names will be used interchangeably in this study.

14. See *New York Times*, October 1, 1988, p. 6; *New York Times*, October 9, 1988, p. 11.

15. *New York Times*, October 9, 1988, p. 11.

16. See the April 24, 1989, report of talks by Tehran Domestic Service in FBIS-NES-89–077, April 24, 1989, p. 69.

17. See report of Baghdad Iraqi News Agency (INA) in FBIS-NES-89–077, April 24, 1989, p. 17.

18. See Editorial, "Peace Talks Still on the Same Old Track," *Tehran Times*, April 26, 1989, p. 2, in FBIS-NES-89–085, May 4, 1989, p. 52.

19. For a useful background and analysis of the Iran-Iraq boundary, see U.S. Department of State, Bureau of Intelligence and Research, *Iran-Iraq Boundary*, International Boundary Study no. 164, July 13, 1978.

20. See discussion of Velayati's letter to the Secretary-General reported by Kuwait News Agency (KUNA) March 10, 1989, in FBIS-NES-89–048, March 14, 1989, p. 61.

21. Ibid.

22. For example, see interview with Deputy Foreign Minister Besharati, Tehran Domestic Service, January 1, 1989, in FBIS-NES-89–02, January 4, 1989, pp. 53–54.

23. For example, Acting Commander in Chief Hojjatolislam Hashemi Rafsanjani declared, "The Iranian revolutionary nation would neither accept occupation of an inch of its territory by the enemy nor intends to hold any part of the Iraqi soil." See his comments in Tehran IRNA, February 4, 1989, in FBIS-NES-89–023, February 6, 1989, p. 69.

24. See text of Velayati's September 8, 1988, news conference, Tehran IRNA, September 8, 1988, in FBIS-NES-88–175, September 9, 1988, pp. 35–36.

25. Ibid.

26. Ibid.

27. See text of message broadcast by Baghdad Domestic Service, February 14, 1989, in FBIS-NES-89–030, February 15, 1989, p. 36.

28. Ibid.

29. Ibid.

30. Ibid.

31. Reportedly Tariq Aziz attached eight maps to his message to the Secretary-General. These identified the areas of Iranian occupation. See report of Kuwait KUNA, March 10, 1989, in FBIS-NES-89–048, March 14, 1989, p. 61.

32. See reference to Khomeini's June 21, 1982, speech in "Middle East and South Asia Review," June 22, 1982, p. ii, Daily Report, V, June 22, 1982.

33. See Saddam Hussein's interview in Basra with Uthman al-'Umayr, March 8, 1989, in FBIS-NES-89–048, March 14, 1989, p. 34.

34. See Tariq Aziz's statement, reported by the Iraqi News Agency on April 18, 1989, in FBIS-NES-89–074, April 19, 1989, p. 19.

35. See statement by Mohammad Hoseyn Lavasani, deputy foreign minister, reported by the Islamic Revolution News Agency, May 6, 1989, in FBIS-NES-89–088, May 9, 1989, p. 53.

36. Ibid.

37. See *Rapport sur le mauvais traitement des captifs Iraniens en Iraq* (Tehran: Centre d'information de la guerre, Conseil supreme de la defense, 1985).

38. See also War Information Headquarters, *Animosity to Peace* (Tehran: Kayhan Press, 1987).

39. The nature of Iraq's human rights abuses and actions bordering on genocide against the Iraqi Kurds goes far beyond Iranian actions against Kurdish groups that assisted Iraq during the war. For the horror of Halabja, see the exceptional issue of *Information and Liaison Bulletin of Institut Kurde de Paris* entitled *Halabja: A Martyr Town* (Paris: Institut Kurde, no date). See also *The Proliferation of Chemical Warfare: The Holocaust at Halabja* (Washington, D.C.: People for a Just Peace, n.d.).

40. See text of Aziz's letter to the U.N. Secretary-General, February 6, 1989, in FBIS-NES-89–024, February 7, 1989, p. 21.

41. The International Progress Organization is a nongovernmental, humanitarian organization based in Vienna. On May 29–30, 1989, it sponsored a meeting of experts in Geneva to discuss the POW problem. For a report of the meeting by the Iranian News Agency, see FBIS-NES-89–104, June 1, 1989, p. 56.

42. See Iraqi News Agency report, March 12, 1989, in FBIS-NES-89–047, March 13, 1989, p. 25.

43. For the Iranian position, see the commentary presented by the Islamic Revolution News Agency, January 25, 1989, in FBIS-NES-89–016, January 26, 1989, p. 60.

44. For the Iraqi position, see the text of Tariq Aziz's February 6, 1989, letter to the U.N. Secretary-General in FBIS-NES-89–024, February 7, 1989, p. 24. For the Iranian position, see Islamic News Agency Commentary, January 25, 1989, in FBIS-NES-89–016, January 26, 1989, p. 60.

45. See FBIS-NES-89–024, February 7, 1989, p. 24.

46. See "Acutest Torture Continues in Iraq," *Tehran Times*, April 26, 1989, in FBIS-NES-89–086, May 5, 1989, p. 50.

47. See report in FBIS-NES-89–068, April 11, 1989, p. 51.

48. For a background on the boundary treaty, see U.S. Department of State, "Iran-Iraq Boundary."

49. See Iraqi News Agency commentary, April 12, 1989, in FBIS-NES-89–069, April 12, 1989, p. 24. For an earlier Iraqi News Agency commentary on an *al-Jumhuriyah* article that similarly lists Iranian violations of the 1975 agreement as reason for the voiding of the agreement, see FBIS-NES-89–009, January 13, 1989, p. 35.

50. See Velayati's interview in *Keyhan*, April 19, 1989, in FBIS-NES-89–083, May 2, 1989, p. 46.

51. Ibid.

52. For a discussion of Iranian abrogation of the treaty, see Tareq Y. Ismael, *Iraq and Iran: Roots of Conflict* (Syracuse: Syracuse University Press, 1982), p. 19. See also Ramesh Shanghvi, *Shatt al-Arab: The Facts Behind the Issue* (London: Transorient Press, 1969).

53. For Iraqi diversion possibilities, see Saddam Hussein's interview on March 8, 1989, in FBIS-NES-89–048, March 14, 1989, p. 29.

54. For a discussion of Khomeini's Islamic world order, see Farhang Rajaee, *Islamic Values and World View: Khomeini on Man, the State, and International Politics* (Lanham, Md.: University Press of America, 1983), p. 72.

14

Peace and Security in the Persian Gulf

A Proposal

R. K. Ramazani

One overarching lesson to be learned from the destructive Iran-Iraq War is that there is a need for lasting peace and security in the entire Persian Gulf region. To meet this need, it is necessary to devise an international strategy involving the participation not just of the Gulf states, but also of the interested outside powers. Just as the regional states have an interest in the peace and security of the region, the international community has an interest in secure access to Gulf oil supplies. Before proposing how such an international strategy can best protect and promote both these two fundamental sets of interests, we shall consider three alternative scenarios about how else peace and security in the Gulf region can be maintained. Theoretically, the first two scenarios reflect the concept of preponderance of power, while the third one partakes of the idea of the balance of power. My own proposal represents a bridge between these notions and the concept of collective security.

A NEW IRANIAN POLICEMANSHIP

One scenario suggests that Iran can rise again as the superpower of the Persian Gulf. Neither revolution nor war robbed Iran of its single most important asset relative to all the other Gulf states, that is, its easy and long access to the high seas through the Gulf waters. Iranian territory stretches along the entire eastern shore of the Gulf; it abuts the Gulf of Oman and the Arabian Sea and dominates the strategic Strait of Hormuz. Nor did revolution and war diminish the overwhelming size of Iran's population relative to all the other Gulf states. The population of Tehran alone may surpass that of all the six Arab states of the Gulf Cooperation Council (GCC) put together. During nearly eight years of war the Iranian population increased by more than 10 million. Today's total population of about 52 million nearly doubled in a little more than a decade.

Nor have revolution and war decreased Iran's hydrocarbon power. Although its proven oil reserves rank third in the Gulf, after Saudi Arabia and Iraq, its natural gas resources are the second largest in the world, after the Soviet Union. Furthermore, revolutionary Iran's commitment to conserving resources may well prolong the life of its 93 billion barrels of oil reserves relative to Iraq's 100 billion barrels. In the short term, at any rate, Iran is no worse off than other Gulf oil producers; they are all dependent on the oil industry that generates over 90 percent of their foreign-exchange earnings.

No one knows for sure the cost of the Iranian Revolution and the Gulf War in financial terms. Iran perhaps lost some $30 billion of earnings as a consequence of the revolutionary upheaval in 1978–79. The war may have cost Iran anywhere from $100 billion to $150 billion. If so, Iran's reconstruction and economic development, a kind of double *perestroika*, will require at least $200 billion above Iran's revenues in the next decade. They will also require borrowing money abroad in a way that will be acceptable in Islamic terms, such as borrowing in the guise of project financing. It is estimated that the unprecedented economic deals concluded between Iran and the Soviet Union during the visit to Moscow of Speaker, and now President, Hashemi Rafsanjani during June 20–23, 1989, will cost $7 billion to $8 billion, or about twice as much if combined with the necessary capital expenditures in Iranian currency between now and the year 2000. The revolutionary government has accorded the reconstruction of the oil industry—the goose that lays the golden egg—a high priority, with tangible results. For example, the war-damaged Abadan oil refinery, with a capacity of 600,000 barrels a day, resumed operation on April 1, 1989 after undergoing repairs. By early July it had refined nearly 10 million barrels of oil.

That is no necessary indication, however, that Iran will be able to easily regain its prerevolutionary superpower status in the Gulf region. The country's overall economy is in shambles. Iranian factories are currently working at 20 to 40 percent of their capacity, and about 4 million people are out of work. The inflation rate ranges between 30 percent and 40 percent, and the government has to import about $2 billion worth of food a year. On top of all these and other economic problems, social malaise, as indicated by drug addiction and corruption, is on the rise.

The ability of the new Iranian leaders to cope with such social and economic problems will make a major difference as to whether Iran will be able to regain its prerevolutionary superpower status. As a matter of fact, since no Iranian leader enjoys the religious and revolutionary legitimacy of the late Ayatollah Ruhollah Khomeini, the new Iranian leaders will have to combine successful performance in the social and economic fields with their revolutionary credentials if the regime is to enjoy a reasonable degree of political stability. The abolition of the position of the prime minister, the concentration of vast powers in the hands of the president, and above all, the de facto subordination of radical ideology to political realism may bode well for the new Iranian leaders, but this all remains to be seen.

No assessment of the prospects of Iran's ability to become again the premier power in the Gulf can overlook its military weakness. The revolution and the war have taken an extremely heavy toll. Revolutionary purges and executions before the war never really "decimated" the Iranian military, but the war almost did. Most of the 1 million or so war dead were Iranians. In the 1987 Karbala–5 offensive alone, 45,000 members of the Revolutionary Guards lost their lives. No less important, today Iran has the single largest number of war-disabled youth of any country in the world. In addition, the Iranian air force was for all practical purposes crippled by the end of the war, while Iraq possessed 500 aircraft by then. Iranian leaders boast about their country's indigenous arms manufacturing capability, suggesting that Iran will eventually be self-sufficient in arms production. Although Hashemi Rafsanjani, during his visit to Moscow, similarly played up Iran's capability, he also admitted Iran's need for foreign military technology. The new deals with the Soviet Union probably involve the transfer of arms as well as the establishment of economic ties. To diversify its sources of arms supplies, Iran will continue to buy arms in the West as well, particularly after its relations with Britain and the United States improve.

IRAQ AS THE GULF GENDARME

A second scenario posits the emergence of Iraq as the new policeman of the Gulf. Equipped with the most sophisticated military hardware and the most battle-tested army in the Arab world, it is currently the strongest military power in the Gulf. As against Iran's near-defunct air force, Iraq increased its air force by one-half in the course of the war to 500 aircraft. Its missile power is considerable. Iraq fired most of the 500 missiles launched during the war. Within three years of Iran's firing

Scud B's at a distance of only 80 miles from Baghdad, Iraq developed the so-called al-Hussein and al-Abbas missiles capable of lobbing a high-explosive warhead 400 and 560 miles respectively. In less than two months in February–April 1988, Iraq fired 180 al-Hussein missiles at Tehran, 300 miles away, and at four other Iranian cities, killing about 2,000 civilians and injuring three times as many. All of Iran's antitank, surface-to-surface, and antiship missiles put together, including the Chinese-manufactured Silkworm missiles, were no match for Iraqi missile power.

Besides Iraq's air and missile capability, its use of chemical weapons adds an ominous element to Iraq's overall military power. With its chemical complex at Samarra, Iraq has demonstrated both the resolve and capability of using chemical weapons not only against military targets, but also against civilian population centers and even against its own citizens. The universal condemnation of the use of chemical weapons on the Kurdish village Halabja on March 16, 1988, failed to deter Baghdad from using them again immediately after the cease-fire took effect. By early September 1988 some 60,000 Kurdish refugees had fled to Turkey. Less than a year later Iraq deported some 300,000 Kurds from Iraqi towns, allegedly in order to settle them in more modern areas, but in reality to create a cordon sanitaire against Iran.

This mass depopulation of the Kurdish areas reflects a major element of demographic weakness in the overall Iraqi power position. Iraq has the largest percentage (25 percent) of Kurds of any Middle Eastern nation, including Iran, Turkey, and Syria. It also has had the most continuously rebellious Kurdish population of any of these countries. Coupled with the fact that the majority of the Iraqi population is Shi'a (about 60 percent), the Sunni minority that rules Iraq considers the Kurdish nationalist movement as a serious threat to its security. Although the Iraqi Shi'as demonstrated their loyalty to the Baathist regime during the war, the Shi'a underground opposition, the Da'wa movement, survives despite thirty years of persecution.

Could it be that at least partly because of continuing uncertainty about the loyalty of the Shi'as as a whole, President Saddam Hussein has made the Shi'a-dominated port city of Basra the major showcase of Iraq's postwar reconstruction efforts? The war-battered city nearly fell to Iran in 1986 when about half of the population fled, making it a virtual "ghost town." Backed by a $5 billion project, the rebuilding of roads, homes, canals, and other buildings and facilities destroyed in Basra by the war has absorbed much of the Iraqi work force. The Iraqi leaders seem determined not to take for granted the loyalty of the Basrans in spite of the failure of Khomeini's Iran to export its revolution to Iraq.

Like Iran, Iraq is giving the reconstruction of its oil industry and ports the highest priority. The Basra oil refinery, like the Abadan oil refinery, has resumed operation, although neither is yet refining oil at full capacity. Iraq is also returning to operating its oil terminals, Mina al-Bakr and Khor al-Amaya, which were destroyed by Iran in the first week of the war. Perhaps the most remarkable feature of Iraq's efforts to cope with its limited access to the high seas is the increase of oil exports by pipeline through Turkey and Saudi Arabia after Hafiz Assad closed the trans-Syrian pipeline. Today Iraq is exporting about 2.5 million barrels of oil a day, and its export capacity will probably increase by about half that much since another pipeline under construction in Saudi Arabia has become operational.

Yet Iraq's seriously limited access to the high seas creates the prime obstacle to its achieving a superpower status in the Gulf. This lies at the heart of Iraq's historic concern with the control of the Shatt al-Arab; it was a prime cause of the war and the principal obstacle to peace. When the war broke out, Iran sank or bottled up the small Iraqi navy in this strategic waterway. After the cease-fire Iraq began freeing some of the ships stuck in the upper reaches of the river where both banks are in Iraqi territory. To goad Iran into accepting Iraq's "full sovereignty" over the waterway, Baghdad has threatened to make the river useless to both sides by building an alternative access to the Gulf further to the west. Iraq also has plans for improving its access to the Gulf through its ports of Umm Qasr and Zubair, located on Khor al-Zubair. But implementing these plans would cause Kuwait concern in two respects: Iraq would have to deepen and widen the channel of Khor Abdallah, which links up with Khor al-Zubair and over which Kuwait shares control with Iraq. Furthermore, Iraq's larger presence in its own ports would bring it too close for comfort to the Kuwaiti Bubiyan and Warba islands, both coveted by Iraq.

Perhaps next only to its limited access to the high seas, Iraq's potential political fragility puts a damper on its prospects of becoming the most powerful state in the Persian Gulf. Saddam Hussein's "great victory" blunted the export of the Iranian Revolution to Iraq, but it did not destroy the revolutionary regime; it strengthened it. Nor did battlefield successes result in full Iraqi control over the Shatt al-Arab waterway. To be sure, Saddam Hussein has emerged from the war as an even stronger and more confident political leader, but it is doubtful that his cult of personality will ensure political stability in the long run. It is also doubtful that coercive methods such as the recent mysterious disappearances of ambitious generals in aircraft and helicopter accidents will protect the Iraqi regime against other attempts at military coups d'état. Similarly, it is doubtful that the demand of the middle classes for participatory politics can be satisfied by such institutions as the National Assembly, which is filled with regime loyalists.

The demonstrated patriotism of the Iraqi people and the resolve of the Iraqi regime to resist Iran augment the current favorable perception of Iraq's international prestige. But deterrence does not simply reflect resolve; it is largely a function of capability. This is why any objective assessment of overall Iraqi power must take into account the incontestable fact that Iraqi power was a "borrowed capability" from the start to the end of the war.

For its economic needs, Iraq borrowed $70 billion—about $30 billion to $40 billion from Saudi Arabia, Kuwait, and the UAE, possibly $10 billion from the Soviet Union and East European countries, and about $26 billion from Western commercial banks. Although the loans from the Arab states are reputedly grants that are not to be paid back, it certainly does not seem that this is the case, at least so far as Kuwait is concerned. Given the revived Iraqi-Kuwaiti border dispute, Kuwait would like to use Iraq's indebtedness as leverage. In his February 6, 1989, trip to Iraq, the Kuwaiti prime minister brought up the border dispute in the context of the rescheduling of Iraq's $8 billion debt to Kuwait. For years Iraq has generally been rescheduling its debts because it is broke. At the moment it has less than one-third of the cash on hand necessary to meet its worldwide financial obligations of $7 billion debt-service payments.

Iraq's military bravado in the name of defense of Arabism also needs to be demythologized if Iraq's true power potential as a future Gulf superpower is to be objectively assessed. Given Iran's self-imposed international isolation beginning with the taking of American hostages, Iraq was superbly positioned to exploit worldwide anti-Iranian sentiments, not only diplomatically within and outside the United Nations, but also militarily. Armed with its 1972 treaty of friendship and the less known arms agreement of 1978 with the Soviet Union, Iraq received most of its arms from Moscow, especially after the Iranian foray into Iraqi territory (July 13, 1982). France was Iraq's biggest Western arms supplier. The Reagan administration's "Operation Staunch" proved to be somewhat less than staunch. The administration allowed the sale of transport planes and furnished intelligence assistance to Iraq, not to mention the scandalous arms deal with Iran. Above all, Washington sided unmistakably, albeit indirectly, with Iraq in its tanker war against Iran. For nearly a year between July 1987 and July 1988, in fact, the U.S. forces engaged in a controversial quasi-war with Iran in the Persian Gulf. If one were to add to the military backing of Iraq by these Eastern and Western powers the Saudi, Kuwaiti, and Jordanian logistical help, the Egyptian military sales and manpower support, and other kinds of aid from around the world, Iraq's military indebtedness would surpass even its staggering financial debt to the rest of the world.

In both these scenarios, whatever the relative power position of Iran and Iraq is today, there is every reason to believe that each of them has the will and potential capability to assign itself the role of future police-man of the entire Persian Gulf. From ancient times to the present the Iranian leaders have believed that their country is *primus inter pares*. The Shah used to insist on expanding Iran's "security perimeter," and at the height of the war then Speaker Hashemi Rafsanjani, in opening what he called Iran's "security umbrella" over the entire Gulf region, said unequivocally: "We declare once again that the security of the Persian Gulf is more important to us than any other party and we will strive to maintain the Gulf's [security] as much as we can." Today President Hashemi Rafsanjani continues to believe in holding the same Iranian security umbrella over the Gulf, but unlike his militant counterparts, he wishes to do so by pursuing a "good-neighbor" policy rather than by exporting the Iranian Revolution.

Insofar as Iraq is concerned, the same ambition for leadership in the Gulf and the Arab world that partly contributed to Saddam Hussein's decision to invade Iran underpins his desire to control not only the entire Shatt al-Arab, but also the sealanes of the Gulf. His air power is already poised to control the Gulf skies. Emboldened by his "great victory," he believes that he succeeded in getting his claim to the whole waterway endorsed by the Arab leaders at the Casablanca summit on May 26, 1989, when they declared their "full solidarity with Iraq" in preserving "its historic rights in its sovereignty over the Shatt al-Arab." In 1979 Vice President Saddam Hussein took the lead in expelling Sadat's Egypt from the Arab fold because of its peace treaty with Israel. In 1989 President Hussein took the initiative to readmit Mubarak's Egypt to the Organization of Arab Petroleum Exporting Countries (OAPEC) as a prelude to Egypt's maiden participation in the Casablanca summit ten days later. Furthermore, besides projecting Iraqi power into Lebanon in support of the Christian forces and against the Iranian and Syrian presence there, he seeks to assert a larger Iraqi role in the Arab world by joining Egypt, Jordan, and North Yemen in a new grouping, the Arab Cooperation Council (ACC). Even more revealing, Iraq plans to build a sophisticated arms industry with Egypt in hopes of achieving "strategic parity" with Israel in advanced weaponry. If this parity includes nuclear weapons capability, Israel's reaction may well be predictable; it will do what it did in June 1981 when it knocked out Iraq's Osirak nuclear reactor.

GCC: THE GULF BALANCER OF POWER

A third and final scenario would posit that the GCC can maintain future peace and security in the Persian Gulf with the help of interested outside powers. They would presumably be able to do so by playing the role of the balancer between Iran and Iraq. This proposition stems from the experience of the Western powers, particularly the United States, at the height of the tanker war between July 1987 and July 1988. Not since the Korean War had the West deployed anywhere in the world such a massive array of naval forces as in the Persian Gulf during that period. The cooperation of the GCC states facilitated the deployment of Western forces and in the end appeared to contribute to the maintenance of a balance, or more accurately, preponderance, of forces in favor of Iraq.

Yet such a scenario suffers from three flawed assumptions. First, it assumes that the GCC states have, or will soon have, the requisite power to play the role of a balancer between Iran and Iraq. But this seems to be a highly questionable assumption. If power and influence simply grew out of the barrels of guns, and in the case of the GCC states, also out of the barrels of oil, then the six nations together, and some would say even Saudi Arabia alone, could play such a role. Arguably, after all, these nations are in possession of the world's single largest pool of oil reserves. Transformed into the biggest single macroeconomic force in the world after the Arab-Israeli October war in 1973, OPEC's quadrupling of oil prices gave the world its "first oil shock." This was followed in 1979 by the "second oil shock" amidst the fury of the Iranian Revolution. The two oil shocks reflected a fifteenfold rise in oil prices, making the present GCC states the world's richest group of nations. Saudi Arabia alone earned $120 billion in 1980. But this proved to be a pyrrhic oil power.

The dramatic collapse of oil prices reversed the shock from oil consumers to oil producers. The GCC was born in the twilight of the transformation of the world oil market from a seller's into a buyer's market. Saudi Arabia's oil revenues tumbled from $120 billion in 1980 to an estimated $18.7 billion in 1989, a fall of more than 80 percent since 1981. The oil income of all the GCC countries together was estimated at no more than $34 billion in 1989. The ensuing economic recession has gripped all the GCC states. It may be that the GCC countries began to reemerge from recession by June 1989 when OPEC raised its production ceiling from 18.5 to 19.5 millions of barrels per day. But it seems unlikely that OPEC will reemerge as the kind of world-class macroeconomic force that it was in 1979.

The military power of the GCC is no less problematic than its economic power. Saudi Arabia is the military as well as the economic giant among the six GCC nations. By spreading its security umbrella over its junior partners, it seems to have achieved a unified defense and deterrent system. Between the eruption of the Iranian Revolution in 1978 and the end of the Iran-Iraq War, Saudi Arabia spent more than $31 billion on buying arms. Economic recession has made no dent in Saudi Arabia's military buildup. As a matter of fact, on July 3, 1988, Saudi Arabia signed its single largest arms purchase ever at the height of the pervasive economic recession. According to the Saudi information minister, this purchase of arms from Britain is worth $68 billion over a 20–year period.

Yet military hardware is not the same as military power. Saudi Arabia and its GCC partners have serious manpower problems. In addition to the paucity of troops, partly because of a population base too small for effective military recruitment, the presence of expatriates in the GCC armed forces such as those of Oman, the lack of battle-tested troops as against those of Iran and Iraq, and the diversity of military training as well as weapons systems all place serious limits on the creation of an integrated defense and deterrent system. Even assuming that such a system can be created and can be made effective, it cannot be simply assumed that the GCC states would necessarily want to play the role of the balancer between Iran and Iraq in the future. Unlike both those countries, the GCC states' primary security interest is to maintain stability and security in the Arabian Peninsula and its immediate vicinity, not in the entire Persian Gulf region.

The second flawed assumption stems from a misunderstanding of the attitudes of the GCC states toward cooperation with the United States. Because Kuwait requested the reflagging of its ships by the United States and because the GCC states, by and large, cooperated with the United States in performing its mission of escorting 11 reflagged Kuwaiti tankers, it is simplistically assumed that the GCC states would be willing to act as an American surrogate in maintaining Gulf security. Unlike Iran and Iraq, however, the GCC states have no desire to play the role of the policeman of the entire Persian Gulf, either by themselves or with the help of the United States. They strongly believe that Gulf security must be maintained by Gulf states. To stress this principle, the Kuwaiti leaders made an important distinction between the responsibility for Gulf security and the responsibility for the safety of navigation in the international waters of the Persian Gulf. The security of the Gulf is the responsibility of the Gulf states, but according to Kuwaiti Prime Minister Shaykh Sa'd al-Abdallah, the freedom of navigation in the Gulf international waters is "the responsibility of the international community, the maritime countries, and those benefiting from freedom of navigation in this international passageway."

The third flawed assumption is rooted in a misunderstanding of the nature of the U.S. commitment in the Persian Gulf. The Carter Doctrine committed the United States in 1980 to the defense of the uninterrupted flow of Gulf oil supplies to world markets, not to the security of the Persian Gulf. The Pentagon's *Defense Guidance* declared unequivocally that the United States was prepared "to introduce American forces directly into the region should it appear that the security of access to the Persian Gulf [oil] is threatened." Because the United States did not wish to step into Britain's imperial shoes, the Nixon administration anointed the Shah's Iran as America's surrogate policeman of the Gulf. That surrogacy partly contributed to the eruption of the Iranian Revolution.

AN INTERNATIONAL STRATEGY

If neither a new Iranian or Iraqi policemanship nor a U.S.-supported balancing role by the GCC states can ensure peace and security in the whole Persian Gulf region, then what can? Given the fact that the underlying conflicts between Iran and Iraq, and for that matter between Iran and other Gulf Arab states and among the Arab states themselves, cannot be conclusively resolved, a way must be found to minimize the danger of armed conflict and maximize the opportunity for cooperation across the Gulf region. Perhaps this is the only realistic way to try to achieve the overriding goal of meeting the legitimate need for peace and security of the Gulf states and simultaneously to protect the interest of the international community in the unimpeded flow of Gulf oil supplies to world markets. This requires an international strategy aimed at (1) a lasting peace between Iran and Iraq; (2) freedom of navigation in the international waters of the Persian Gulf; and (3) measures to enhance the stability and security of the Gulf region as a whole.

Iran-Iraq Peace

Clausewitz called war the continuation of politics by other means. In the Middle East, the *Economist* says, politics is the continuation of war by other means. Nowhere has this been so true as in the peace negotiations between Iran and Iraq, which began at Geneva on August 25, 1988. Having failed to achieve the control of the Shatt al-Arab by invading Iran, Iraq has sought to achieve that same objective through peace negotiations. It claimed "full sovereignty" over the waterway the day after the negotiations began. The Iranian foreign minister rejected the Iraqi demand, saying, "No bargaining, no compromise," and drew what he called a "red line." Ever since this unexpected revival of the ancient Shatt al-Arab dispute by Iraq, the U.N.-brokered peace process has, for all practical purposes, been deadlocked. Even the cease-fire, the only item of Resolution 598 that has been in effect since August 20, 1988, has not escaped the underlying conflict between Iran and Iraq. The United Nations Iran-Iraq Military Observer Group (UNIIMOG) has so far received nearly 2,000 complaints about violations of the cease-fire, although only about 800 of them have been confirmed by the U.N. group. UNIIMOG has also confirmed that the two nations have exchanged some artillery, small arms, and rocket fire. Furthermore, except for a token exchange of sick and wounded POWs, there are still about 100,000 awaiting repatriation. About two-thirds of them are Iranian nationals and one-third Iraqis.

To break the deadlock, the Secretary-General, among other things, presented his own plan on October 1, 1988. Although there is no mention of the Shatt al-Arab dispute in Resolution 598, his plan calls on Iran to allow the reopening of the waterway as an inducement to Iraq to come to terms but suggests that the issue of sovereignty over the river be put off until after a peace treaty is signed. According to the Secretary-General, the two sides have agreed in principle on the "usefulness . . . of restoring the Shatt al-Arab to navigation," but the waterway continues to be closed. Furthermore, no progress is being made on the withdrawal of "all forces to the internationally recognized boundaries without delay" as required by Article 2 of Resolution 598. As a matter of fact, 2,600 square kilometers of Iranian territory still remain under Iraqi occupation. Iraq claims that "military necessity" compels such occupation.

Under the circumstances, the complacency of the Gulf states, the outside powers, and the Security Council is incomprehensible. It is time to act. Between July 20, 1987, when the United Nations adopted Resolution 598, and July 18, 1988, when Iran finally accepted it, the United States led a campaign against Iran, threatening a follow-on resolution for an arms embargo as a means of pressuring Iran into compliance with the resolution's call for a cease-fire. Now is the time for consideration of a follow-on resolution unless some progress is made in peace negotiations. Resolution 598 has a binding character under Articles 39 and 40 of Chapter VII of the U.N. Charter, to which the resolution specifically refers. Furthermore, under Article 10 of the resolution, the Security Council is bound to take appropriate measures to ensure compliance with the terms of Resolution 598. Before a follow-on enforcement resolution is considered, however, the Soviet Union and the United States should try to persuade Iran and Iraq to get off dead center. Moscow played a major part in inducing Iran to accept Resolution 598. In the instant case both Washington and Moscow should persuade Iraq to put off the Shatt al-Arab issue, as suggested by the Secretary-General, until after a peace treaty is signed.

The really tough question is how to persuade Iraq to withdraw its forces to "the internationally recognized boundaries." This would necessarily require Iraq's observance of the boundary line, the *thalweg*, the middle of the navigable channel, under the 1975 Algiers agreement, which Iraq abrogated on September 17, 1980, and continues to consider "null and void." One way of persuading Iraq to accept the Secretary-General's suggestion mentioned earlier is for the Secretary-General to seek the authorization of the Security Council to establish a permanent U.N. peacekeeping force, regardless of how the Shatt al-Arab issue is eventually settled. Such a force could help assuage Iraq's sense of insecurity about its access to the high seas under the terms of the 1975 Algiers agreement.

In paving the way for the Algiers agreement, the U.N. Security Council failed to insist on the need for a permanent peacekeeping force. When it called for a cease-fire on March 7, 1974, after prolonged border skirmishes between Iran and Iraq, it merely asked for bilateral negotiations and hence left the parties to their own devices. The Algiers agreement of March 6, 1975, and the relevant protocols of June 13, 1975, the dredging agreement of December 26, 1975, and other related legal instruments that resulted from negotiations provided the most elaborate regulations for land and river boundary security. But the parties failed to provide for any third-party impartial group to monitor the observance of the terms of their agreement. Even five years later and before the start of the war, Iraq complained that the Shah's Iran had refused to withdraw its forces from certain areas of Iraqi territory. Ten days before Iraq launched its full-fledged attack on Iran, General Khairallah said that Iraq had by then recovered these areas by military force.

The creation of a permanent observer group as proposed here would require a new Security Council resolution. Resolution 619 of August 9, 1988, which set up UNIIMOG for an initial period of six months, is primarily a "cease-fire–keeping" force (my appellation). It is entrusted merely with such tasks as establishing cease-fire lines, monitoring compliance with the cease-fire, supervising the withdrawal of all forces to the internationally recognized boundaries, and so on. But the primary mission of the peacekeeping force suggested here would be to ensure the compliance of Iran and Iraq with all the terms of their agreements, whether they concern land and river boundary lines, freedom of navigation in the Shatt al-Arab waterway, dredging operations, or cross-border infiltration. Such a permanent observer group could draw its troops from the same group of countries that are participating in UNIIMOG. As in the case of UNIIMOG, the proposed group should exclude participation by the superpowers.

Freedom of Navigation

Who should maintain the freedom of navigation in the international waters of the Persian Gulf? Given the overwhelming dependence of the economies of the Gulf states on oil revenues, they have a vital interest in the seaborne export of their oil, notwithstanding the expansion of overland oil export by means of pipelines, particularly by Iraq. Furthermore, besides oil exports, the Gulf states depend heavily on the Gulf sealanes for their overall international trade. But few other waterways in the world are stamped so graphically by the interests of the international community at large as is the Persian Gulf. The main reason, of course, is that the industrialized democracies, particularly Japan and the West European countries, significantly depend on Gulf oil supplies. This is why the Strait of Hormuz at the entrance of the Gulf has been characterized as the "global chokepoint."

The U.S. deployment of massive forces in the Persian Gulf at the height of the tanker war stimulated suggestions for the involvement by the United Nations in maintaining freedom of navigation in the Gulf. In 1987 former Secretary of State Cyrus Vance and former Secretary of Defense Elliot L. Richardson proposed that the United Nations should reflag "nonmilitary vessels in the gulf." This proposal would not require a U.N. flotilla for patrolling the Gulf. But subsequently their proposal envisaged "lightly armed patrol boats." In the same year, the Soviet Union suggested in the U.N. General Assembly that the "safety of navigation in the Gulf can and must be ensured by the entire world community, in whose behalf the United Nations will be acting. If necessary, appropriate and sufficient forces should be made effectively available to it."

Five years earlier, in 1982, as a consultant to the U.N. Secretary General on the Persian Gulf region, this author proposed the creation of a "U.N. Patrol Authority." Anticipating at the time that armed hostilities between Iran and Iraq might eventually threaten the freedom of navigation, this proposal aimed at minimizing such a threat. Two years later, in 1984, the start of the tanker war in earnest began to disrupt oil transportation, a disruption that in fact increased after the U.S. forces began to escort the reflagged Kuwaiti ships. In the light of this experience, the idea of a U.N. Patrol Authority all the more deserves consideration.

As proposed here, such an authority should be established by the U.N. Security Council with the objective of maintaining the freedom of navigation in the international waters of the Persian Gulf in the interest of the international community. Under the auspices of this authority, a United Nations Gulf Flotilla (UNGF) should be formed having the specific objective of monitoring ship movements in the international waters of the Gulf. In principle, all Gulf states should contribute vessels to this monitoring flotilla. Furthermore, Britain, France, Italy, Holland, and Belgium should contribute ships and minesweepers to this flotilla. These five maritime Western nations demonstrated interest in the safety of ship movements during the Iran-Iraq War. Japan could help to finance this force. The ships of the United States and the Soviet Union should be excluded from this seaborne monitoring force as their troops should be from the permanent UNIIMOG proposed earlier. In peacetime this flotilla should be unarmed, but if a war breaks out again, it should be armed. Moreover, since the breach of peace concerns all the permanent members of the Security Council, the authority could ask the Soviet Union and the United States as well as the other permanent members of the council to provide appropriate forces as a means of enhancing the monitoring capability of the flotilla.

Gulf Security

No doubt both the permanent UNIIMOG and UNGF proposed here can contribute to the stability and security of the Persian Gulf. But the region is as rich in conflict as it is in oil. Although the conflict between Iran and Iraq is the single greatest cause of tension in the area, other conflicts—between Iran and Saudi Arabia and also other Gulf Arab states—cause regional strains. The Saudi-Iranian conflict over the Hajj issue simmered for years and finally led to a diplomatic break after the death of hundreds of Iranian pilgrims at Mecca in 1987. The psychological wounds of this tragic incident continue to fester, although President Hashemi Rafsanjani's new "good-neighbor policy" may eventually help to improve relations between Tehran and Riyadh.

Furthermore, inter-Arab relations are by no means immune to friction and dispute. Before the Iranian Revolution Iraq's subversive activities were the prime cause of tension in the Gulf region. But during the Iran-Iraq War the threat of the contagion of the Iranian Revolution and the spread of the war overshadowed the threat of Iraq in the face of the greater Iranian threat. Despite all the diplomatic, logistical, and financial aid of the GCC states to Iraq, the fear of Iraqi ambitions reemerged after the cease-fire. The ancient Iraqi-Kuwaiti border dispute has been revived, while the tiny city-state is trying to counterbalance Iraq's postwar pressures by upgrading its diplomatic relations with Iran. In a rare move to forestall any ambitious southward thrust in the Gulf by the Baathist regime in a flush of postwar overconfidence, King Fahad visited Baghdad and on March 22, 1989, signed a noninterference accord with Iraq that forbids the use of force between the two states and also initialled a security-coordination agreement. The latter may have been signed with the possibility of a future Iranian threat in mind.

The creation of the GCC has no doubt helped to ease tension among the six like-minded monarchies, but active and potential conflicts continue. The Kuwaiti-led GCC mediation has helped to minimize the conflict between South Yemen and Oman, but the underlying tension continues. The Saudi-led GCC intercession has helped to reduce the armed skirmishes between Bahrain and Qatar over the Fasht al-Dibal dispute, but the matter is yet to be settled by the International Court of Justice.

These examples of regional conflicts suffice to indicate why the international strategy for peace and security in the Persian Gulf proposed here calls for measures in addition to those suggested earlier. It is precisely because of this need that Resolution 598 requests the Secretary-General in its Article 8 "to examine in consultation with Iran and Iraq and with other states of the region measures to enhance the security and stability of the region." The creation of a permanent UNIIMOG and UNGF proposed here are two such measures, but they cannot prevent the active and potential conflicts that were just mentioned from festering and leading to armed conflict. The need for additional measures is all the more urgent in view of the unprecedented arms race and the dramatic change in the nature of warfare in the region since the Iran-Iraq War.

The wisdom of involving the U.N. Secretary-General in consultation with the Gulf states regarding the stability and security of the region can be easily seen from the historical record. The Shah spoke often of the need for regional stability and security through regional cooperation, but in practice he sought to dominate the Gulf region, and hence his pleas fell on deaf ears among the suspicious Gulf Arab states. The settlement of the Shatt al-Arab dispute in 1975 led to a short-lived period of unprecedented interest in regional cooperation, so much so that the Shah and Saddam Hussein consulted each other on regionwide security issues. The Gulf states' foreign ministers meeting after the Islamic Conference in Jidda in 1975 was a failure partly because the agenda included too many diverse and sensitive issues, such as the fate of the islands of Abu Musa and the two Tunbs and the Bahrain-Qatar dispute over the Hawar Islands, as well as the "division" of Gulf waters, domestic coups, foreign fleets, and so on. The less sensitive issue of combatting pollution in the Gulf, however, did become the subject of a major treaty in 1978, which is to date the sole basis of the only Gulf-wide forum for cooperation among the littoral states, including Iraq and Iran.

THE BALANCE SHEET

In considering the measures needed for enhancing the stability and security of the Gulf region, the U.N. Secretary-General and the Gulf states should be guided by the following principles:

1. Respect for the territorial integrity and political independence of all Gulf states, particularly by observing the principle of noninterference in internal affairs

2. Nonproliferation of chemical, biological, and nuclear weapons, including the destruction of existing chemical weapons stockpiles and prohibition of the sale of chemical agents or "precursors"

3. Prohibition of the use of missiles of any type against civilian populations and oil tankers, including the abandonment of all permanent missile sites either planned or under way

4. Reduction of arms in all categories and denial of military bases to any and all non-Gulf states

5. Peaceful settlement of regional disputes by means of negotiations, fact-finding, mediation, conciliation, and adjudication

Agreement on some of these principles may be more difficult to achieve than others. The most important example is the issue of the nonproliferation of chemical weapons. At the international conference on chemical weapons in Paris in January 1989, Arab countries argued that they were entitled to develop and possess chemical weapons as long as Israel was allowed to have nuclear arms. Iraqi Foreign Minister Tariq Aziz led the Arab chorus. Yet the Soviet Union's reported acceptance of inspection of chemical weapons stockpiles would seem to facilitate the eventual signing of a U.S.-Soviet treaty banning chemical weapons. If such a treaty is signed by many nations, the chances for its acceptance by the Arab states may improve.

By contrast, agreement on the principle of peaceful settlement of regional disputes may be easier to achieve. If so, the U.N. Secretary-General could point out to the Gulf states under Article 8 of Resolution 598 that the Gulf states may wish to consider the creation of a U.N. Gulf Mediation Board (UNGMB). Such a mechanism could help to nip regional quarrels and skirmishes in the bud before they get out of hand and lead to a breach of peace and threats against the stability and security of the Persian Gulf.

Selected Bibliography

Bryan R. Daves

DIPLOMACY

Axelgard, Fred. *U.S.-Arab Relations: The Iraqi Dimension*. Jacksonville, Ill.: National Council on U.S.-Arab Relations, 1985.
———. "U.S.-Iraq Relations: A Status Report." *American-Arab Affairs*, Summer 1985, 1–9.
Hamdoon, Nizar. "Iraq-U.S. Relations." *American-Arab Affairs*, Fall 1985, 95–97.
King, Ralph. *The United Nations and the Iran-Iraq War*. New York: Ford Foundation, 1987.
Nakhleh, Emile A. *The Gulf Cooperation Council: Policies, Problems, and Prospects*. New York: Praeger, 1986.
Peterson, Erik R. *The Gulf Cooperation Council: Search for Unity in a Dynamic Region*. Boulder, Colo.: Westview Press, 1988.
Ramazani, R. K., with Joseph A. Kechichian. *The Gulf Cooperation Council: Record and Analysis*. Charlottesville: University Press of Virginia, 1988.
Sindelar, H. Richard, III, and John Peterson, eds. *Crosscurrents in the Gulf*. London: Routledge, 1988.
United Nations Backgrounder. *Chronology of United Nations Negotiations to End the Iran-Iraq War*. New York: United Nations, 1988.
United Nations Backgrounder. *Chronology of United Nations Negotiations to End the Iran-Iraq War since the Cease-Fire*. New York: United Nations, 1989.

INTERNATIONAL LAW

Amin, S. H. "The Iran-Iraq Conflict: Legal Implications." *International and Comparative Law Quarterly* 31 (January 1982): 167–89.

Boczek, Boleslaw A. *Flags of Convenience: An International Legal Study*. Cambridge, Mass.: Harvard University Press, 1962.

Caron, David. "Ships: Nationality and Status." In *Encyclopedia of Public International Law*, vol. 11, edited by R. Bernhardt, 289–97. New York: North-Holland, 1989.

Fenrick, W. J. "The Exclusion Zone Device in the Law of Naval Warfare." *Canadian Yearbook of International Law* 24 (1986): 91–126.

Gray, Christine. "The British Position in Regard to the Gulf Conflict." *International and Comparative Law Quarterly* 37 (April 1988): 420–28.

al-Izzi, Khalid. *The Shatt al-Arab Dispute: A Legal Study*. London: Third World Centre for Research and Publishing, 1981.

Jenkins, Maxwell. "Air Attacks on Neutral Shipping in the Persian Gulf: The Legality of the Iraqi Exclusion Zone and Iranian Reprisals." *Boston College International and Comparative Law Review* 8 (Summer 1985): 517–49.

Kaikobad, Kaiyan Homi. *The Shatt-al-Arab Boundary Question: A Legal Reappraisal*. Oxford: Clarendon Press, 1988.

Leckow, Ross. "The Iran-Iraq Conflict in the Gulf: The Law of War Zones." *International and Comparative Law Quarterly* 37 (July 1988): 629–44.

McConnell, Moria M. " 'Business as Usual': An Evaluation of the United Nations Convention on Conditions for Registration of Ships." *Journal of Maritime Law and Commerce* 18 (July 1987): 435–49.

Phillips, Tod. "Exchanging Excuses for Uses of Force: The Tug of War in the Persian Gulf." *Houston Journal of International Law* 10 (Spring 1988): 275–93.

Sanghvi, Ramesh. *Shatt al-Arab: The Facts behind the Issue*. London: Transorient Press, 1969.

Schiller, Thomas S. "The Gulf War and Shipping: Recent Developments." In *Violence at Sea*, edited by Brian A. H. Parritt. Paris: ICC, 1986.

Tucker, R. W. *The Law of War and Neutrality at Sea*. Naval War College International Law Studies. Vol. 50. Washington, D.C.: Government Printing Office, 1955.

POLITICS

Abdulghani, Jasim. *Iraq and Iran: The Years of Crisis*. Baltimore: Johns Hopkins University Press, 1984.

Ali, Sheikh R. "Holier Than Thou: The Iran-Iraq War." *Middle East Review* 17 (Fall 1984): 50–57.

El Azhary, M. S. *The Iran-Iraq War: An Historical, Economic, and Political Analysis*. New York: St. Martin's Press, 1984.

Bakhash, Shaul. *The Reign of the Ayatollahs: Iran and the Islamic Revolution*. New York: Basic Books, 1984.

Bradley, C. Paul. *Recent United States Policy in the Persian Gulf 1971–1982*. Grantham, N. H.: Thompson and Rutter, 1982.

Chubin, Sharam, and Charles Tripp. *Iran and Iraq at War*. Boulder, Colo.: Westview Press, 1988.

Cottrell, Alvin J. ed. *The Persian Gulf States: A General Survey*. Baltimore: Johns Hopkins University Press, 1980.

Cottrell, Alvin J., and Michael L. Moodie. *The United States and the Persian Gulf: Past Mistakes, Present Needs*. New York: National Strategy Information Center, 1984.

Fukuyama, Francis. "Patterns of Soviet Third World Policy." *Problems of Communism* 26 (September–October 1987): 1–13.

Ghareeb, Edmund. "The Forgotten War." *American-Arab Affairs*, Summer 1983, 59–75.

Grummon, Stephen R. *The Iran-Iraq War: Islam Embattled*. New York: Praeger, 1982.

Heller, Mark A. *The Iran-Iraq War: Implications for Third Parties*. Tel Aviv: Jaffee Center for Strategic Studies; Cambridge, Mass.: Harvard University, Center for International Affairs, January 1984.

Helms, Christine. "Taha Yasin Ramadham: The Future of Iraq and the Ruling Party." *Middle East Insight* 6 (Spring 1989): 16–20.

———. *Iraq: Eastern Flank of the Arab World*. Washington, D.C.: Brookings Institution, 1984.

Hiro, Dilip. "Impact of the Gulf War on Iran." *Atlantic Community Quarterly* 25 (Summer 1987): 129–44.

Hunter, Shireen. "Arab-Iranian Relations and Stability in the Persian Gulf." *Washington Quarterly* 7 (Summer 1984): 67–76.

Ismael, Tareq Y. *Iraq and Iran: Roots of Conflict*. Syracuse: Syracuse University Press, 1982.

Khadduri, Majid. *The Gulf War: The Origins and Implications of the Iraq-Iran Conflict*. New York and Oxford: Oxford University Press, 1988.

Limbert, John W. *Iran: At War with History*. Boulder, Colo.: Westview Press, 1987.

Marr, Phebe. *The Modern History of Iraq*. Boulder, Colo.: Westview Press, 1985.

Martin, Lenore G. *The Unstable Gulf: Threats from Within*. Lexington, Mass.: Lexington Books, 1984.

Nyrop, Richard F. *Iraq: A Country Study*. Foreign Area Studies Handbook. Washington, D.C.: Government Printing Office, 1979.

Patrizia, Charles A. "U.S. Policy in the Arabian Gulf: A Long-Term View." *American-Arab Affairs*, Fall 1987, 45–55.

Penrose, Edith and E. F. *Iraq: International Relations and National Development*. Boulder, Colo.: Westview Press, 1978.

Peterson, J. E. "The GCC States after the Iran-Iraq War." *American-Arab Affairs*, Fall 1988, 96–106.

Quandt, William. *Saudi Arabia in the 1980s: Foreign Policy, Security, and Oil*. Washington, D.C.: Brookings Institution, 1981.

Ramazani, R. K. "Iran: Burying the Hatchet." *Foreign Policy* no. 60 (Fall 1985): 52–74.

————. *Revolutionary Iran: Challenge and Response in the Middle East*. Baltimore: Johns Hopkins University Press, 1986.

————. "The Iran-Iraq War and the Persian Gulf Crisis." *Current History* 87 (February 1988): 61–64.

Ross, Dennis. "Soviet Views toward the Gulf War." *Orbis* 28 (Fall 1984): 537–46.

Rubinstein, Alvin Z. "Perspectives on the Iran-Iraq War." *Orbis* 29 (Fall 1985): 597–608.

Sick, Gary. "Trial by Error: Reflections on the Iran-Iraq War." *Middle East Journal* 43 (Spring 1989): 230–46.

U.S. Congress. Senate. Committee on Foreign Relations. *U.S. Policy in the Persian Gulf*. 100th Cong. 1st Sess., 1988. Washington, D.C.: Government Printing Office, 1988.

Whelan, Joseph G., and Michael J. Dixon. *The Soviet Union in the Third World: Threat to World Peace?* Washington, D.C.: Pergamon-Brassey's, 1986.

Yodfat, Aryeh Y. *The Soviet Union and the Arabian Peninsula*. New York: St. Martin's Press, 1983.

SECURITY

Amirsadeghi, Husain, ed. *The Security of the Persian Gulf*. London: Croom Helm, 1981.

Chubin, Shahram. *Security in the Persian Gulf: The Role of Outside Powers*. London: International Institute for Strategic Studies, 1982.

Ciarrocchi, Robert J. *U.S., Soviet, and Western European Naval Forces in the Persian Gulf Region*. Congressional Research Service Report 87–956F, December 8, 1987.

Darius, Robert G., John W. Amos, and Ralph H. Magnus. *Gulf Security into the 1980s: Perceptual and Strategic Dimensions*. Stanford, Calif.: Hoover Institution Press, 1984.

Entessar, Nader. "Superpowers and Persian Gulf Security: The Iranian Perspective." *Third World Quarterly* 10 (October 1988): 1427–51.

Faksh, Mahmud. "Saudi Arabia and the Gulf Crisis: Foreign and Security Policy Dilemma." *Middle East Review* 19 (Summer 1987): 47–53.

Hameed, Mazher A. *Arabia Imperilled: The Security Imperatives of the Arab Gulf States*. Washington, D.C.: Middle East Assessment Group, 1986.

Hasnat, Sayed Farouq. "Iran-Iraq and the Regional Security System of the Persian Gulf." *Strategic Studies* 11 (Summer 1988): 52–74.

Hickman, William. *Ravaged and Reborn: The Iranian Army, 1982*. Washington, D.C.: Brookings Institution, 1982.

Irfani, S. "The Iran-Iraq War and Its Implications for the Region." *Strategic Studies* 11 (Winter 1987): 38–59.

Jaber, S. "American Security Measures in the Arab Gulf." *Arab Gulf Journal* 5 (Winter 1985): 31–38.

Johnson, Maxwell O. *The Military as an Instrument of U.S. Policy in Southwest Asia: The Rapid Deployment Joint Task Force, 1979–1982*. Boulder, Colo.: Westview Press, 1983.

Karsh, Efraim. *The Iran-Iraq War: A Military Analysis*. London: International Institute for Strategic Studies, Spring 1987.

Kechichian, Joseph. "The Gulf Cooperation Council: Search for Security." *Third World Quarterly* 7 (October 1985): 853–81.

Kupchan, Charles. *The Persian Gulf and the West: The Dilemmas of Security*. London: Allen and Unwin, 1987.

Levran, Aharon. "The Iran-Iraq War: The Military Balance, Major Developments, and Repercussions." *Global Affairs* 1 (Summer 1986): 67–89.

McNaugher, Thomas L. *Arms and Oil: U.S. Military Strategy and the Persian Gulf*. Washington, D.C.: Brookings Institution, 1985.

Naff, Thomas, ed. *Gulf Security and the Iran-Iraq War*. Washington, D.C.: National Defense University Press, 1985.

Noyes, James H. *The Clouded Lens: Persian Gulf Security and U.S. Policy*. 2d ed. Stanford, Calif.: Hoover Institution Press, 1982.

O'Ballance, Edgar. *The Gulf War*. London: Brassey's, 1988.

Peterson, J. E. *Security in the Arabian Peninsula and Gulf States, 1973–1984*. Washington, D.C.: National Council on U.S.-Arab Relations, 1985.

———. *Defending Arabia*. London: Croom Helm, 1986.

Ross, Dennis. *Considering Threats to the Persian Gulf*. Washington, D.C.: Wilson Center for International Scholars, 1981.

———. "Considering Soviet Threats to the Persian Gulf." *International Security* 6 (Fall 1981): 158–80.

Sabin, Philip A. G., and Efraim Karsh. "Escalation in the Iran-Iraq War." *Survival* 31 (May/June 1989): 241–54.

Schahgaldian, Nikola. *The Iranian Military under the Islamic Republic*. Santa Monica, Calif.: Rand Corporation, 1987.

Tahir-Kheli, Shirin, and Shaheen Ayubi, eds. *The Iran-Iraq War: New Weapons, Old Conflicts*. New York: Praeger, 1983.

Tripp, Charles, ed. *Regional Security in the Middle East*. New York: St. Martin's Press, 1984.

U.S. Congress. House. Committee on Armed Services. *National Security Policy Implications of United States Operations in the Persian Gulf*. Report of the Defense Policy Panel and the Investigations Subcommittee. 100th Cong., 1st sess., July 1987.

———. Senate. Committee on Foreign Relations. *War in the Persian Gulf: The U.S. Takes Sides*. Staff Report. Washington, D.C.: Government Printing Office, 1987.

Wells, Samuel F., Jr., and Mark Bruzonsky, eds. *Security in the Middle East*. Boulder, Colo.: Westview Press, 1987.

Wizart, Talat Ayesha. "The Role of the Gulf Cooperation Council in Regional Security." *Strategic Studies* 11 (Winter 1987): 69–78.

STRATEGY

Axelgard, Fred. *A New Iraq? The Gulf War and Implications for U.S. Policy*. New York: Praeger, 1988.

Cordesman, Anthony H. *The Gulf and the Search for Strategic Stability*. Boulder, Colo.: Westview Press, 1984.

———. *The Iran-Iraq War and Western Security, 1984–1987*. London: Jane's, 1987.

Heller, Mark A. "The War Strategy of Iran." *Middle East Review* 19 (Summer 1987): 17–24.

Karsh, Efraim. "Military Power and Foreign Policy Goals: The Iran-Iraq War Revisited." *International Affairs* 64 (Winter 1987–88): 83–96.

Katz, Mark. "The U.S.S.R. and the Iran-Iraq War: Short Term Benefits, Long Term Risks." *Middle East International* 5 (January/February 1987): 8–13.

King, Ralph. *The Iran-Iraq War: The Political Implications*. London: International Institute for Strategic Studies, 1987.

Matinuddin, Kamal. "Geo-political and Geo-strategic Survey of the Gulf." *Strategic Studies* 11 (Winter 1987): 11–28.

Ramazani, R. K. *The Persian Gulf and the Strait of Hormuz*. The Hague: Martinus Nijhoff, 1979.

———. "Iran's Foreign Policy: Contending Orientations." *Middle East Journal* 43 (Spring 1989): 202–17.

Rubinstein, Alvin Z. *The Great Game: Rivalry in the Persian Gulf and South Asia*. New York: Praeger, 1983.

Segal, David. "The Iran-Iraq War: A Military Analysis." *Foreign Affairs* 66 (Summer 1988): 946–63.

Index

Contributors

ANTHONY CLARK AREND is assistant professor of government at Georgetown University. He is a former articles editor of the *Virginia Journal of International Law* and senior fellow at the Center for Law and National Security at the University of Virginia School of Law. His publications include *Pursuing a Just and Durable Peace: John Foster Dulles and International Organization* (1988), *The United States and the Compulsory Jurisdiction of the International Court of Justice* (editor and contributor, 1986), and *The Falklands War: Lessons for Strategy, Diplomacy, and International Law* (coeditor and contributor, 1985).

BOLESLAW ADAM BOCZEK, professor of political science at Kent State University, has been invited as visiting professor of international law to several international universities, including those in Frankfurt, Mexico City, Leuven, Warsaw and Utrecht. The author of the classic study on the *Flags of Convenience* (1962), he has written several other books, among them *The Transfer of Marine Technology to Developing Nations in International Law* (1982) and *The International Law Dictionary* (1987). Professor Boczek has contributed numerous scholarly articles to professional publications, including the *American Journal of International Law*, *Ocean Development and International Law*, and *Ocean Yearbook*.

DAVID D. CARON is acting professor of international law at the School of Law (Boalt Hall), University of California at Berkeley. A former editor-in-chief of *Ecology Law Quarterly*, he served as legal advisor to the United States arbitrators at the Iran-U.S. Claims Tribunal in The Hague from 1983 to 1986 and was a senior research fellow at the Max Planck Institute in Heidelberg during 1986. The author of numerous law review articles on the law of the sea and dispute settlement, Professor Caron has co-edited two volumes, *Law of the Sea: U.S. Policy Dilemma* (1983) and *Perspectives on U.S. Policy Towards the Law of the Sea* (1985). He thanks Peter Root for his very able research assistance.

BRYAN R. DAVES, a M.A. candidate in political science at the George Washington University, has authored several articles on the Middle East. He is the coeditor of Congressional Quarterly's *The Middle East* (6th ed., 1986) and editor of the *Defense and Foreign Affairs Handbook, 1987–88* (1988).

EDMUND GHAREEB, a specialist on Middle East affairs and media issues in Washington, D.C., is an adjunct professor at the George Washington University and the University of Virginia. He has authored or edited several books, including *Split Vision: The Portrayal of Arabs in the American Media* and *The Kurdish Question in Iraq* (1981).

ERIC HOOGLUND is visiting associate professor of political science at the University of California, Berkeley, and an editor of *Middle East Report*. He was senior analyst (1986–88) for the Iran Revolution Project at the National Security Archive in Washington, D.C. His major works include *Land and Revolution in Iran* (1982), *The Iranian Revolution and the Islamic Republic* (1986), *Crossing the Waters: Arabic-speaking Immigrants in the U.S. to 1940* (1987), and a forthcoming volume on Reagan administration policy toward Iran and the Persian Gulf.

MAXWELL ORME JOHNSON, director of international marketing for Tacoma Boatbuilding Company, formerly served as country director for the Persian Gulf region in the Office of the Assistant Secretary of Defense for International Security Affairs. The author of *The Military as an Instrument of U.S. Policy in Southwest Asia, 1979–1982: A Study of the Rapid Deployment Joint Task Force* (1983), Col. Johnson has traveled extensively throughout the Middle East and has published numerous articles on military strategy and international security considerations affecting the Persian Gulf region.

CHRISTOPHER C. JOYNER is associate professor of political science and a member of the Elliott School of International Affairs at the George Washington University. Formerly senior editor of the *Virginia Journal of International Law*, he has published more than one hundred articles and notes on international legal issues in scholarly books and journals, including the *American Journal of International Law, International and Comparative Law Quarterly, International Lawyer, Harvard International Law Journal*, and *Ocean Development and International Law*. Professor Joyner serves on the editorial boards of several publications, including *International Legal Materials, Virginia Journal of International Law*, and *Terrorism: An International Journal*. He has edited five volumes, most recently *The Antarctic Legal Regime* (1988), and is completing a study on Antarctica and the law of the sea.

MARK N. KATZ, professor of public affairs at George Mason University, served during the 1989–90 academic year as a fellow at the U.S. Institute of Peace. He is the author of *The Third World in Soviet Military Thought* (1982), *Russia and Arabia: Soviet Foreign Policy toward the Arabian Peninsula* (1986), and *Gorbachev's Military Policy in the Third World* (1989).

JOSEPH A. KECHICHIAN, former assistant dean of international studies at the University of Virginia, is author of the forthcoming volume *The Arab Search for Security in the Persian Gulf*. He has published several articles in professional journals, including *Conflict Quarterly, Third World Quarterly*, and *International Journal of Middle East Studies*, and is a regular contributor to *Encyclopaedia Iranica*.

CHARLES G. MACDONALD is professor of international relations and chairperson of the Department of International Relations at Florida International University. The author of *Iran, Saudi Arabia, and the Law of the Sea* (1980), Professor MacDonald has also contributed to several professional journals, among them *Foreign Affairs, Journal of South Asian and Middle Eastern Studies, Middle East Insight, Middle East Journal, Naval War College Review*, and *Middle East Review*.

PHEBE MARR is a senior fellow at the Institute for National Strategic Studies at the National Defense University in Washington, D.C. Currently on the Advisory Board of the *Middle East Journal*, she served formerly as an associate professor of history at the University of Tennessee and chairperson of the Middle East Studies Program at the Foreign Service Institute. The author of *The Modern History of Iraq* (1985), Dr. Marr has also contributed several works on Iraqi politics and security policy to scholarly books and journals.

THOMAS L. MCNAUGHER is a senior fellow in the Foreign Studies Program at the Brookings Institution and a professorial lecturer at the Johns Hopkins School of Advanced International Studies. A former policy analyst for the Rand Corporation, Dr. McNaugher is the author of *Arms and Oil: U.S. Military Strategy and the Persian Gulf* (1985), *The M16 Controversies: Military Organizations and Weapons Acquisitions* (1984), and *New Weapons, Old Politics: America's Military Procurement Muddle* (1989).

R. K. RAMAZANI is the Harry Flood Byrd, Jr., Professor of Government and Foreign Affairs at the University of Virginia. A member of the Board of Governors of the Middle East Institute and the editorial board of the *Middle East Journal*, Professor Ramazani has authored numerous works on Iran and Middle East politics, including *The Persian Gulf: Iran's Role* (1972), *The Persian Gulf and the Strait of Hormuz* (1979), *The United States and Iran: The Patterns of Influence* (1982), *Revolutionary Iran: Challenge and Response in the Middle East* (1986), and *The Gulf Cooperation Council: Record and Analysis* (1988).

BERNARD REICH is professor of political science and international affairs at the George Washington University. He is chairman of advanced area studies at the Department of State's Foreign Service Institute, a member of the Advisory Council of the International Security Studies program of the Woodrow Wilson International Center for Scholars, and on the Advisory Board of Editors of the *Middle East Journal*. Professor Reich has authored or edited several works, among them *Quest for Peace: United States–Israel Relations and the Arab-Israeli Conflict* (1977), *The United States and Israel: Influence in the Special Relationship* (1984), *Government and Politics of the Middle East and North Africa* (2d ed., 1986), and *The Powers in the Middle East: The Ultimate Strategic Arena* (1987).